Politics and Religion in tl Kingdom

This important new volume seeks to provide significant contribution to our understanding of religion and politics, demonstrating through comparisons with other countries the unusually complex nature of the interaction of religion and politics in the United Kingdom.

Bruce provides a detailed and comprehensive analysis of the field, covering key topics including:

- Religion and violence in Northern Ireland
- A UK–US comparison of the relationship between the church and the nation state
- Links between Protestantism and the rise of modern democracy
- The relationship between Methodism and Socialism
- The impact that ethnic minority status and religious values have on political alignment

This work will be of great interest to students and scholars of religion, politics and religious sociology.

Steve Bruce has been Professor of Sociology at the University of Aberdeen since 1991. In 2003 he was elected a Fellow of the British Academy and in 2005 he was elected a Fellow of the Royal Society of Edinburgh. He is the author of 24 books and some 140 journal articles and essays in edited collections.

Routledge studies in religion and politics

Edited by Jeffrey Haynes
London Metropolitan University, UK

This series aims to publish high quality works on the topic of the resurgence of political forms of religion in both national and international contexts. This trend has been especially noticeable in the post-cold war era (that is, since the late 1980s). It has affected all the 'world religions' (including, Buddhism, Christianity, Hinduism, Islam, and Judaism) in various parts of the world (such as, the Americas, Europe, the Middle East and North Africa, South and Southeast Asia, and sub-Saharan Africa).

The series welcomes books that use a variety of approaches to the subject, drawing on scholarship from political science, international relations, security studies, and contemporary history.

Books in the series explore these religions, regions and topics both within and beyond the conventional domain of 'church-state' relations to include the impact of religion on politics, conflict and development, including the late Samuel Huntington's controversial – yet influential – thesis about 'clashing civilisations'.

In sum, the overall purpose of the book series is to provide a comprehensive survey of what is currently happening in relation to the interaction of religion and politics, both domestically and internationally, in relation to a variety of issues.

Politics and the Religious Imagination
Edited by John Dyck, Paul Rowe and Jens Zimmermann

Christianity and Party Politics
Keeping the faith
Martin H. M. Steven

Religion, Politics and International Relations
Selected essays
Jeffrey Haynes

Religion and Democracy
A worldwide comparison
Carsten Anckar

Politics and Religion in the United Kingdom

Steve Bruce

Routledge
Taylor & Francis Group

LONDON AND NEW YORK

First published 2012
by Routledge
2 Park Square, Milton Park, Abingdon, Oxon OX14 4RN

Simultaneously published in the USA and Canada
by Routledge
711 Third Avenue, New York, NY 10017

Routledge is an imprint of the Taylor & Francis Group, an informa business

First issued in paperback 2012

British Library Cataloguing in Publication Data
A catalogue record for this book is available from the British Library

Library of Congress Cataloging in Publication Data
Bruce, Steve, 1954–
    Politics and religion in the United Kingdom/Steve Bruce.
    p. cm. – (Routledge studies in religion and politics)
    Includes bibliographical references and index.
    1. Religion and politics–Great Britain. 2. Great Britain–Religion. 3.
    Great Britain–Politics and government. 4. Christianity and politics–
    Great Britain. 5. Great Britain–Church history. I. Title.
    BL65.P7B79 2011
    201′.650941–dc23
                                                            2011019612
ISBN: 978-0-415-64367-2 (pbk)
ISBN: 978-0-415-66492-9 (hbk)
ISBN: 978-0-203-18126-3 (ebk)

Typeset in Times
by Wearset Ltd, Boldon, Tyne and Wear

Contents

Preface

Although I am probably best known as a sociologist of religion who specialises in documenting and explaining the decline of religion in Western liberal democracies, I have also maintained a parallel interest in places where religion is sufficiently popular to remain politically significant. As a Scot who began his teaching career at The Queen's University of Belfast, I have long had an interest in Protestant–Catholic conflict. My first book was *No Pope of Rome: Militant Protestantism in Modern Scotland*, a subject I returned to in 2004 with the jointly authored *Sectarianism in Scotland*. My time in Belfast produced four studies of Protestant politics in Northern Ireland: *God save Ulster! The Religion and Politics of Paisleyism* (1986), *The Red Hand: Loyalist Paramilitaries in Northern Ireland* (1992). *The Edge of the Union: The Ulster Loyalist Political Vision* (1994) and *Paisley: Religion and Politics in Northern Ireland* (2009). Along the way my interests gradually broadened and became more comparative with *The Rise and Fall of the New Christian Right: Protestant politics in America, 1978-88* (1988), *Conservative Protestant Politics* (1998) and *Politics and Religion* (2003). They stretched even further with *Fundamentalism* (2007).

When Jeff Haynes originally suggested I contribute to the Routledge series on Religion and Politics, the proposal we discussed was a volume that drew together various essays originally published in specialist journals that would benefit from being placed side by side, and that deserved a more general readership. As I worked through potential candidates for inclusion, I realised that, paradoxically, the virtues of the original essays became clearer the more I revised them and that, with the addition of new material, the reworked versions formed a coherent monograph. In the end only Chapter 5 survived from the original concept. All the other chapters were written for this volume. My hope is that together they form a coherent general account of religion and politics in the United Kingdom.

Acknowledgements

Over a period of 33 years the obligations mount up. Although none of the chapters reports a specific externally funded research project, the Economic and Social Research Council, the Nuffield Foundation, and the Carnegie Trust for the Universities of Scotland have all supported my work over the years. I am extremely grateful to them and to the Leverhulme Trust, which awarded me a senior research fellowship for 2007–09. That and generous research leave from the University of Aberdeen allowed me to complete this project. Both Queen's University of Belfast (from 1978 to 1991) and the University of Aberdeen (from 1991 to the present) have been generous in supporting my research with small grants and with time free from teaching and administration. The Universities of Edinburgh and Virginia were kind enough to give me house room during periods of research leave in the 1980s when I worked on sectarianism in Scotland and the New Christian Right in America.

I have been extremely fortunate in recently enjoying research and writing partnerships with two first-rate social statisticians. David Voas of the University of Manchester has been a major source of inspiration and encouragement for the last decade, as has Tony Glendinning of the University of Aberdeen, who co-wrote the conference presentation that evolved into Chapter 10. Most of the material presented in Chapter 4 comes from joint work done with Michael Rosie of the University of Edinburgh, Iain Paterson, who works for Glasgow City Council, and Tony Glendinning, and I am extremely grateful to them for their permission to benefit from our collective endeavours.

One of the most pleasant features of my profession is the generous spirit in which colleagues share information and ideas. I have incurred so many debts doing the research that informs this book that I am sure to have forgotten many signal acts of kindness that should be acknowledged. I can only ask that those who expect to see their names in the following list, but do not, to accept that omission represents forgetfulness rather than ingratitude. I know that, in addition to those colleagues already mentioned, I am beholden to John Anderson, Peter Brierley, John Curtice, Clive Field, Anthony Heath, Siobhan McAndrew, David McCrone, John Madeley, Lindsay Paterson and Maria Sobolewska.

Finally, I am grateful to Taylor and Francis for permisison to reprint 'Did Protestantism Create Democracy?', *Democratization* 11(14), as Chapter 5.

1   British Gods

Introduction

In 1996, the Methodist church on Oxford Road in Reading was sold to the Church of God Worldwide Mission Pentecostal Church, which previously met round the corner in Waylen Street. The Pentecostal premises were sold to the Bangladeshi Association for use as a mosque and community centre.[1] In that one property chain we can see three of the defining features of religious life in modern Britain. The Methodists, the largest group of English Protestants outside the state church in the nineteenth century, had declined to the point where large churches were a liability rather than an asset. A black Pentecostal church had grown out of its small hall. A British Asian Muslim group was taking its place at the foot of the ecclesiastical housing ladder.

This chapter has three main purposes. It offers a very brief history of Christianity in the United Kingdom and it explains the many divisions within the Christian churches. It is a social scientist's summary, intended to provide just enough background so that novices can make sense of the political correlates and consequences of UK religion. Those who wish to know more will find guides in the footnotes; those who already know more may wish to move direct to the second part of the chapter, which describes the origins of the UK's non-Christian populations. The third part summarises the current religious composition of the United Kingdom.

The reformation

Speculation is a more common response than reticence to a lack of information and there is no shortage of fiction to fill the blank space between the death of Christ and the appearance of reliable records about the Church in the British Isles: the infant Jesus visiting Glastonbury, the Holy Grail, King Arthur. Fun though such fictions are, I will start with the Reformation in the sixteenth century.[2] Prior to this, the four countries of the British Isles were pretty well united in their allegiance to a common form of Christianity as a belief system and to a relatively unified and extremely powerful Christian Church. The first point that needs stressing for the modern reader is the close connection between the Church and temporal power. It is little exaggeration to say that the Christian Church formed the backbone of both the national and the local state. Senior church officials held what would now be described as government offices. Thomas Wolsey (1473–1530) was both Archbishop of York and, as Lord Chancellor, Henry VIII's most senior advisor and functionary. Insofar as they were provided at all, activities such as health care, education, social welfare and public administration, for which we now have departments of state and local government offices, were once the work of religious institutions. What makes the subject of this book possible is the gradual separation of religion and politics as two distinct spheres and the Reformation was a major cause of that separation.[3]

The Reformation was not a single event. It was a series of long-drawn-out arguments (and some equally long-drawn-out wars) that eventually divided the Western European Christian world into Catholics and Protestants (who further divided amongst themselves). The issues were many and complex but they can be summarised around a few simple principles.

At the heart of what troubled Reformers such as Martin Luther, John Calvin and Huldrych Zwingli was the notion, common to most religions, that religious merit can be transferred from the Godly to the less Godly. So the man who feared for his soul could leave money in his will to pay others to say masses on his behalf after death. The very rich man who feared for his soul could buy himself eternal assistance by endowing a chantry, a hospital or school, the inmates of which would say prayers for his soul in perpetuity. Against this the Reformers argued that each of us was individually responsible before God for the state of our souls and could not borrow the piety of others. The Reformers were also opposed to the idea that the Church's officials could remove the stain of sin. Most world religions have assumed that most of us will at times fall short of what is required by God and have provided periodic rituals for restoring the sinner to a pristine condition. In the pre-Reformation Christian Church this was done by the sinner confessing his or her sins, the clergy setting some appropriate sanction, and the sinner performing such punishments in the right penitential spirit. Even when ritual re-purification and doing religious work on behalf of others had not degenerated into a simple cash transaction that allowed the sinner to buy him or herself out of trouble, the Reformers objected that such practices discouraged proper attention to religious duty and consistent moral behaviour.

For similar reasons the Reformers were opposed to a division of the population into the pious and the ordinary: they wished everyone to be equally pious. As the world would grind to a halt if everyone became a monk, nun or priest, the solution was to broaden the notion of a vocation or calling. Instead of displaying piety by forsaking mundane work for religious exercises or contemplation, the true Christian could glorify God through a secular occupation, provided it was performed honestly and diligently. The sixteenth century English Puritan Matthew Perkins was clear about the importance of work:

> Whatsoever is not done within the compass of calling is not faith ... [and] every man must do the duties of his calling with diligence. [There are] two

damnable sins that are contrary to this diligence. The first is idleness, whereby the duties of our callings and the occasions of glorifying God are neglected or omitted. The second is slothfulness, whereby they are performed slackly or carelessly.

However, not all jobs are callings. Unsurprisingly, Perkins excluded making one's living 'by usury, by carding and dicing, by maintaining houses of gaming, by plays and suchlike'.[4]

A crucial element of dissolving the boundary between what David Martin has called God's athletes and his also-rans was the Reformers' rejection of the special status of the clergy.[5] Pre-Reformation theory held that Jesus had passed his powers to the apostle Peter, who became the first Bishop of Rome (or Pope). Through correctly performed rituals those powers passed down to successive Popes. Some of the powers were also passed down the church's hierarchy so that a properly ordained priest (even if he was unpleasant and impious) could turn the wine and wafer into the blood and flesh of Christ and administer other sacraments. 'Sacrament' is derived from the Latin *sacramentum*, which means to 'make sacred'. Different branches of Christianity believe in different sacraments. Almost everyone accepts two: Baptism and Holy Eucharist (or Mass or Communion). The Catholic and Orthodox Churches add confirmation, confession, marriage, holy orders (that is, the various statuses of the clergy) and anointing of the sick. The Reformers argued against the magic of ordination and against the idea that descent from Peter in an 'apostolic succession' ensured divine insight. They argued for an essentially democratic theory of access to the will of God. Anyone who read the Bible in the right spirit was as capable as the Pope of knowing, and hence doing, the will of God. Some Reformers rejected entirely the idea of religious officials while others thought that training, experience and personality made officials useful but neither group thought that the clergy possessed spiritual powers that set them apart from the laity in the eyes of God.

All of this amounted to a fundamental change in the perceived relationship between the people and God and hence in the role for the church. Where pre-Reformation the church had been seen as placating God on behalf of the entire people, now the true church was just those souls who had the correct beliefs and who voluntarily aligned themselves with fellow believers. That is, religion shifted from being an organic community matter to being a matter for associations of individuals. As we will see, this posed a fundamental challenge to the idea of a national church.

The Reformation proceeded at different speeds in different parts of Europe and it inevitably became tangled up in secular local disputes. In Italy, France, Spain, Portugal and parts of Germany and the Netherlands, the Reformers lost and the Church became 'Roman Catholic'. Scandinavia and parts of Germany saw the triumph of Lutheran Protestantism, which rejected the authority of Rome but retained some pre-Reformation ritual, a hierarchical structure, and a sense of national mission. The Netherlands and Scotland became radically 'Reformed'. Thirty years of religious warfare was eventually settled by the Peace of

Westphalia of 1648, which is often taken as a convenient founding date for the modern nation-state system because it established the principle that each sovereign state should follow the religion of its monarch and accept the right of its neighbours to do likewise.

Diversity

Crucial to understanding the complexities of religion in the British Isles is the multi-national nature of the UK state. In the period after the Roman occupation, a number of kingdoms were formed in what is now called Wales but none was able to unite the area for long and gradually the English and then the Normans brought Wales under the English crown.[6] The Welsh periodically rebelled, most latterly under Owen Glendower in the early fifteenth century. Wales became part of the Kingdom of Great Britain in 1707, and then the United Kingdom of Great Britain and Ireland in 1801. Despite considerable English influx (especially in the border regions and later in industrial South Wales) the Welsh retained their language and culture. Although the English regularly disputed its independence, Scotland managed to maintain an independent kingdom until first the Union of the Crowns in 1603 (when James VI of Scotland became also James I of England, Wales and Ireland) and the Union of the Parliaments in 1707 brought the two parts of the island into a common political unit.[7] However, Scotland retained its own legal and education systems and most importantly its own church.

The English presence in Ireland dates from the twelfth century but it was not until the Reformation period that English monarchs began to impose direct control. The problem was that the Irish were largely resistant to the Reformation. In an era when rulers were fearful of anything that might provide grounds for rejecting their authority, the response to such obstinacy was increased direct imposition through military campaigns and the 'plantation' of loyal English and Scots in Ireland.

It was not only in Ireland that the uneven impact of the Reformation had political consequences. In Scotland the Reformation was genuinely popular; almost all the lowland population was converted to its principles. Remnants of the old religion lived on in the Gaelic-speaking and still-feudal highlands and islands and later monarchs tried to impose the English church model on Scotland but the mass of Scottish Christians became Presbyterians. What distinguished the Presbyterians from the Cromwellian 'Roundheads' of the Civil War period is that instead of permitting congregational autonomy (the preference of the Independents aka Congregationalists), they organised their congregations in a representative hierarchy of discipline and insisted on a common liturgical order.

The Reformation in England, and thus in Wales, which the English controlled in a way they could not control Scotland, was initially elite-led and the first changes were organisational rather than ideological. Between 1533 and 1540 Henry VIII broke with Rome because it would not approve his spouse disposal plans and, in the greatest property transfer since the Norman Conquest, he dissolved the monasteries and transferred much of their land to the parish churches and the rest to his loyal supporters.[8] Thereafter the English church was at times more or less Reformed depending on the wishes of the monarch and the court and the monarch's ability to act on these wishes.

Conflict over religious principles and the power of the monarchy led to three civil wars in England. In the first two, supporters of Parliament fought supporters of Charles I, who was executed in 1649. In the third, the Parliamentarians fought the supporters of his son and won a decisive victory at the Battle of Worcester in 1651. The exile of Charles II saw the replacement of the monarchy with first the Commonwealth of England (1649–53) and then with a Protectorate of Oliver Cromwell. It also saw the consolidation of English rule in Ireland and the establishment of the precedent that an English monarch could not govern without Parliament's consent. Although the victory of the Parliamentarians should have brought the Protestants of Scotland and England together, the United Kingdom had one state church for only a few months during the 1640s when the Westminster Parliament accepted the various templates for the beliefs, structure and ritual of a national church prepared by the Westminster Assembly of Puritan Divines. Those documents became the standards of the Church of Scotland and inform Presbyterianism to this day but the English quickly rejected them: Presbyterianism was too centralising for the English Independents and not ritualistic or hierarchical enough for those who regretted the Reformation.

With the Restoration of the monarchy in 1661, the Church of England reversed a lot of the Reformation. It did not return to Rome but it brought back episcopacy (or rule by bishops) and a good deal of pre-Reformation liturgy. The next hundred years saw systematic attempts to coerce religious conformity. The Corporation Act of 1661 required all public office holders to take communion in the Church of England. The Act of Uniformity required all clergy to be episcopally ordained. The Conventicle Act of 1664 banned dissenting religious gatherings of more than five people. The Five Mile Act of the following year banned any clergyman from going within five miles of a town from which he had been excluded for refusing to conform to the Church of England. The most mean-spirited law gave magistrates the power to take children from dissenters and give them into the care of Anglican families. Fortunately, the operation of the penal laws was never as severe as the theory. In many parts of the country dissenters were numerous or powerful enough to deter persecution and to protect those officials who declined to implement fully the penal laws. Gradually they fell into disuse and then the tide turned and they were gradually repealed.

The attempt to coerce people into the state churches (and the plural is needed because dissent from the Church of Scotland was initially met with the same reaction) was gradually abandoned for two reasons: it did not work and it was not needed. When Graham of Claverhouse shot dead Andrew Hislop in the village of Eskdalemuir in 1685 for refusing to renounce his Covenanter beliefs, he just gave the Covenanters another martyr and did little or nothing to stem either criticism of, or defection from, the Church of Scotland.[9] And it proved unnecessary, because the fear behind the desire for religious conformity proved false.

Justifying imposition was the belief that a single uniform church was essential to the stability of the state: hence the attempt to make the Irish conform to the Episcopalian Church of Ireland. To this was added a subsidiary proposition: a hierarchical church was necessary both to legitimate a hierarchical society and to sustain the institution of monarchy. As James VI succinctly put it to the Hampton Court Conference: 'I approve the calling and use of bishops in the Church, and it is my aphorism "No Bishop, no King" '.[10] In fact, rebellious Ireland aside, the British state was to prove remarkably resilient despite the lack of a common faith binding its subjects. When in 1715 James the 'Old Pretender' (the son of the James VII who had been deposed in the Glorious Revolution in favour of the Protestant Dutch Prince William) led the first Jacobite rebellion, it was crushed relatively easily, as was the attempt by his son Charles Edward Stewart 30 years later. From 1789, the French Revolution provoked new fears of political unrest and hence new demands for religious uniformity to buttress the monarchy but the state endured.

What makes the history of religion in the British Isles especially complicated is the fact that the Reformation did not, as was intended, purify but leave intact the single Christian church. Like alcohol, schism proved addictive. By encouraging individual judgement, Luther's dictum of 'every man his own monk' became 'every man his own Pope' and Protestants split repeatedly over a series of theological and organisational quarrels. The issue of congregational autonomy (which divided Presbyterians from Congregationalists/Independents) has already been mentioned. A further fault line concerned the best way to worship God: should there be a common liturgical order or should people praise God as the Holy Spirit moved them? Sects further divided over minor versions of that argument. Could instruments be used in worship? Could human words be used or, as conservative Scots Presbyterians insisted, should singing be confined to metrical translations of the divine words of the Psalms of David? Baptism was contentious. Was it actually a sacrament: that is, an act with supernatural power that radically changed the status of the person being baptised? And should it be administered to infants or should it be confined only to those old enough to understand the commitment implied?

Scots Presbyterians, who agreed about infant baptism and church order, split repeatedly over the principle of state imposition. First zealots rejected the state Church because it was not pure enough to justify it being imposed on the populace. Later, liberals split because, like the English Quakers, they could not support the principle of imposition. By imitation and migration, the Protestants of the north of Ireland acquired the English and Scottish sects and generated a few of their own.

In summary, the consequence of the Reformation was a Catholic majority in Ireland and small pockets of Catholics in England, Wales and Scotland; a semi-Protestant state church in England (where it was popular) and in Wales and Ireland (where it was not); a popular and thoroughly Protestant state church in Scotland; and a very large number of dissenting Protestant sects.

The nineteenth century

The expansion of the franchise brought religion into the electoral arena in two ways: through agenda and through class identity. Waves of religious dissent had always recruited along pre-existing lines of social division (though in some cases the class divide coincided with and was reinforced by regional interests). It was always those who enjoyed some degree of economic independence who were most free to disagree with the national church and they were the first people outside the gentry who were given the vote. Hence the general pattern that, as the proportion of the population that was allowed to express a political preference increased, support for the national churches among those expressed preferences went down. So the Reform Act of 1832, which extended the franchise to about one in six adult males, brought significant numbers of dissenters into the House of Commons, as did the 1867 act, which extended the vote to all adult male householders. Five years later the power of landlords to coerce their tenants was drastically reduced with the introduction of the secret ballot. Finally, the 1884 act extended the vote to 60 per cent of adult males.

This expansion of the electoral base gave new power to those who objected to two aspects of the state church system. Repeal of the worst of the penal laws had liberated people from the obviously punitive parts of state support for the national churches but there was still the issue of social status: the status both of a particular church and by implication of those who adhered to it. This was an especially sore point in Ireland and Wales, where the Anglican Church was typically seen as the ideological arm of English oppression. Second, there was the universal problem of funding. Essentially the Church of Scotland and the Church of England (and thus the Church of Wales and the Church of Ireland) were funded by a land tax: a tithe payable either in agricultural produce or in money equivalent. Naturally the dissenters objected to financing a religion they rejected on principle. Gradually, at various points in the nineteenth century and early twentieth, the most pressing elements of these irritants were removed. The Church of Ireland was disestablished in 1871, its sister church in Wales was disestablished in 1914, and gradually the financial burden of the Church of England and Church of Scotland was shifted from the population at large to their adherents.[11] That the state churches had their tax revenues turned into very large capital sums that generated considerable interest gave them a financial advantage over their competitors and they retained symbolically important privileges but the gradual process of changing religious affiliation from a national characteristic to a personal preference was pretty well complete by the end of the nineteenth century.

The Lutheran Church of Sweden was until 2000 the national church in the sense that every Swede was treated as a member, paid for it through taxation, and was entitled to its services. The 1860 innovation of allowing Swedes to leave it was hedged by the requirement to join another of a short list of acceptable Christian bodies: an obstacle not removed till 1951. Until 1964 the position of the Lutheran Church in Norway was similar. As an international body the Roman Catholic Church rejected the formation of autonomous national bodies and favoured protecting its local interests through a system of concordats with individual states. However, because most European Catholic states are overwhelmingly Catholic, the Church has managed to exert considerable influence on political and social life, even in France with its history of anti-clerical republicanism. The British system of two different national churches and a great deal of tolerated dissent set it apart from its European neighbours but, for a short period in the late nineteenth century, it did manage to produce something of a harmonic coincidence of religious and national identity. Once the major grievances of dissenters had been dealt with, the Church of Scotland, its Presbyterian rivals, most Welsh and English dissenters, and the 'low' or Protestant end of the Church of England could find, if not exactly common cause, then at least a vague sense of common identity in evangelical Protestantism, Imperial mission and a sense of British self-aggrandisement. In some respects the reign of Queen Victoria was a period of great intellectual turmoil, with Darwinism apparently threatening religion and Low Church (that is, really Protestant) and High Church (quasi-Catholic) Anglicans battling for the soul of the Church of England. Nonetheless there was a sense among the middle classes that the Greatness of Great Britain was a consequence of the British character: commonsensical rather than philosophical, practical rather than emotional, self-reliant but loyal. This was the common religion expressed in coronations and state burials and in the war memorials that were erected in every town, village and hamlet after the First World War.[12] But lacking a common church framework and any serious theological under-pinning, it was a very weak sense of identity and those who wished to deepen it were regarded with suspicion as 'enthusiasts'. Victoria herself was opposed to making public professions of faith. When Edward Benson became Archbishop of Canterbury in 1883, he was approached by a group of aristocratic ladies to lead a weekly prayer meeting at Lambeth Palace. The Duchess of Leeds and her friends were concerned about the moral decay of London and thought that the upper classes should set an example. When invited to attend these services, the Princess of Wales felt obliged to consult her mother-in-law.

> The Queen did not like the idea, for in spite of her own firm religious convictions and the faith of which she was the Defender, religion was not a thing to be mixed up with life, nor could she, by any possible elasticity of terms, be called devotional. To go to church or chapel on Sunday mornings with unfailing regularity, to ask God's blessing on launched ships, docks, regimental colours and foundation-stones, to attend all family christenings, marriages, funerals and anniversary services compris the dəsum of public religious observances ... 'I can't understand', she said, 'why princesses should want to go to Lambeth meetings. It's all sacerdotal. I can't think what it's all about ... most extraordinary'.[13]

The twentieth century

The departure of the Irish Free State in 1922 removed a large part of the UK's Catholic population. What was now formally the United Kingdom of Great

Britain (that is, England, Wales and Scotland) and Northern Ireland was an over-whelmingly Protestant Christian state. In 1930, over 80 per cent of the popula-tion had been baptised and about 30 per cent of the adult population was in membership of some church. The Anglicans were the largest community at four million, Catholics and Presbyterians each had around two million, and other Protestant denominations and sects (of which there were a very large number) totalled something similar.[14] The one innovation was the arrival, in that ruck of small sects, of Pentecostalism. The label refers to an event described in the New Testament book of the *Acts of the Apostles* when the Holy Spirit gave the apos-tles the gift of being simultaneously comprehensible to people from a wide variety of different language backgrounds. Pentecostalists believe that such 'gifts of the Spirit' as speaking in tongues, healing and prophesying, which most Christians believe were confined to the contemporaries of Jesus, are available today for those who believe in them. The modern Pentecostal movement began in the USA in 1910 and by the 1930s was present in the UK in the shape of the Elim Four Square Gospel Church, the Assemblies of God, and the Apostolic Church.[15] Although the movement was small, it was a precursor of the 1970s charismatic movement and the rise of the black Pentecostal churches.

In the early twentieth century, Christianity's reach was considerably greater than the membership figures suggest. Far more people regularly attended church than were members. With an enrolment that was around 50 per cent larger than the number of adult church members, Sunday schools clearly attracted the chil-dren of non-churchgoers as did para-church organisations such as the Boys Brigade, the Scouts and the Girl Guides. Naturally Catholic and Anglican day schools promoted Christianity but so too did the state schools.

Generally speaking the national fringes were more religious than England, and within England, the peripheries were more religious than the Home Counties and the industrial centre. Partly this reflected the uneven impact of the social forces that caused secularisation.[16] Partly it was a function of various local ten-sions. In Northern Ireland religious affiliation was high because it was tied up with the long battle over Irish independence. Scotland (and parts of the North West of England) had minor versions of Ulster's Protestant–Catholic conflicts. Scotland's religious culture was also stimulated by enduring and bitter argu-ments over the status of the national church, as was that of Wales, which had the added dimension of ethnic conflict between the Welsh (and Welsh speakers) concentrated in various Protestant sects and the recently dis-established Church of Wales. That their own arguments caused the national fringes to be more reli-gious than England was reinforced by a reflexive awareness of that difference. Many Scots, Northern Irish and Welsh saw themselves as more religious than the English, and built that into contrasting stereotypes of national character.

From the 1930s to the 1960s, the two main changes were secularisation and the growth of Catholicism. The precise dating of the decline of the main Christian churches remains contentious because scholars use different measures of religious interest and variously report gross figures or percentages of the available population.[17] However, the general picture is clear. Church attendance had been declining as a proportion of the available population since at least 1851, when the Census of Religious Worship showed that between 40 and 60 per cent attended church on Sunday 30 March. We cannot be more specific because the census recorded attendances rather than attendees and so we have to allow for people attending twice or even three times. If we take membership (and that notion is a little difficult to apply to Anglicans and Catholics, who regard all those who have been baptised, even if they subsequently do nothing to maintain a connection, as members), the peak is around the first decade of the twentieth century. Nonetheless, most of those who were not members and never attended still claimed some church identity. In the Oxfordshire market town of Banbury in the 1950s, for example, although church membership was only a quarter of the adult population and attendance less, over 97 per cent of survey respondents claimed some church connection.[18] And if they had no particular church connection, people still expected to be able to avail themselves of the services of the church for baptisms, weddings and funerals.

Although it never came close to compensating for the decline in the state churches and nonconformist sects and denominations, the other major change in the first half of the century was the increase in Catholic numbers. Some of this was due to conversion. Among a narrow slice of the English upper classes, Catholicism, with its incense, arcane ritual, furtiveness and emphasis on sin, had a certain almost smutty appeal; parts of Evelyn Waugh's *Brideshead Revisited* catch the tone. And the Catholic Church's insistence on its superiority brought in a regular stream of converts from what would otherwise have been mixed marriages. But the main source of Catholic growth was Irish migration. In 1911, 1 per cent of the residents of England and Wales were Irish-born; a proportion that grew steadily with every census. This migration allowed the Catholic community to grow from about 5 per cent of the population in 1851 to around 11 per cent in 1971. Most importantly, the Irish were more religious than their British coreligionists and considerably more conservative in their general attitudes.[19]

The migration of West Indians to the UK from the late 1950s added a little variety to the country's religious composition – many West Indians were Pentecostal Christians – but it was not till the 1970s that the backwash of the Empire made Britain what we know call multi-cultural. Britain's only pre-Empire non-Christian population, the Jews, were few in number. The first British Jews had been expelled in 1290. Their return dates from the 1660s but the largest settlement came in the 1880s with Jews escaping persecution in Russia. In the late nineteenth century there were 46,000 Jews in England; by 2001 there were 267,000 in an ageing community, many of whose members married out and secularised.[20] The majority of Muslims and Hindus came originally from the Indian sub-continent. In the late 1950s and 1960s migration from Pakistan and India was encouraged to provide labour shortages in the British steel and textile industries (which explains the high concentrations in the North West of England) and in the National Health Service.[21] Some Muslims and Hindus came to Britain via Africa. In the heyday of Empire, Asians settled in East Africa; some staffing imperial offices; others running businesses that supported the Imperial presence.[22] These communities became increasingly threatened as newly independent African governments in Tanzania, Kenya and Uganda sought a scapegoat for their economic and political failures. In 1971, 50,000 Ugandan Asians were expelled from the country by the military dictator, Idi Amin, and half of them settled in Britain.

The pattern of Sikh migration was similar. In the late 1950s and 1960s single men came direct from the Punjab to Britain to work in manufacturing and textile industries. Although initially intending to return, many stayed and brought their families before the 1968 tightening of immigration laws. There was also two-step migration as Sikhs were among those Asians expelled from East Africa.[23]

Religion in 2001

Although Irish censuses had asked for religious identity since 1861 and there had been a census of attendance at places of worship in 1851, the 2001 census was the first to ask the British their religion and the topic was considered sufficiently sensitive that the religion questions were the only ones that were optional. Fortunately, at 7 per cent, the number who chose not to answer is small enough that we can suppose the overall results, described in Table 1.1, to be reasonably accurate.

Britain remains a nominally Christian country. The second largest group after the Christians are those who declared they had no religion, who at 15.5 per cent dwarf any religious minority. The third largest bloc are the Muslims, with 1.6 million nominal adherents.[24] Quite what these nominal figures represent is not at all obvious. It certainly does not mean, as many unscrupulous church representatives now claim, that Britain is Christian in the sense that my local Baptist Church is Christian.

There are three good reasons for being sceptical about these nominal identifications. First, although all Christian churches require or most strenuously

Table 1.1 United Kingdom population by religion, Census, 2001

	Thousands	*(%)*
Christian	42,079	71.6
Buddhist	152	0.3
Hindu	559	1.0
Jewish	267	0.5
Muslim	1,591	2.7
Sikh	336	0.6
Other religion	179	0.3
All religions	*45,163*	*76.8*
No religion	9,104	15.5
Not stated	4,289	7.3
All no religion/not stated	*13,626*	*23.2*
Base	*58,789*	*100*

Source: Census, April 2001, Office for National Statistics.

encourage their adherents to attend, the number of census Christians is ten times the number that attends Christian churches. Second, the number is considerably higher than that suggested by large-scale and well-run social surveys. Third, the relative proportions of Christians in the various parts of the United Kingdom do not match the relative proportions of church attendees. Although the figures have been converging as they decline, church attendance is more common in Scotland than in England and Wales but the census showed a higher Christian proportion for England and Wales (at 72 per cent) than for Scotland (at 67 per cent).

The first point to note about the 2001 census is that the forms were normally completed by a single 'household reference person' (or HRP). As it would be a surprise if the HRP did not impute his or her religious identity to all members of the family (irrespective of their levels of commitment) and as old people are more likely to be religious than young people, we must expect that the system exaggerates the popularity of the major religious traditions and under-estimates the size of both the non-religious population and those who belong to non-ethnic minority religions.

The explanation for the national discrepancies almost certainly lies in a combination of technical differences in the census forms and important differences in the social background to the administration of the census. The person completing the census form in England and Wales was asked in Question 8 'What is your ethnic group?' and offered the options of White, Mixed, Asian or Asian British, Black or Black British, and Chinese or other Ethnic group, with each of those headings further sub-divided. That question was immediately followed by 'What is your religion?', with the choices 'None, Christian (including Church of England, Catholic, Protestant and all other Christian denominations), Buddhist, Hindu, Jewish, Muslim, Sikh, Any other religion (please write in)'. The wording, placing and prompts for the religion question seems to have encouraged HRPs to read it as an extension of the question about ethnicity. In the Scotland form, the religion question did not follow the ethnicity one and it asked, 'What religion, religious denomination or body do you belong to?' and offered the prompts: 'None, Church of Scotland, Roman Catholic, Other Christian (please write in), Buddhist, Hindu, Jewish, Muslim, Sikh, Another religion (please write in)'. That wording and placement seems much more likely to cause HRPs to think of religion as an acquired rather than as a genetically transmitted characteristic: an expression of personal commitment rather than of heritage.

The second major difference is context. One reason why fewer non-churchgoing Scots may have felt impelled to assert their nominal Christian identity is that there are far fewer non-Christians in Scotland (less than one-third of the proportion in England) and they are so concentrated as to be a significant part of the cultural landscape only in one part of Glasgow. Scottish problems with identity are focused more on relations with the English than on relations with Muslims.

Moving from nominal identification with a religious tradition to a narrower and more active notion of affiliation is not simple. There are no structures for Islam, Hinduism or Sikhism comparable to Christian denominations that collect data on collective worship numbers or 'members'. Hence we are reliant on surveys, with their attendant problem of respondents exaggerating expected or socially desirable responses. The largest and most reliable survey asked in 2005 'What is your religion even if you are not practising?' and 'Do you consider you are actively practising your religion?' Of the Muslims, Hindus and Sikhs, just over 70 per cent were actively practising; for Christians the figure was only 31 per cent.[25] Such a high figure for religious observance is generally not repeated in polls that ask more specific questions. For example, a 2006 NOP poll found that, although 78 per cent of British Muslims said their religion was 'very important' to them, 48 per cent said they never attended a mosque, with another 6 per cent saying they only attended for special occasions.[26] A 2009 poll of Muslims in Birmingham found that only 10 per cent consistently prayed five times a day, 67 per cent did not and 23 per cent said they did so 'sometimes'.[27]

We are on surer ground with the Christian nominals. A series of censuses of church attendance show that the proportion of the British population that attended church on a typical Sunday in May 2005 was 6.8 per cent, down from 12 per cent in 1979, 10 per cent in 1989 and 8 per cent in 1998.[28] We lack comparable data for Northern Ireland, though we can be sure both that it is higher and that is shows the same downward trajectory.

The relative popularity of different strands of Christianity in England and Wales is shown in Table 1.2. There are two novelties in this spread worth noting. First the Pentecostal sector has grown considerably, largely because of migration from West Africa and from Nigeria in particular. Second, the charismatic and independent evangelical sector has grown. Its churches often pointedly reject association with previous denominations by giving themselves generic names such as the Deeside Christian Fellowship or the Banbury Community Church. Although autonomous, they are often linked in loose networks and they are defined as much by their informality of dress, demeanour and worship styles – the electronic pop group having replaced the organ – as by their theology. This sector grew during the 1980s, mostly by recruiting from more traditional conservative Protestant sects, but contracted towards the end of the 1990s.

Table 1.2 Church members by church type, England and Wales, 2007

	Church members (%)
Anglican	28
Catholic	27
Charismatic and Independent Evangelical	10
Other	9
Methodist	9
Pentecostal	9
Baptist	8
Total	100

The decline in the core of British churchgoers has been accompanied by a related change that has considerable implications for the social and political influence of religion: the faster decline of Christianity's penumbra. In 1900 the institutional churches were the centre of a web of influence. Non-members attended sporadically. A majority of children would have attended Sunday school and all would have been introduced to Christian beliefs at school. Almost everyone would have been involved in the religious legitimisation of rites of passage: children were baptised in church and couples were married in church. By the end of the twentieth century, Sunday schools taught only the children of church members and state schools taught about competing religions in even-handed terms. In 1933, the number of babies baptised in the Church of England was more than three-quarters of live births. In 2000 it was 22 per cent; a decline nowhere near offset by the growth of other churches.[29] In 1900, 84 per cent of marriages were religious ceremonies; in 2007 it was just 34 per cent.[30]

This decline in popular engagement with organised religion has had the expected effects on the nation's stock of religious capital. Almost three-quarters of Britons may describe themselves as Christian, but very few of them can put any religious content to that term. Opinion polls and attitude surveys show large numbers willing to say they believe in a wide variety of supernatural entities and experiences but very little of this is Christian.

Secularisation, secularism and secularity

At the risk of scandalising historians I will summarise the above history of religion in Britain by forcing it into three periods. The internal complexities prevent us fixing identifying clear dates for those periods but we can recognise the following sequence of types of dominant religious culture. The first period, which ended around 1800, was an era of communal organic religion, the property of an ethnic, national or regional group, imputed to or imposed upon all those born into the group. By the nineteenth century, for most people religion had become a matter of voluntary association and, with varying degrees of enthusiasm, most people voluntarily chose one. By the third quarter of the twentieth century, Britain was a largely secular society with a culture of wide-scale religious indifference, enlivened by residues of the first two periods. Although communal organic Christianity has gone, migration has brought significant minorities of people whose faith is still of the communal organic kind. And if we double the number of regular churchgoers to include occasional visitors to church, the voluntary association type of religion continues to engage perhaps 10 to 12 per cent of the population. With around 80 per cent of the population showing no interest in any form of religion, it seems entirely sensible to describe the United Kingdom as a largely secular society.[31]

However, it is important to distinguish secularity as 'the condition of being secular' from secularism as an ideological commitment to promoting secularity. The decline of religion in Britain (and the associated relegation of religion to the private sphere) owes almost nothing to anti-clerical sentiment. As we will see in

Chapters 8 and 10, Christian leaders often complain about the 'marginalisation' of religion as though some agent has been doing the marginalising. There is not space here to explain secularisation but if we are to understand the relationship between religion and politics, it is important to appreciate how little of Britain's secularity is due to secularism. The anti-clericalism of the French Revolution was almost entirely absent from British arguments about religion, which were concerned primarily with the privileges of particular churches and not with the virtue of religion per se. It was not rationalists and secular humanists who dismantled the structure and the philosophy of a state-imposed national religion. That was done by dissenting Christians, and many of those were not liberals. Most Scottish sects were perfectly happy with the idea of enforcing religious uniformity when they hoped that they would be in a position to do the enforcing. Each gradually found virtue in religious toleration when it became clear that they were not going to win. The increasingly neutral state was not the conscious work of atheists; it was the unintended consequence of religious schism and religious self-interest.

This chapter has been intended as a brief explanation of the current religious composition of the United Kingdom. The next will consider the political correlates and consequences of religion.

2   The politics of religion

Introduction

An elderly friend pastors a Welsh-speaking chapel in Liverpool. He is originally from Llangollen, Bala. He is a Welsh speaker and a Welsh nationalist and has always regarded his Welshness and his Methodism is inexorably inter-twined and thus he leans towards Plaid Cymru. As a Christian he is opposed to free market economics and is thus attracted to the social reform politics of the Labour party but he is also keen on individual responsibility and firmly opposed to drinking and gambling, which set him against the last Labour government's plans for a 'super-casino' in Liverpool and for continental drinking hours. Furthermore, his dislike of Islam, which he traces both to his progressive attitude to gender roles and to his preference for Christianity, makes him suspicious of much of the last government's multi-culturalism.

That one example alone gives us some idea of the complexity of the possible links between religion and politics. But complexity is no friend of clarity and to give some shape to this chapter, I will press a wide range of material into three headings. I will consider the part that religion has played in ethnic or national identities, the role of religion in ethnic minority politics, and the politics of religious values.

Ethnic identity and Christian religion

One of the most common ways in which religion becomes politically significant is through identifying and legitimating a large social unit such as a people sharing a common language. It is not an accident that nations (or populations bidding for nation status) tend to share a common religion. Religions generally spread through but not beyond a population that has some common characteristics (such as a shared language, tribal identity or governmental structure). Once a faith becomes part of what distinguishes one people from another, it can do the important ideological work of making those people feel justified. For a dominant population, religion can provide a satisfying explanation of privilege and power. People feel better if they can attribute their position to divine approval rather than greater firepower. A shared faith can also console a subordinate people by promising them that they will eventually be rewarded. The Afrikaans settlers in southern Africa used their common Calvinism in both ways: to justify their domination over the various African tribes with which they competed and to comfort themselves when they were dominated by the British.[1]

While interviewing Tony Blair in 2003, an American journalist asked a question about his religion. Blair's famously aggressive press secretary Alistair Campbell quickly cut in with 'We don't do God. Sorry. We don't do God,' and the matter was dropped.[2] Actually Blair was rather partial to doing God. Once he left office he converted to Catholicism and took to presenting himself as a defender of the social virtues of religion in general. In this new role he inadvertently produced one piece of self-refutation so perfect that, though it has no relevance to this chapter, it must be repeated. In November 2010 Blair debated the merits of faith with the well-known atheist and journalist Christopher Hitchens. While listing all the good works that religious people did, Blair referred to the efforts religious groups in Northern Ireland made 'to bridge the religious divide'![3] Hitchens left a long pause for the audience to work it out before asking who created the religious divide.

Whatever Blair's personal preferences, his press secretary had a better understanding of modern British political culture. Unlike their American counterparts, twentieth-century British premiers have not been personally pious nor have they been fond of linking religion and national identity. Matters were different in the eighteenth and nineteenth centuries, especially if Britain was at war with Catholic powers. As noted in the previous chapter, in the second half of the nineteenth century, most dissenting churches were happy to join the state churches in promoting a vaguely Protestant piety as part of a sense of Britishness, especially when it was presented to the world as Imperialism.[4]

The most enthusiastic carrier of this popular Protestant identity was the Orange Order, a fraternal association of mostly working-class men, that was popular in such parts of Britain as Liverpool and Glasgow where there was significant Irish settlement.[5] More significant for the country as a whole was the enthusiastic work done by the major Christian churches, which competed with each other to provide a very large number of para-church associations and activities. The churches created Sunday schools, temperance associations, boys' clubs, penny savings banks, mutual insurance clubs, lending libraries, male voice choirs, brass bands, operatic societies, and associations to improve every imaginable aspect of modern life. With Victoria on the throne, the second half of the nineteenth century saw a boom in national state ceremonies (often repeated in local communities) that ritually linked Protestantism, the monarchy and the nation.[6]

With the churches apparently flourishing, it was easy to overlook the fact that religious diversity was eroding the structural basis for a shared religio-ethnic British identity but some important institutions could see which way the wind was blowing. For the Conservative party, the great challenge of the nineteenth century was to manage the consequence of the Great Reform Act and one of its most popular responses was the Primrose League (so-named after Benjamin

Disraeli's favourite flower).[7] The League sponsored a wide range of social activities that were easily accessible to ordinary people and proved very successful in convincing large numbers of middle-and working-class people to identify a common interest with the ruling parliamentary elite as members of a British patriotic nation. In the early 1890s, it had well over a million members and at the time enjoyed more support than the trade union movement.[8] What is remarkable is that the League went out of its way to avoid militant Protestantism. Although serving God figured in its list of aims, it very deliberately shunned the Orange Order, which it saw as far too disruptive. As well as courting Nonconformists, the League worked hard to incorporate Catholics and Jews. An important signal was sent by the involvement of the Duke of Norfolk, England's leading Catholic. In an attempt to rise above the more recent religious and political divisions and to imply an ancient and enduring British unity that predated the Reformation, the League adopted archaic language. Its members were known as 'Dames' and 'Knights' and its branches were 'Habitations'.

Andrew Bonar Law, who became Conservative party leader in 1911 and was briefly Prime Minister in the early 1920s, was the last Conservative leader who had any sort of sentimental attachment to the idea of the United Kingdom as a political unit defined by a common religion. And he was not English. He was born in New Brunswick, Canada, where his father, an Ulsterman from Coleraine, was a Presbyterian minister. After his mother died he was raised by her sister, who brought him back to the family home in Glasgow. The Kidstons were wealthy bankers; they were also senior figures in the Conservative party. Bonar Law's roots were in Ulster-Scots Presbyterianism. It is no surprise that late in life he wrote, 'Before the war there were only two things which I really cared for as matters of conviction, the rest was mainly a game. One of these was tariff reform; the other was fair play for Ulster, and I feel as strongly about it as I did then'.[9] Subsequent Conservative leaders – Neville Chamberlain, Winston Churchill, Harold Macmillan, Alex Douglas Hume, Edward Heath – showed no interest in religion. Margaret Thatcher had no particular Christian faith and her closest ally, Norman Tebbit, was a professed atheist.[10] When John Major struggled to explain what England meant to him, his only mention of religion came in a quotation from something George Orwell had said 50 years earlier. In 1993, Major told fellow Conservatives:

> Fifty years from now Britain will still be the country of long shadows on county grounds, warm beer, invincible green suburbs, dog lovers and pools fillers and, as George Orwell said, 'old maids bicycling to Holy Communion through the morning mist' and, if we get our way, Shakespeare will still be read even in school.[11]

Major could not simply assert the importance to the country of the continuity provided by the Book of Common Prayer offices performed daily in the state church; his Anglicanism seems to have been largely nominal. Instead he made the point in a roundabout way, without committing himself to it, by quoting a humorous remark (albeit an affectionate one) made by a famous socialist.

British nationalist sentiment to the right of the Conservative party has been equally devoid of religion. Sir James Goldsmith, the millionaire founder of the UK Referendum Party, launched to contest the 1997 general election on a platform of demanding a referendum on membership of the European Union, was Jewish by birth but was not known to have any particular faith.[12] His daughter, Jemima, married a famous Pakistan cricketer and converted to Islam for the duration of her marriage. The Referendum Party made no mention of religion in its reasons for wanting to preserve Britain from Europe. The *Daily Telegraph*, the best-selling serious conservative newspaper, now has considerable trouble sorting out a consistent attitude towards Christianity. On the one hand it mourns the decline of the Church of England and the loss of ancient churches, which the Church cannot afford to maintain. On the other hand, most of its readers and most of its staff are not personally religious and, significantly, leading columnists such as Simon Heffer now feel free to say so. When launching its *Save Britain's Churches* campaign it made its pitch, not on religious grounds but on some vague notion of social cohesion. Like the pub and the village shop, the church is presented as the centre of community life. Unfortunately – for all three institutions – this is empty rhetoric. The pubs and post offices are closing because people no longer use their services; and the same is true of the churches. If they were indeed the centre of community life, there would be no need to campaign for their preservation.

One powerful mark of the secularisation of the general culture is the declining role of religion in chauvinism. Let us consider responses to two waves of immigration separated by about a century. From the middle of the nineteenth century large numbers of Irish people migrated to Britain. Lots of native Britons objected to the immigrants and accused them of a variety of social and economic vices. They were stealing our jobs and they were undercutting trade union power by working for less money than the natives were being paid or they were a drain on social welfare or both.

What was distinctive about anti-Irish sentiment was that much of it was also anti-Catholic. Organisations campaigned against the immigrants on the grounds that their corrupt faith would subvert the religion that since the Glorious Revolution had made Britain great. For a brief period in the 1930s anti-Catholic and anti-Irish parties won seats in the local councils in Glasgow, Edinburgh and Liverpool and it seemed that anti-Catholicism would be as popular in Britain as fascism was in continental Europe. But the Scottish Protestant League and Protestant Action fell as quickly as they had risen and by the end of the 1930s, anti-Catholicism was a spent force.[13]

Move forward to the end of the twentieth century. In the late 1950s and 1960s West Indians migrated to Britain. In the 1970s they were joined by large numbers of Hindus, Sikhs and Muslims. There was a great deal of hostility. Racist parties such as the National Front were formed and, as with the Irish, there were calls for repatriation but this time the bigots did not try to enlist God. That most of the West Indians were Christians meant there was no opportunity to mobilise religious sentiments against them but the Asian sub-continent immigrants were followers of strange Gods. Some racists joined liberal Christians and secularists in criticising *secular* aspects of Muslim culture but the British National Party (BNP) did not campaign against Pakistanis on the grounds that they worshipped the wrong God. According to its 2003 manifesto: 'the BNP takes no particular religious position. The BNP would protect the British tradition of separating church and state'.[14] In 2006 one BNP activist ordained himself and founded the Christian Council of Britain but he seems to have been the only member.[15] That Richard West had to fabricate a movement of racist Christians rather makes my point.

The absence of an effective British religio-ethnic identity is simply explained. Those classes most attracted to chauvinism and xenophobia are least likely to be religious and the major churches are by and large liberal. That is, the social-structural circumstances for creating and maintaining a sense of Britain as one of God's most favoured peoples are missing.

If we move down a level from the UK to its component parts, we find circumstances better suited to the promotion of a shared religio-ethnic identity but internal divisions remain a problem, as does the extent of secularisation. Additionally, as is explained in detail in Chapter 7, the centralised nature of British politics meant that locally significant groups in the peripheries lacked the power to turn local preferences into actions that would increase religio-ethnic animosity. Northern Ireland is the exception. There, the argument over the constitutional status of Ireland and the relative power and status of groups identified by religion has reinforced opposing sectarian identities. The relative autonomy of the Stormont state from 1928 to 1972 (when the parliament was closed down by the Westminster government) gave Ulster Unionists the power to exacerbate grievances and to maintain the structural divisions that supported competing identities.[16] With the exception of the tiny Alliance party, all of Northern Ireland's indigenous political parties are sectarian, in composition if not in intent.[17] But even here we can see the effect of a lack of sovereign power. The British government was able to close the Stormont parliament and it was able eventually to impose on Northern Ireland's politicians a settlement that very few of them would have freely chosen.

Scotland's ability to create and sustain a shared religio-ethnic identity was fatally undermined by internal divisions. The social, political, economic and cultural gulf between the Anglophone modern Lowlands and Gaelic-speaking feudal Highlands has kept the two parts of Scotland out of step at every stage in religious evolution. In the seventeenth and eighteenth centuries, when the Lowlands were Protestant, the Highlands were Catholic. The armies of the 1715 and 1745 Jacobite risings found support in the Highlands but the towns of the Lowlands were barred against them. By the time the Highlands converted to evangelical Protestantism in the nineteenth century, the Lowlands were giving it up. The migration from Ireland in the later nineteenth and early twentieth centuries brought the seeds of Ireland's sectarian conflict but, as we will see in Chapter 4, they fell on rather stony ground. The majority of those who possessed the right religion to actually care about Popery were in the Highlands and Islands, remote from the areas where the papists settled. The majority of those who competed with the immigrants and hence might blame them for their poverty and job insecurity were not serious Christians. The lack of internal cohesion was exacerbated by Scotland's subordination to England. Many Scots Unionists were temperamentally anti-Catholic but their party nationally was not. In addition, on grounds similar to the English nonconformist support for the Liberal party, many evangelical Scots were Liberals rather than Unionists.

When Scottish nationalism became a serious force in the 1970s, it was clear that it could not make Presbyterianism a central plank of its image of Scotland. To succeed the Scottish National party (SNP) had to win seats in the industrial Lowlands and that meant accommodating Catholic Scots and Scots of no religion. Billy Wolfe, who had been SNP leader during its 1970s breakthrough, was party president in 1982. He was also an elder of the Church of Scotland. Wearing that hat, he voiced his opposition to the impending Pope's visit to Scotland in the Kirk's magazine. Leading SNP figures were appalled.

> The row then died down, although the SNP lost its deposit in the Hillhead by-election. Then, the following month, Wolfe wrote another letter, this time to the *Scotsman*, expressing concern that the predominantly Protestant Falkland islanders might fall under the control of a 'cruel and ruthless Fascist dictatorship of a Roman Catholic State'. Coming as it did on the eve of elections to Scotland's regional local authorities, the SNP was once again plunged into crisis. Alan McKinney, the SNP's National Organiser, told Wolfe that his 'continuing attack on the Roman Catholic Church is causing great concern within the Party'. 'I have spent the last three hours,' he wrote, 'dealing with telephone calls from Press, ministers, Nationalists and members of the public attempting to staunch the wound you have opened' …

Gordon Wilson, the SNP Convenor, was also furious, writing to Wolfe to condemn his 'bigoted anti-catholic views' and asking him to resign as party president. Wilson also wrote to Cardinal Gray to apologise.[18] It took many years of hard diplomacy, particularly by Alex Salmond when he became party leader, to win the confidence of Scots Catholics. It is an ironic sign of the times that Wolfe later gave up Christianity altogether, married a Catholic, and spent his final years promoting alternative spirituality.

Welsh nationalism was similarly constrained in any reliance on religion. In the evangelical revivals of 1859 and 1904 religion benefitted considerably from its attachment to Welsh (or at least anti-English) sentiment but the relationship did not work the other way round. Much of the drive of Welsh dissent was secularised and diverted into support for the Labour party. The disestablishment of the Episcopalian Church of Wales freed it from its role as representative of the English and of landed interests and allowed it to become a genuinely Welsh institution. The lines of religious division, of language, and of party affiliation no longer matched so that the Welshness that Plaid Cymru promotes no longer has a religious component.[19]

Although it may seem obvious, it is worth stressing the importance of homogeneity for the maintenance of a shared religious identity. It is useful if the 'other' against which a people habitually defines itself has a competing religious identity but it is essential for the people to share a single religion and to be reasonably committed to it. This is especially the case if the religion in question is Protestant rather than Catholic or Orthodox. Because Catholicism and Orthodoxy permit the transfer of religious merit and see themselves as serving the entire people, degrees of religious observance are not necessarily an embarrassment to the claim that the people enjoy particular favour in the eyes of God. That many of those people have an attachment to the church that is at best nominal is not such a problem if the Church sees itself as doing religious work on their behalf. The Protestant insistence that only individuals, not communities, can be saved makes it difficult to believe that the Scots or the Welsh are, as a whole, favoured by God.

It may seem ironic but it follows logically that the most religious people tend to have the greatest trouble believing in the divine election of a nation or a race. In the nineteenth century, when about half the adult Protestants of Ulster were churchgoers, very large numbers of clergymen were active in the Orange Order. As churchgoing declined (and even more pointedly, when the nominal Protestants of the loyalist terror groups matched the IRA for violence) it became harder for religious officials to remain in an organisation that claimed religious grounds for valorising an ethnic group. Hence there are now very few Church of Ireland or Irish Presbyterian clergy in the Orange Order. There was a very pointed division within the senior ranks of Ian Paisley's supporters in Northern Ireland: his party activists were Orange but his clergy were not. In 2005, three-quarters of the Democratic Unionist members of the Stormont Legislative Assembly, but just one-tenth of the ministers of his Free Presbyterian Church were members of the Orange Order.[20] As religion declines those who remain religious become ever more critical of those who share their ethnicity or nationality but not their faith. Pastor Jack Glass of Glasgow, who to his intense annoyance was often described as 'Scotland's Ian Paisley', was a gifted anti-Catholic preacher. Although he fully supported the Orange Order's political agenda, he was often highly critical of the Orange Order's failure to live up to its religious rhetoric. Typical of his critique was the following: 'See the Bible? The Orangemen carry it on parade. Up at the front. And they have a plastic cover on it. They say it's to keep the rain out. Well, it isnae. It's to keep the Orangemen out!' And if religiously inspired militant Protestants such as Glass hesitate to criticise those who only nominally share their faith, they are quickly accused of hypocrisy.

To summarise, the internal divisions of the United Kingdom, and the even greater divisions within the religious culture of its constituent parts, have prevented religion playing any great part in modern British identity. Of the provincial and national fringes, only in Northern Ireland has religious identity played any enduring role in community identities. In Wales and Scotland modern nationalism has been largely secular.

Migrant minority politics

The characteristic feature of the politics of Britain's migrant religious minorities is that their position in the social structure has disposed them to support the wrong party. As we see with European Christian Democrat parties, Catholics at home, in the majority, tend to the Right.[21] When homogenously Catholic states such as France, Spain, Portugal and Italy divided, the Church and the faithful were on the conservative side. In France in the 1790s they supported the *Ancien Régime*; in Spain in the 1930s they supported General Francisco Franco and the Falange; in Portugal they supported António de Oliveira Salazar and the Estado Novo; and in Italy they supported Benito Mussolini's Fascists. Although there were notable exceptions in what was called 'liberation theology', in most Latin America countries in the 1950s and 1960s, as Billy Wolfe of the SNP observed to his party's cost, the Church and it most loyal supporters were to be found in the side of the military dictators.

In part this reflects the organisational interests of the Catholic Church. As a major social institution that claims to encompass and represent the entire people, the Church is generally on comfortable terms with other centres of power such as the armed forces, capital, and the major landowners and generally in favour of the status quo. It may sympathise with the poor and dispossessed but that sympathy will generally take the form of charity rather than encouraging the poor to rebel.

The naturally conservative stance of the Church is reinforced by the anti-clericalism of the political Left. This is not just a matter of relative placing: because the Church is on the Right, left-wing forces become anti-clerical and vice-versa. There are also independent ideological components. Marxists have always had a clear theoretical objection to religion as the opiate of the masses; less doctrinaire radical groups have simply seen the Catholic Church as an obstacle to change. The core demands of the Left – initially for democratic representation and later for social controls on the market – are typically accompanied by a range of innovative demands: greater sexual freedom, the liberation of women from constraining gender roles, respect for religious, ethnic and linguistic minorities, greater artistic licence, freedom of the press and the like. Many of those demands will conflict with the Catholic Church's teachings. All of the above explains Catholicism's general leaning to the Right.

When Catholics were a migrant minority, they adopted a very different political posture. Irish migrants to the USA, entering the labour market at the bottom, with little capital and few professional skills, aligned themselves with the labour unions and with the Democratic party. The political power they thus acquired offered a channel of upward social mobility that eventually saw John, Ted and Robert Kennedy, Daniel Moynihan, Tip O'Neill and others rivalling the WASP hegemony represented by the Bush family.

The political history of the Irish in Britain shows the same process in a minor key. Once the Irish Free State had been created in 1922, there was no point in the Irish in Britain voting for Irish parties and they pursued their interests through the trade unions and the Labour party. The pull of common class inter-ests was accompanied by a definite push in that direction. The long Irish crisis had reinforced the Protestant sympathies of what was now the Conservative and Unionist Party, and despite their support for Irish independence, many Liberals were evangelical Protestants. The one clearly religious interest was the state funding of Catholic schools. Once this was achieved there was little that one could call a distinctive Catholic politics but there was nonetheless an effect. That Catholics were disproportionate part of the leadership of the Labour movement explains its grim reluctance to support progressive causes. Such Catholic social-ists as John Wheatley campaigned for employment rights and decent housing; they were not interested in what would later be called 'identity politics'.[22] The notion of women's rights, for example, was as alien to Catholic trade unionists in the Scottish Labour party as it was to the Scottish landed gentry in the Con-servative and Unionist party.

The political positioning of Muslim, Hindu and Sikh migrants was similar to that of the Irish. Their status as members of minorities, often located at the bottom of the labour market, led them to associate most strongly with the 'wrong' party. Culturally most Asian migrants had more in common with Con-servatives than with Labour. They were strongly in favour of the family with tra-ditional patriarchal gender roles. They saw private initiative rather than class action as the route to improved material circumstances. Many were self-employed in small businesses and hence favoured low rates of taxation and a small state. However, many Asian immigrants worked in heavily unionised industries and settled in what became areas of high unemployment and depriva-tion: the old mill towns of the North West and the East End of London. Conserv-ative hostility to immigration was a clear push.

Over 80 per cent of Pakistanis (almost all of whom are Muslims) supported Labour in the 1970s. This fell to just over 50 per cent in the 1990s.[23] It rose to two-thirds in the 1997 landslide victory but then fell sharply at the 2005 gen-eral election, when many Muslims switched to the Liberal Democrats (the only major party to oppose the Iraq war). Fifty-seven per cent of Muslims said they intended to vote Labour in 2010.[24] Underneath those fluctuations is an enduring shift of loyalties powered by upward social mobility and made possible by the Tory party largely purging itself of its racist past and ensuring the selection of ethnic and religious minority candidates. The gradually broad-ening of preferences can be seen in the council chambers. In 1996 there were 160 Muslim local councillors of whom 153 were Labour and precisely one sat in the Conservative interest. By 2001, the total had risen by 57 but only eight of those gains went to Labour. The rest were evenly divided between the other two parties.[25] Detailed research in 2010 showed considerable complexity within the non-white electorate. It found a clear difference between genera-tions, with younger members of ethnic and religious minorities being con-siderably more varied in their preferences than their parents and it rejected 'the hypothesis of anything distinctive, in turnout or Labour voting, about adherents to Islam'.[26]

Religious values

As well as defining a community of interest, religion can be politically significant as a source of distinctive values. The Liberal party in the nineteenth century enjoyed the support of nonconformists not just because it represented their sectional interests in matters such as removing the privileges of the state churches but also because it was in tune with the social ethics of most nonconformist denominations: egalitarian rather than hierarchical, independent-minded rather than deferential, self-disciplined rather than indulgent. Correspondingly, the Tory–Anglican association was a product not just of self-interested support for the status quo but also of a more generalised belief in the importance of tradition and of hierarchy. As David Bebbington puts it: 'so general was the liberal allegiance of the nonconformist congregations that by 1880 their regional organisations, forswearing all inhibitions about the worldliness of politics, were unreservedly partisan'. For example, in 1881 the Shropshire Baptist Association resolved: 'that the ministers and delegates now assembled, recognise with pleasure and gratitude, the principles of Her Majesty's Government, believing they are directed to promote generally the best interests of the country morally, socially, financially, and internationally'. In praises fulsome enough to make a Soviet leader blush, the resolution concluded: 'the efforts of our high principled Premier and his worthy colleagues will have the hearty support of the masses of our people and the blessing of Almighty God'.[27]

The great nineteenth century two-party contrast is, of course, a simplification. It was smudged by the largest nonconformist body. The Wesleyan Methodists were always the most conservative and hierarchical of the main dissenting groups; indeed they had always been somewhat reluctant dissenters. The Wesleyans did not leave the Church of England: they were expelled. Of the three chapels in the North Yorkshire fishing village of Staithes, it was the Wesleyan chapel that in 1865 invited the local grandee, the Marquis of Normanby, to lay the foundation stone for their new chapel and schoolroom. A contemporary press summary of his speech neatly expressed his interest in evangelical religion:

> the Marquis was at pains to point out that as a member of the Established Church, he entertained a sincere veneration for the Anglican tenets, but he did not think it proper to interfere with those who sincerely differed from him in their mode of worshipping God.

He was especially keen on the civic consequences of the Wesleyan chapel: 'He trusted that the children might learn in the schoolroom lessons of veneration and subordination which would be of benefit to them even in this life and that in the chapel they would be instructed in the truths of our common Christianity'.[28]

Historians argue over the precise details of when the shift occurred but it is widely agreed that during the second half of the nineteenth century – the first period of general enfranchisement – religion was the best predictor of voting preference, that religion and class interacted in the first quarter of the twentieth, and that post-1945 politics followed a 'class-stratified configuration' partly because denomination–party links weakened and partly because the proportion of the electorate with any denominational affiliation declined.[29] Even if all Anglicans voted Conservative, this would have had less effect in 1980 than in 1900 because there were fewer Anglicans.

To what extent does religious affiliation shape political choices now? It is certainly hard to imagine any church, denomination or sect being as uncritical of any prime minister as the Shropshire Baptists were of their hero Gladstone. Nonetheless religious values do still have some effect on general political orientations. As the data in Table 2.1 show, the Church of England may no longer 'represent the Conservative Party at prayer', as Maude Royden put it, but Anglicans are still more likely than the population at large to vote Conservative.[30] We can also see a strong pattern of Catholic support for Labour. Despite the decline of the Catholic fortress mentality, considerable inter-marriage and upward social mobility (in 2005 Catholic respondents were more likely to describe themselves as middle class than Church of England respondents), Catholics still show a strong preference for voting Labour.[31] From a series of MORI polls, we can compare the stated voting intentions of Catholics with those of the total sample. In 1992, Catholics were 48 per cent pro-Labour as against the total figure of only 41 per cent. In 1997 and 2001, the corresponding figures were 53 to 50 and 60 to 52 per cent. When overall support for Labour slumped in 2005 to 36 per cent, Catholic Labour support was at 53 per cent; as high as it had been in the Labour landslide of 1997.[32]

That Catholic support for Blair grew between 1997 and 2001 may reflect gratitude for his efforts to advance the peace process in Northern Ireland but overall, given that there is very little about the Labour party's programmes that would make it more attractive to Catholic values than those of the Conservatives, we have to suppose that much of this is a residue of the patterns formed on class grounds in the 1930s.

Despite this section being apparently concerned with the political consequences of religious values, in some of the above analysis religion is being treated as a community characteristic. That surveys commonly use nominal religious identification rather than any measure of personal faith is in part a consequence of secularisation. In a sample survey of 1,000 people, only 100 will be

Table 2.1 Voting by religion, British general election, 2010

	Conservative (%)	Labour (%)	Liberal Democrat (%)	Other (%)	Total (%)
Anglicans	45	25	20	10	100
Catholics	30	40	23	7	100
Other Christians	33	30	26	11	100
Other religions	31	28	31	10	100
Not religious	29	28	33	10	100
Election result	36	29	23	12	100

'religious' in any strict sense of the term. Once we start to divide those people by denomination and by age and gender (which we know to be important determinants both of religiosity and of political preferences) we often end up with too few people in any category for meaningful comparison.

Where it has been possible to consider the effects of religious identification, religious behaviour and religious belief on voting behaviour, the results are complex. Analysing data from the 1991 and 1992 waves of the British Household Panel Study, Laurence Kotler-Berkowitz finds residues of the old connection between religious identification and party support: 'For Catholics and dissenting Protestants – particularly the middle-class members of these groups – contemporary electoral divisions from Anglicans reflect the highly structured cleavages of an earlier era, though in tempered form'.[34] Middle-class 'non-religious' people are also less likely to vote Conservative. Working-class members of the Church of Scotland (of whom there are very few) are disproportionately Conservative. Not surprising given the value positions implied, churchgoing consistently reduces support for Labour. It is perhaps surprising that it increases Liberal Democrat support. The effects of religious belief are less clear and sometimes run counter to the effects of religious behaviour. For example, while churchgoing for Catholics is associated with stronger support for Labour, strong religious belief has the opposite effect. Some of the lack of clarity may stem from the weak and not entirely appropriate measures of religious belief available. Some of it may reflect the absence in contemporary elections of religiously salient issues on which the parties take clearly distinctive stances.

A more recent survey suggests that party alignment may have been displaced by political engagement as the key variable to be explained by religion. Siobhan McAndrew sorted the British Social Attitudes (2008) respondents into three groups based on responses to 14 items, which included claimed religious affiliation, church attendance, self-perception as religious or not, and a variety of religious beliefs: the religious, the unreligious and a middle category of the 'fuzzy faithful'.[35] The results are shown in Table 2.2. Here the party differences are small and the largest difference is not in party preference but in having voted at

Table 2.2 Party voted for in 2005 General Election, by religiosity

Party voted for	Religiosity			All (%)
	Religious (%)	'Fuzzy faithful' (%)	Unreligious (%)	
Did not vote	28	28	36	31
Conservative	22	23	17	21
Labour	31	27	27	28
Liberal Democrat	10	7	9	9
Nationalist parties	1	3	2	2
Other	1	3	3	2
Not answered	6	8	5	7
Base	302	388	318	1,008

all. The unreligious were significantly more likely than the religious and the middling group to have abstained. That is, the largest effect of being religious is to be minimally politically active, irrespective of one's political preferences.

As well as providing a general value orientation, religious organisations often give specific ethical and moral teaching that has political implications. As the traditional Cork folk singer Jimmy Crowley noted in praise of drinking: 'And what does the Salvation Army shout down/Boozing bloody well boozing/Against what are they preaching in every town/Boozing, bloody well boozing'.[37] Until the 1960s many Methodists would also have been members of the temperance organisation Christian Endeavour and redundant chapels were sold with the condition that there were not to be used for the consumption of alcohol or gambling. The Catholic Church has been a vocal opponent of artificial contraception and abortion. Most conservative Christians are opposed to homosexuality. We might reasonably expect that such mores will lead conservative Christians to support the Conservative party. Medhurst and Moyser's study of members of the Church of England's General Synod showed a clear link between holding conservative (i.e. hostile) views on homosexuality, abortion and euthanasia and favouring the Tory party.[38] However, for reasons discussed at length in Chapters 7 and 8, the socio-moral value preferences of British Christians have not been *directly* politically influential since the present party system took shape. When the Thatcher government was engaging in what now seems a petty, even petulant, crusade against gay rights, it is hard to imagine many homosexuals voted Conservative but the behaviour of her own ministers prevented the Tories being convincingly presented as the moral party. The convention of leaving socio-moral issues of particular intensity (such as abortion and capital punishment) to an 'unwhipped' vote allows the main parties to avoid taking a stance and thus deprives voters of the sort of choice (pursued in Chapter 7) that conservative Christians in the USA voters enjoy.

Of course elections are not everything. There are many other ways in which leaders of religious communities and organisations are able to influence governments and state agencies. From its foundation, the British Broadcasting Company (later Corporation) gave sympathetic attention to the views of church leaders.[39] Even now, when churchgoing is unpopular, it is still routine for broadcasters to invite religious leaders to opine on a wide range of contentious issues. Abortion, euthanasia, in-vitro fertilisation, cloning, stem cell research, homosexuality; almost any news item involving such matters will 'balance' the views of those in favour of an innovation with the views of some conservative church leader.

The language of civil society is new but the value of the churches as sources of social stability and of social value has long been recognised. Governments have generally been receptive to lobbying by church leaders (probably more receptive than is merited by the numbers such leaders represent). The Catholic Church very effectively lobbied Scottish and Westminster officials and politicians in support of the state funding of Catholic schools. Church of England bishops have enjoyed even better access because, as well as representing a very large and prestigious social institution, they also shared a common class back-ground with senior politicians and civil servants. During the 1980s, church leaders became somewhat alienated from the Thatcher government's right-wing policies: the rift symbolised by the Church of England's refusal to claim divine approval for the victory over Argentina in the Falklands war.[40] But for most of the twentieth century, the churches could count on having the ear of government, and during the Blair years the churches were courted as potential partners in delivering social improvements.

Although the corporatist model of states negotiating with churches fits contin-ental Europe better than the UK, the lack of national representative bodies has been an obstacle to Muslims, Hindus and Sikhs advancing their collective inter-ests.[41] As religio-ethnic minorities have grown, politicians and civil servants have become increasingly sensitive to their interests but, as with the earlier development of race relations law, such sensitivity has been dramatically height-ened by violence (both from and, more often than not, towards minority com-munities). For example, the most intensive attempts by the government to create a representative body of British Muslim leaders with which it could negotiate followed the 2005 London bombings.

Conclusion

This chapter has been intended as a brief overview of some of the main ways in which religion can have political consequences and, with the first chapter, it serves as an introduction to the detailed studies that follow. In providing a con-text for what follows, I have been keen to make five general observations.

First, much that is interesting about the interaction of religion and politics in the United Kingdom stems from the multi-national nature of the UK. As we will see in Chapter 7, the UK was until very recently governed by a remarkably cen-tralised polity. Yet much of its religious history has been shaped by the continu-ing salience of the four nations of Ireland, Scotland, England and Wales. Britain managed to produce British political parties but it never had a single state church.

Second, much that is interesting about the political consequences of religion in the UK stems from the fact that its dominant religion was Reformed (rather than Lutheran) Protestantism. Although the Churches of England and Scotland tried to impose a Lutheran style of national church, neither succeeded in prevent-ing frequent waves of religious dissent. The initial responses to dissent were always punitive and oppressive but the failure of theocratic imposition and the success of the state in surviving the absence of a common religious legitimisa-tion allowed a rapid transition from penal laws to toleration to full religious freedom. Although most European states now accept the principle of religious freedom, even many of the long-democratic states of Western Europe have not entirely given up the idea that the state should decide what counts as acceptable religion. For example, the French response to concerns about the recruitment tactics of some new religious movements was to issue a list of dangerous 'cults' (which managed to include a number of established Protestant bodies as well as the usual suspects). In contrast, the religious diversity of the UK forced it to become one of the lead states in accepting that religious affiliation is a private matter.

Third, it is important to appreciate the secularity of British public life. Much confusion is caused by the fact that the Church of Scotland and the Church of England are allowed privileged access to the institutional equivalent of the dressing-up box.[42] Royalty visits them and their leaders enjoy prominent places in national ceremonies. But pageantry should not be mistaken for power. If the monarch being the head of two very different churches really meant anything, the arrangement would have been changed shortly after the 1851 Census of Religious Worship showed that there were more dissenters than members of the national churches. The formal status of the established churches is no more a sign of their influence than the formal status of the monarch is a sign of her power. What matters is the strength of religious belief, and the vast majority of the citizens of the United Kingdom have little or no religion.

The previous two paragraphs add up to my fifth general observation. Because almost all the attention to immigrant religious minorities is framed in claims of discrimination and arguments about integration, it is easy to miss sight of the ease with which Irish Catholics, West Indian and African Pentecostalists, Muslims, Hindus and Sikhs have settled in the UK. There have been no formal restrictions on the free exercise of religion and, for the most part, the major Christian churches have been active in promoting inter-faith dialogue and in broadening access to institutional religious rights (such as prison and hospital chaplaincies). Most importantly, since the failed 1920s Scots Presbyterian campaign to whip up fear of the threat of the Irish to the Scottish race, no church leaders of any significance have offered any encouragement to racist and xenophobic opposition to religious minorities.

3 Religion and violence in Northern Ireland

Introduction

Structural differentiation is commonly associated with modernisation. In the life-world of the small and simple society it is hard to separate religion from the economy or the polity. The point was made to me as an undergraduate with the (probably apocryphal) story that the first Europeans to contact the inhabitants of Australia reported that they had no religion: a mistake based on the fact that their religion, although all-pervasive, was not institutionally distinct. In the industrial societies of modern Europe it is possible to identify religion as a separate sphere, with its distinct patterns of behaviour, beliefs and values; hence it is possible to ask how religion affects other parts of such a society. But even in complex, functionally differentiated society, the divisions of the life-world are rarely abrupt. Although in practice the following distinctions are hard to maintain, it might be helpful to identify four ways in which religion can be implicated in political conflict.

First, religious beliefs might be central. Although mundane considerations are never absent, crusades and holy wars are primarily religious struggles. For example, principles of the Reformation were so central to the conflict in France between the 1550s and the Edict of Nantes in 1598 that it was quite properly called 'the Wars of Religion'.

Second, religion may be heavily implicated in conflict because it defines and legitimates national or ethnic group identities. Many of the borders of modern European nations marked the edges of competing religious confessions (or of significantly different traditions within them) and many sub-populations that have tried to secede from their states are distinguished by religion. For example, it would be difficult to describe the fragmentation of Yugoslavia without noting that Serbs were Orthodox Christians, Croats and Slovenes were Roman Catholics, and Bosnians were Muslims. The salience of the religious element of ethnic identity will always vary with secular concerns. The break-up of Yugoslavia certainly made Bosnians more conscious of their Muslim heritage than they had been during the relative quiet of Tito's rule. But it is often a significant source of social cohesion even in quiet times.

Third, competing religious beliefs and institutions can generate rather different ways of seeing the world which have political consequences: the communal organicism of the Catholic and Orthodox strands sometimes produce very different political visions and preferences to those encouraged by the individualism of the non-Lutheran strands of Protestantism.

Fourth, within any particular society or group that shares a common religious culture, degrees of commitment to the dominant religion may produce different values and hence different orientations to conflict when it occurs. That is, the attitudes and behaviour of the religious virtuosi may differ markedly from those of the common people.

I will present my conclusion at the start: crusade or jihad has played little part in the Irish conflict. All combatants have been prone to claim divine approval but rarely do we find a desire to eliminate heresy or to impose the will of God. Religion figured first through the medium of ethnic identity: it helped create divisions in the sixteenth and seventeenth centuries, it discouraged inter-marriage (and thus froze those divisions), and it provided some ideological justification for the development of competing political agendas in the nineteenth and twentieth centuries. Secondly it has figured to the extent that religious institutions and movements have played a role in supporting secular constitutional positions. And thirdly it has played an important role restraining the violence. I will argue that, although leading political actors on both sides of the Protestant–Catholic divide (sometimes inadvertently) encouraged division by strengthening the association between political preference and religious identity, religious virtuosi played a significant part in damping down conflict. This will be my somewhat ironic conclusion. Religion is implicated in the divisions that generated the conflict, but the most violent protagonists have been the personally least religious members of their respective communities: the religious virtuosi have acted to confine the competition to the legitimate channels of liberal democracy.

Historical Foundations of Contemporary Divisions

The enduring nature of the Irish question owes much to the partial success of the Reformation and to subsequent patterns of political conquest and settlement. Had Ireland followed England, Scotland and Wales in becoming Protestant (or had Britain remained unreformed), subsequent history would have been very different. That the majority of the Irish remained Catholic, and hence liable to assist co-religionists in France or Spain, meant that Britain had a foreign policy interest in subjugating Ireland. That the native Irish remained of a different religion to the English (Episcopalian Protestant) and to the Scottish (Presbyterian Protestant) settlers discouraged the degree of mixing that would eventually have turned settler–native relations into more fluid social class relations. With the rise of representative democracy, the movement for Irish Independence became a largely Catholic movement and the threat from the Catholic majority forced Episcopalians and Presbyterians into a sense of shared Protestant identity (expressed, for example in the fraternal Orange Order). Although significant Catholic and Protestant populations were left on the wrong side of the border, the 1921 division of the island into two parts reinforced the place of religion in ethnic identity.

For Irish nationalists the Free State was properly a Catholic country: an assertion that was given prominence in Eamonn De Valera's 1937 constitution for the renamed Irish Republic. The Unionist party administration that dominated Northern Ireland from its foundation to the suspension of the devolved Stormont Parliament in 1971 ensured that Protestantism enjoyed pride of place in the public culture.[1] Not all Ulster unionists were anti-Catholic bigots but the structure of the conflict made it difficult to avoid having religious, social and political divisions reinforce each other. For example, in order to ensure dominion over its people, the Catholic Church insisted on maintaining a separate school system. In Scotland and England such a posture was not terribly contentious because, by the time a nation-wide state education system was being constructed, religious affiliation had ceased to have any great political salience. But in Northern Ireland, such separatism reinforced unionist perceptions that the Catholic minority would not accept the partition settlement.

Partition was followed by a brief period of intense violence but Northern Ireland settled down and the Border campaign of the Irish Republican Army (IRA) in the 1950s was not popular with nationalists, did not create a popular unionist backlash, and was easily contained by the state.[2]

The Troubles

The origins of the Troubles can be summarised simply. Inspired by the black Civil Rights movement in the USA and frustrated by the apparent determination of the Unionist government to ensure that the benefits of 1960s economic growth went disproportionately to 'loyal' Protestant areas, Catholics became increasingly forceful in their demands for an end to various forms of discrimination.[3] Terence O'Neill, prime minister from 1963 to 1969, made small gestures towards the Catholic nationalist community.[4] This in turn provoked hostile responses from unionists. Caught between its own voters, the nationalist minority, and the sovereign London government (which had little sympathy for the unionist cause), the devolved Stormont government alternated between accommodation and repression in a manner that encouraged the extremes on both sides to become ever more demanding and violent in the pursuit of those demands. The initial Catholic demand for greater equality *within* Northern Ireland was quickly replaced by old-fashioned anti-partitionism and the response of the Protestant working class (usually called 'loyalists') was to take up arms to defend the Union. The British army was sent on to the streets of Northern Ireland to keep the peace. Although initially welcomed as defenders by nationalist communities, British soldiers quickly became the targets for IRA violence.

In 1971 republicans killed 93 people; loyalists 21. In 1972 republicans killed 257 people; loyalists killed 103.[5] On top of the deaths there were thousands of shootings, bombings and arson attacks. By the late 1970s, the level of violence had fallen to a steady 80–120 casualties a year and, although each death was an atrocity to the family and friends of the dead, the Province had been pulled back from the brink of collapse. Over the next two decades political initiatives came and went but beneath the apparent chaos of failed solutions there was a clear trend. With changes in the religious composition of the voting age population, Catholics came sufficiently close to Protestants in number to be seen, not as a minority, but as a bloc with interests on a par with those of unionists. The British government gave the Irish government a considerable role in representing northern nationalists. And on both sides of the divide the more extreme party made gains. The IRA's political wing, Sinn Fein, gradually built a powerful base in community and local politics and on the unionist side, the Democratic Unionist party (DUP), led by the Reverend Ian Paisley, challenged the Ulster Unionist party (UUP), the traditional representative of unionists.[6]

In the mid-1990s there was a significant breakthrough. The IRA called a ceasefire and the loyalist terror organisations reciprocated. With a few hiccups those ceasefires have held. Although the terror organisations have remained intact, their violence has been scaled down drastically and is now used mainly to support criminal activities, to police their own members – what one man euphemistically called 'housekeeping' – and to impose on their own communities.

The political settlement faltered. The devolved assembly was suspended a number of times and there was a dramatic shift towards the political extremes on both sides. Sinn Fein became the majority nationalist party and the DUP displaced the UUP. In 2007 the IRA finally renounced violence and the DUP agreed to form a government with Sinn Fein. The main loyalist terror groups also stood down and disarmed. That the ceasefires have now held for over a decade gives us hope that we can talk of the Troubles in the past tense.

The role of religion

What part did religion play in the violence of the period 1971 to 1994? Although some parts of the answer will be the same for each side, it helps to distinguish Catholic and Protestant actions and reactions.

The Catholic-nationalist bloc

With its long traditional of political caution and its obligations to Catholics in all states, the Catholic Church did not throw itself into the Troubles by, for example, declaring the destruction of Northern Ireland to be a legitimate crusade: it did not declare *jihad*. But indirectly it played a major part in the political instability of the Troubles. During the Home Rule period the Church campaigned on behalf of the Nationalist party. It condemned the 1916 Easter Rising but sided with the Irish in the war for independence. The close relationship between the Church and the Irish Republic was signalled in the 1937 constitution, which accorded it the status of the 'guardian of the Faith professed by the great majority of its citizens'.[7] In Northern Ireland, the Church was the major social institution for nationalist rejection of the state and its leaders often represented its people's political interests. A 1968 survey showed all the priests interviewed being opposed to partition.[8] Senior church leaders were usually careful to avoid directly supporting any particular political party, but even when they spoke an apparently universalistic language of 'justice and reconciliation' their political interventions were first and foremost on behalf of the Catholic nationalist people and hence the Church was seen by both its adherents and its critics as a promoter of nationalism.

Those who took up the armed struggle were not, by and large, particularly religious and they did not couch their struggle in religious language. The IRA of the 1970s did not repeat the language of 1916 Easter Rising proclamation, which said: 'we place the cause of the Irish Republic under the protection of the Most High God, whose blessing we invoke upon our arms'.[9] Although most IRA activists had been raised as Mass-going Catholics (and among the rural cells of the IRA Mass-goers remained common), the contemporary IRA drew its inspiration from secular national liberation movements in Africa, Asia and Latin America and its rhetoric was leftist. The fact that the Irish Republic existed meant that nationalists could be inspired by an entirely secular nationalist rhetoric: all people had a right to be ruled by their own sort and hence the Irish had a right to an Ireland completely free of Britain.

There is little evidence of republicans deploying religious rhetoric in support of their cause. The one example that comes to mind may have been largely inadvertent: less a direct bid for Christian legitimisation and more the general iconography of martyrdom. The republican prisoners who died as a result of a hunger strike in 1981 were emaciated and haggard, had long uncut hair and, because they had been refusing to wear prison clothes, were often naked except for a blanket. When photographs of the hunger strikers were blown up to poster size or painted on wall murals, the result often looked strikingly like the classic portrayals of Christ on the cross.

A small number of priests were active in supporting the IRA. Father James Chesney is reputed to have been the leader of the South Derry IRA unit that killed nine people and seriously wounded a further 40 when it bombed the village of Claudy in July 1972.[10] Former IRA man Sean O'Callaghan claimed that other priests were involved.[11] A study of Catholic policemen reports a number of incidents that suggest considerable low-level clergy support for republicans. In reflecting on his school days, one Catholic police officer recalls a priest justifying Catholic girls using their sexuality to trap British soldiers into a fatal ambush. Another reports a priest telling his fiancée: 'I'd rather see you in the cemetery than marrying that man'. A third remembers a priest offering prayers for the innocent Catholic victims of IRA violence but not for victims who were member of the security forces.[12]

The Church often buried republican terrorists in a manner that looked like legitimising their activities. At a funeral mass for a young man who accidentally blew himself up with a bomb intended to kill a part-time policeman, the priest said:

> When the young man's family and I set out ... for the Tyrone County Hospital, it was for both of us an experience painful beyond description....

Today it has been my duty in the name of Jesus our Saviour to receive this same young man's body with all its hurts and wounds at the door of our parish church. In her liturgy for the dead, the Church treats the bodies of all her children with fitting reverence. ... It is not for any of us to pass judgement; we leave judgement in the hands of Jesus, whom the Father has appointed the just Judge and merciful Saviour of us all.

After the burial, the priest went on to blame the state for the young man's death.[13] That sort of sympathy for republicans did not go down well those on the receiving end of their murderous campaign. A Catholic policeman said: 'Canonising republicans sickened me. I remember [a Catholic priest] speaking at the funeral of [...] about him being a respected local businessman. The truth was that he brainwashed youngsters.'[14] Clonard monastery in Belfast was the venue for a Mass to commemorate the twentieth anniversary of the 1981 hunger strikes. In front of the altar were arraigned very large photographs of the dead. The clergy could defend it as an act of remembrance; to many it looked like endorsement.[15]

As a general proposition, senior clergy always had less sympathy for republicanism than parish priests and curates. The Pope was quite clear in his description of Irish republican violence as 'terrorism' and emphatic in his condemnation of it. The Irish bishops were firmly against the use of violence for political ends and frequently denounced republican murders. In October 1990 the IRA forced a Catholic to drive a lorry load of explosives into a military checkpoint and detonated the bombs while he was still in the vehicle. Patsy Gillespie and five soldiers died. In his address at Gillespie's funeral Edward Daly, the Bishop of Derry, said: 'I believe that the work of the IRA is the work of the Devil. I say that very deliberately and I say it as a Catholic Bishop charged with preaching the gospel and with the pastoral care of the people of this diocese.'[16] Daly came to prominence in one of the key events of the early Troubles. In January 1972 British soldiers fired on an illegal but general peaceful demonstration in Derry, killing 14 people and wounding 17 others. Despite military claims, there is no evidence that the soldiers came under sniper fire. A photograph of Daly administering the last rites to one of the wounded became one of the best known and powerful images of the Troubles.[17] Later returning to the city as Bishop of Derry, Daly spent much of his career battling with republicans for the hearts and minds of the Catholic people. He and other members of the hierarchy were critical of the government and security forces on many occasions but they were persistently critical of the IRA.

Critics have made much of the fact that the Irish Church did not excommunicate republican terrorists. When excommunication was automatic for anyone performing an abortion, profaning the Host, becoming an heretic or joining the Freemasons, and when Pope Pius XII could excommunicate all communists, that the Church did not take the same step with convicted terrorists was taken as a politically significant omission.

However, there is one feature of church involvement that clearly distinguishes the Northern Ireland Troubles from, say, the Ustaše violence in Croatia in 1941.

While officials of all denominations argued for the legitimacy of their people's aspirations, they cooperated in public appeals for civility and an end to violence. It was common for senior Catholic and Episcopalian bishops, presidents of the Methodist Conference and Moderators of the Presbyterian General Assembly to make joint public statements condemning republican and loyalist killings.

Quite how effective such interventions were is impossible to gauge. Sinn Fein managed to build a substantial popular vote while justifying the IRA's use of murder as a political lever, which suggests that a large part of the Catholic population did not share Bishop Daly's view that the IRA was doing the work of the Devil. A 1999 survey shows that while only 7.4 per cent of Catholics had 'a lot of sympathy for' republican violence, 34.6 had 'a little sympathy'.[18] Given the tendency of opinion polls to produce overly moderate responses, this suggests that only parts of the laity were responsive to the official Church perspective.

The Protestant-unionist bloc

The influence of Protestantism on the conflict is less easy to describe because Protestants are divided amongst a number of churches. The Irish Presbyterian Church (IPC) and the Episcopalian Church of Ireland (COI) between them account for 36 per cent of the Ulster population. Very many clergy were members of the fraternal Orange Order and through it they enjoyed considerable influence on the Unionist party, which dominated the Stormont regime from partition to the late 1960s. However, such influence was not sufficient to stop the gradual secularisation of such state institutions as hospitals and schools. Protestants were in a somewhat awkward position. The popular view was that the Catholic-nationalist bloc had got the lion's share with the Irish Free State (later Republic) and that Northern Ireland should be a Protestant state for a Protestant people. But formally it was a secular liberal democracy and most government officials tried to exercise their responsibilities in a non-sectarian manner. The Catholic Church could keep its schools and hospitals 'Catholic' but the state institutions could not be similarly 'Protestant'. This anomaly gave ample ammunition to a small number of conservative Protestant clergy and conservative unionist politicians who collaborated in a variety of associations which nagged and badgered the Unionist government over any weakening of Protestant popular religious culture (such as a ban on gospel singing in the state hospitals) and over anything that could be interpreted as a concession to Irish nationalists. Despite the apparent solidity of the Stormont regime, there were unionists on the fringes who developed a twin vision of betrayal (actual or impending). The ruling elites in the Protestant churches could not be trusted (because they showed signs of doctrinal liberalism and ecumenism) with the gospel and the elites running the Unionist party could not be trusted to save Ulster from Irish nationalism.

Almost every Protestant cleric would have voted unionist and hundreds were active in promoting the alliance of evangelical religion and unionist politics through the Orange Order and the Apprentice Boys of Derry.[19] But a handful were particularly active in trying to prevent political betrayal. In the early 1970s the MP for South Belfast was Robert Bradford, an evangelical Independent Methodist minister who opposed the liberal tendencies of the Unionist party when, under the leadership of Brian Faulkner, it attempted to form a power-sharing government with the moderate nationalist party. When Bradford was assassinated his seat was won by Martin Smyth. Smyth was also a dissident conservative Ulster Unionist. He was also Grand Master of the Orange Order and, although he was a minister of the Irish Presbyterian Church, he was a conservative evangelical and he led the campaign to have the IPC distance itself from the international ecumenical movement.

Ian Paisley

The most prominent politically active Protestant clergyman was the Reverend Ian R. K. Paisley, and his career suggests that religion played a greater part in the politics of Northern Ireland for Protestants than it did for Catholics.

Ian Paisley is remarkable in the history of modern democracy for founding a political party and a church and leading both to success.[20] The party he founded in 1966, initially called the Protestant Unionist Party, then the Democratic Unionist Party or DUP, is now Ulster's major unionist party. The Free Presbyterian Church of Ulster (FPCU), which he founded in 1951, had over 100 congregations 50 years later. Paisley's political career was built on defending the right of the Protestant people of Ulster to remain part of the United Kingdom and on opposing demands from Irish nationalists for the territory of Northern Ireland to be integrated with the Republic of Ireland. His religious career was constructed around the claim that the main Protestant churches have abandoned their historic creeds and hence that separation from Protestant apostasy is necessary to defend the true faith against the encroachments of Catholicism and liberalism. The two careers were united by the belief that northern Irish nationalist demands were a product of Catholic Church scheming and were encouraged by the decline of a biblical Protestant witness.

Religion is implicated in the success of the DUP (and hence in Ulster unionist politics) in a number of complex ways.

First, religion arguably improved the performance of the DUP as a party. The evangelical religious base gave the DUP an unusual degree of fortitude. Since the 1970s all nationalists and many unionists have believed that a united Ireland is inevitable. Even when the Union was not being doubted, Paisley's place in Ulster politics was. At every election from 1969 to 2003 Paisley was written off but his sense of divine mission kept him cheerful. It also gave him a divine trump card. Other unionist leaders have been forced into compromises that hardly persuaded them and would not persuade others. In similar circumstances, Paisley has been able to resist pressure because he has God on his side. He has also been able to remain unusually focused. The sense of divine calling gave Paisley and his associates a certainty of purpose: dogmatism may be a hindrance to a politician in power but it is an advantage to someone in opposition. Finally, the common religious base gave the party cohesion. That most DUP activists were Free Presbyterians (and most of the rest evangelicals) helped hold them together. They spoke a common language, mixed socially, and inter-married. It was this ideological and social cohesion rather than Paisley's personality, powerful though that was, that let the DUP speak quickly with a single voice. In contrast the much larger Ulster Unionist party (UUP) was crippled by a structure designed to incorporate the largest number of groups rather than to produce and enforce agreed policy. In the 1970s, it split over proposals for enforced power-sharing with nationalists. In the 1980s, it was stretched between those who wanted to restore devolved government to Northern Ireland and those who wanted greater integration with Great Britain. In the 1990s it was deeply divided over the post-ceasefire negotiations and the 1998 Belfast Agreement. In the twenty-first century it was all but eliminated as an electoral force.

We can now move to electoral impact. Arithmetic tells us that the DUP attracted votes from well beyond its small evangelical core. What part did Paisley's religion play in making him more popular with the electorate than secular contenders for the leadership of the conservative wing of unionism?

First, it gave the DUP a reputation for certainty and trustworthiness. Even quite radical changes of policy were overlooked as voters saw evangelicals as dependable. As one man put it: 'they're mirthless killjoys but you know where you are with them. Bigots maybe but reliable bigots.' Second, Paisley's faith made him old-fashioned and in a political culture where the past looks better than the future, the man who could present himself as a contemporary reincarnation of the great heroes of the past (many of whom were clergymen) had an advantage over secular rivals in mobilising nostalgia and claiming the unionist heritage. Paisley's religion also tapped into personal nostalgia. Many of those who described themselves by the 1980s as having 'no religion' had been raised with an evangelical church connection. When Paisley spoke the language of the Old Testament, he talked in terms that they had heard before, often enough and in such circumstances as to instil respect.

Perhaps the most important political value of Paisley's religion was the most subtle. Ethnic or national divisions are not just neutral labels: they imply claims to superiority. Each side thinks well of its people and ill of its rival. With varying degrees of self-consciousness, Ulster unionists would claim for themselves such secular virtues as being diligent, hard-working, sober, loyal, and self-disciplined. In contrast Catholics could be derided as slothful, indigent, disloyal, feckless and priest-ridden. Such stereotypes do not need to be true but they do need some kind of justification. Racial stereotypes could be explained and justified by biology but such a defence is not available in Northern Ireland. The one thing that united Protestants and separated them from Catholics was religion. Even 'secular' Protestants found it hard to avoid the conclusion that what made them better than Catholics was having the true faith. What was wrong with a united Ireland? It would be dominated by the Catholic Church. For many unionists the evangelical Protestantism that explained their superiority was a communal memory rather than a personal faith, but there was enough of that memory left to advantage the politician who actually carried the faith. The leadership of the Orange Order resented Paisley as a trouble-making upstart but Paisley embodied the religious culture to which the Orange Order paid lip service.

However, while the evangelicalism of the DUP may have given it some advantage over secular right-wing rivals, it also alienated a considerable part of the unionist electorate. By 1981, after a decade of growth, the DUP had secured a third of unionist votes and there it stuck for a further decade. In theory the most significant target of Paisley's brand of evangelicalism was the Antichrist of the Catholic Church but in practice the most frequent victims of his rhetoric were the other Protestant churches. Paisley's people never had any illusions about the Catholic Church: the focus of their attention was the liberal forces within the Protestant churches that were fatally undermining the gospel from within. From the early 1950s Paisley and his ministers had banged on about sin and apostasy in the Protestant churches. Their case fell on deaf ears until the political uncertainty of the late 1960s and early 1970s brought them a large number of defectors from the main churches. But by 1974 they had recruited all who shared their belief that it was essential to separate from apostasy. For the next 30 years all they did was alienate conservatives in the other churches who shared much of Paisley's right-wing religion and politics but who rejected his separatism. During the 1980s I met very many conservatives in the Church of Ireland and the Presbyterian Church who agreed with all of Paisley's positive preaching and who shared his fears about liberal tendencies in the churches but who remained loyal to their ministers because they were sound evangelical men, and who deeply resented Paisley's claim that their refusal to abandon their traditional churches was the result of cowardice.

The DUP's big breakthrough resulted from a secular rational calculation. In the referendum on the 1998 Belfast Agreement, unionists voted for it by the slimmest of majorities. Over the next few years many of those voters lost faith in David Trimble and the UUP as they concluded that he had conceded too much to Irish nationalists (and especially to Sinn Fein) and got too little in return. The IRA's disarmament and Sinn Fein's conversion to democratic politics were too slow for many UUP voters who either went over to the DUP or abstained. But even though the main dynamic behind the UUP's collapse was unionist frustration, the DUP's triumph was not entirely without a religious component. Extensive conversations with unionists who switched led me to believe that an important background consideration was the temperament of the evangelical puritans in the DUP. Although the party never openly linked trustworthiness and religion, the two themes were often presented side by side in election literature. Candidates said 'I am a staunch and reliable unionist' and 'I am an evangelical Christian' and left voters to work out that, if you have to negotiate unpalatable political changes, you could do worse than put your fate in the hands of narrow-minded dogmatic people.

Anti-Jihad

Just as the Catholic Church is traditionally Irish nationalist in its politics, so the Protestant churches are unionist. Because it has congregations in the Irish Republic, the Irish Presbyterian Church has always been careful not to be theologically unionist but the majority of its members are Northern Irish

Protestants, it supported the partition settlement and it has vigorously opposed attempts to bounce Ulster into a united Ireland. The Church of Ireland is in a similar position. Hence we could say that the Protestant churches have mirrored the Catholic Church in contributing to the conflict by encouraging their members' political preferences. Although the number declined over the course of the Troubles, many clergy have been members of the Orange Order, which very explicitly links religion, ethnicity and politics.

However, like the Catholic Church, the Protestant churches have consistently approached the violence of the Troubles from a legalist position. They have encouraged people to support the institutions of the state and to reject vigilante violence. They have condemned all forms of terrorism. The only significant difference between the two sides is that the Protestant churches have been more enthusiastic in support of the police, the army and the prison service. Although the Catholic Church has not taken the extreme rejectionist positions advocated by some nationalists and all republicans, it has been far more critical of the security services than have been the Protestant churches.

While most analysts would have no difficulty with the above description of the IPC or Church of Ireland, many have argued that Ian Paisley and other members of his Free Presbyterian Church of Ulster have played an active part in encouraging violence.[21] Paisley is such an major figure in Ulster political and religious life that any assessment of the role of religion in the conflict needs to examine his record (and that of his core supporters) in detail.

Although often described as a fundamentalist, Paisley was not a theocrat. His views on the use of force were entirely consistent with the principles of liberal democracy. Like most people in Western democracies, he expected the state to protect its citizens and those citizens to be loyal to the state. He ceded to the state the right to the legitimate use of coercion. Although Paisley frequently cited the Scottish Covenanters as an inspiration, he did not hold to the view that support for the 'civil magistrate', to use the Covenanter term, should be conditional on the state actively promoting the true religion. So long as the state delivers its secular protection, the citizen has no right to use violence for political ends. The following from a 1973 statement succinctly expresses his view:

> it is wrong for Protestants to contemplate taking the law into their own hands and meting out justice to those whom they believe guilty of atrocities ... 'Avenge not yourselves' is the unmistakable teaching of Scripture. Romans 12, verse 19, goes on to remind Christians that 'Vengeance is mine; I will repay, saith the Lord'. This does not mean, of course, that Protestants ought not be ready to defend themselves, their homes and their families from attack. It does mean that the punishment of offenders must and should be left to those holding official authority to judge and punish.[22]

If the state abandons the citizen, the citizen is released from his obligation and may do what is necessary to protect himself, his family and his country. Clearly there is a lot of slack in deciding just when the state has failed but the principle is clear and is clearly opposed to the terrorism used by loyalist groups such as the Ulster Defence Association (UDA) and Ulster Volunteer Force (UVF).[23]

Paisley's response to acts of terror committed by Ulster loyalists – the people on his side – was unequivocal. In response to one of the first loyalist terror acts, in 1966, he said: 'Like everyone else, I deplore and condemn this killing, as all right-thinking people must.'[24] He repeated that sentiment over and over. For example he said:

> What really stuns the decent Ulster Protestant is that a section of his own community would engage under the guise of Protestantism and Loyalty in crimes just as heinous and hellish [as those of the IRA]. As a Protestant leader I once again totally, utterly and unreservedly condemn these atrocious crimes and those who perpetrated them or planned to perpetrate them.[25]

Evangelicals were involved in public disorder but their actions were almost invariably respectable in character. Competing politics were often dramatised with marches and demonstrations. Frequently the police have banned parades in the hope of minimising conflict. Most Northern Ireland politicians at some time of their career have demonstrated their unhappiness with government policy by defying such bans. Evangelical DUP politicians were quite happy to parade illegally or try to cross police barriers. But they did not assault police lines or throw rocks at their opponents. Defying authority to show one's disagreement is acceptable: using violence is not. Being a long-suffering victim of undemocratic government decisions is fine; being the aggressor is not.

Paisley has also come close, in rhetoric at least, to rejecting the state's monopoly of violence. Four times in his long career, Paisley tried to organise a militia. His very first Ulster Protestant Volunteers was a political rather than a paramilitary organisation but its name and structure were intended to remind people of the original 1912 Ulster Volunteer Force. In 1969, he reacted to the disbanding of the Ulster Special Constabulary by calling on members to form a private militia. In 1981, after the British and Irish governments signalled a new closeness in their relationship, Paisley launched what was called the Third Force (the police and the army being the other two). He took five journalists to a secret location in North Antrim to see 500 men in combat jackets wave what were purported to be certificates for legally held firearms. At another rally he announced: 'We have a choice to make. Shall we allow ourselves to be murdered by the IRA, or shall we go out and kill the killers?'[26] As usual there was much militant rhetoric. At one rally Paisley said:

> We demand that the IRA be exterminated from Ulster … there are men willing to do the job of exterminating the IRA. Recruit them under the Crown and they will do it. If you refuse, we will have no other decision to make but to do it ourselves.[27]

That rhetoric was qualified when he later said: 'this force proposes to act entirely within the law and will in no way usurp either the work or the activities of the crown forces.'[28] There was no fighting. The rallies gradually got smaller and the movement died. Five years later Paisley agreed to lead a new third force called Ulster Resistance. There were the usual mass meetings with much hot air: Paisley's deputy said:

> thousands have already joined the movement and the task of shaping them into an effective force is continuing. The Resistance has indicated that drilling and training has already started. The officer of the nine divisions have taken up their duties.[29]

The reality was quite different. There was no mass movement. Ulster Resistance dribbled away to leave a small handful of County Armagh loyalists who collaborated with the UVF and UDA in the bank robbery in Portadown in July 1987 to fund a large purchase of arms from South Africa. Two Resistance men, both DUP activists from the same area and members of Paisley's Free Presbyterian Church, were caught trying to swap a Shorts missile system for small arms with the South African state company Armscor.

Paisley's condemnation of vigilante violence naturally had no effect on the UDA and UVF but it does seem to represent honestly (or to have shaped – causation is impossible to prove) the views of evangelical Protestants. If evangelical Protestantism encouraged political violence, we should see this is in the denominational affiliations of those convicted of serious offences. Allowing for turnover, by resignation or death, Paisley's Free Presbyterian Church has probably had about 10,000 adult and male (the two main demographic characteristics of terrorists) members since 1966. That is a lot of potential terrorists. Apart from a handful of men who in the 1960s tried to dramatise the threat from the then-dormant IRA by damaging public utilities, I can find only three Free Presbyterians who have been clearly involved in terrorism.[30] Membership of other evangelical sects is probably less likely to be mentioned in press reports but as most loyalist terror activity has been the work of the UDA and UVF, data on the religion of their members can stand as a fairly complete assessment of the violence of evangelicals.

If his church is blameless, what of Paisley's party? Again it is hard to know how many adult male members the DUP has had over the course of the Troubles but even if we confine our attention to those active enough to have stood as candidates in elections, we would have to set a figure of at least 500 and given the considerable turnover as people move in and out of parties, the cadre could be much larger; let us guess 3,000. I can find only six DUP activists who have been implicated in serious crimes and none of them involved personal murderous attacks.

Despite the lack of evidence, some people persist in claiming that Paisley secretly supported paramilitaries. A 1999 book review in *Socialism Today* repeated the assertion that Paisley encouraged the formation of the UDA and

UVF and cited as evidence the statement supposedly made by one of the first UVF men convicted of murder (in 1966). Hughie Mclean is quoted as saying: 'I am terribly sorry I ever heard of that man Paisley or decided to follow him. I am definitely ashamed of myself to be in such a position.' This single quotation has been endlessly and uncritically repeated without anyone pausing to think if those words were likely to have been spoken by an uneducated Shankill Road man.[31] Had anyone bothered to check contemporary accounts of the trial, they would have found the implausibly articulate statement was denied by McLean, who asserted that the RUC had invented the quotation.

Although Paisley had no hand in creating the real loyalist terror organisations, he did twice work alongside them. In 1974 Paisley, like every other Ulster unionist politician, supported a general strike that was led by the UDA and UVF. Although there is no suggestion that he or his people approved of UDA and UVF men using intimidation to enforce the strike, he must have been aware of it. Three years later he again worked with loyalists to mount a second and this time unsuccessful strike. It is worth observing Paisley's own conduct in that strike. As though he had been stung by accusations of mixing with hoodlums, he did his best to defuse potentially violent situations. At one confrontation between a large picket and the police, Paisley arranged with the police that they should try to move him, he would resist and then allow himself to be arrested. He would thus make his point and acquire the necessary media coverage. In recognition of this choreography the rest of the picket would disperse quietly. There was no violence. But however properly Paisley and his people behaved, they must have known that the UDA and UVF were responsible for hundreds of sectarian killings yet they were briefly willing to associate with them for political gain.

Having considered Paisley's responsibility for loyalist violence from Paisley's end, we can consider what is known about the religion of the loyalists responsible for that violence. Between 1978 and 1991, I interviewed hundreds of UDA and UVF men and noted the biographies of many more. I can think of only a handful who claimed to be Christians before or during their paramilitary involvement. Among the first generation of loyalist paramilitaries there were many who, although not personally pious, were happy to acknowledge the historical and social importance of evangelical religion by maintaining the elements of religious ritual and symbolism that they had learnt either in the Orange Lodges or in the British Army. If pushed they would claim that Protestants were better people than Catholics because they had the right religion. Many had a household division of religious labour and though they admitted that religion played no part in their lives, they would tell me proudly that 'the wife is God-fearing' and good-living and took the children to church.[32] The next generation, the men who reached adulthood and commanding positions in the UDA and UVF in the late 1980s and 1990s, had no time at all for religion. A well-researched biography of Johnny 'Mad Dog' Adair, a UDA leader from the 1990s, makes no reference to religious sentiment or activity.[33] Presumably because they could not think of anything else that would add a bit of solemnity to their rituals, Adair's generation used a Bible in administering membership oaths but that apart, they were openly scornful of even the limited borrowing of Christian symbolism and rhetoric from Lodge or Army ceremonies that the older generation favoured.

Critics spend so much time trying to establish links between Paisley and the paramilitaries that the reality of their relationship gets missed. In all my years of interviewing members of the UDA and UVF I have yet to meet one person who did not dislike Paisley intensely and this should be no surprise if we remember that Paisley and his people repeatedly described loyalist paramilitaries as being no better than republicans, demonised their political initiatives as 'communist', and tried to have them hanged. In the mid-1990s, when the details of the Belfast Agreement were being developed, the DUP was as opposed to loyalists gaining political representation as it was to Sinn Fein being allowed into the talks, and it consistently opposed the early release of prisoners from both sides of the divide. In this period, leading UDA man Michael Stone was responsible for inviting a variety of politicians to the Maze to address UDA prisoners: 'the only people who did not get an invite were Sinn Fein and the Democratic Unionist Party – Sinn Fein because they were the political wing of our enemy and the DUP because they had repeatedly called for the death penalty.' He adds: 'Loyalist prisoners never referred to ... Ian Paisley by name. They called him "cow head".'[34]

Colin Crawford's study of the UDA contains long interviews with a number of UDA men. Only two of the 17 mention religion in their explanations of how they become involved in terrorism. Stone notes that his family were church people and that as a boy he regularly attended Sunday school and was in the Boy's Brigade but the church in question was not Free Presbyterian. It was the mainstream Church of Ireland.[35] Another man mentions a church background but does so to draw a before-and-after contrast. There was the respectable church life of his family that he consciously rejected and there was his involvement in the UDA. There are only two mentions of Paisley. One is an off-hand reference to having voted for him. The other criticises him for not supporting the campaign for the segregation of loyalist and republican prisoners. Almost every biography identifies republican violence as the cause of violence. Typical is the man who said: 'I suppose the event which changed my life was the murder of a good friend of mine, William Thompson. ... The IRA murdered Billy on the Crumlin Road just outside Everton Girl's School. I was distraught when I heard he'd been murdered.'[36]

In my many interviews with loyalists I have sometimes found a very weak (and somewhat inconsistent) assertion that Paisley should take some of the blame because 'he marched us up to the top of the hill and marched us down again', but the stress is always on the second command and not the first. When they were taking risks to save Ulster, 'that fat bastard did nothing'. When they were serving life sentences, 'the self-righteous Bible-bashing creep was trying to have us executed'. More often, when I have deliberately pressed the issue of whether others encouraged them to become terrorists, I have found a simple honesty. One serial killer from the 1970s said in response to my probing for

Paisleyite influence: 'that's all bollocks. Paisley did not make me go out and kill people. I done that.' Far from taking them as distant support for their work, the real terrorists scorned Paisley's third force efforts. As one later-very-senior UVF man said: 'Waving fuckin fire arms dockets! Fuckin joke. That boy was just an embarrassment.'

Far from being seen as justifying paramilitary violence, evangelical religion was seen by loyalists as justification for former members to 'stand down'. A number of former terrorists became Christians while in prison and their former comrades accepted that as a good reason for disaffiliation. One East Belfast commander of the UDA was deposed for supposedly informing on the organisation and stealing its funds. Conventionally he would have been murdered (or at the very least severely wounded) by his successors. He was not and the explanation was that he had become born again and was now an associate pastor of a Pentecostal church. As one of his former men out it: 'I never trusted that lying bastard. He's safe for now but if we ever find out he's faking he's booked into Roselawn [the local cemetery].' Buried in the general scorn for those who become 'good living', there was often a hint of respect.

The rough and the respectable

Those who are familiar with the UDA and UVF know that their members are not Paisley's people. In evangelical eyes, loyalists are scum who blaspheme, fornicate, drink alcohol, smoke, take drugs and kill people. The evangelical and paramilitary worlds barely touch each other, let alone overlap. The slight exceptions only make the contrast clearer. In the early 1970s there were a number of very small and short-lived organisations that employed some of the trappings of militia organisation without actually engaging in violence. The Down Orange Welfare recruited primarily from farmers and respectable small businessmen in County Down. The 1970s Orange Volunteers was a planning and marching organisation within the Orange Order that collected some weapons, but appears not to have done anything with them. The Vanguard movement within the Ulster Unionist party had its Ulster Vanguard Service Corp but it did little more than parade as a ceremonial bodyguard. There was also the Ulster Special Corp, an attempt by former part-time policemen to retain some sort of organisational structure in rural areas in the west of the province after they were stood down. Like Paisley's various third forces, these ephemeral groups saw themselves as creating a structure and a capacity that would allow effective defence in the case of all-out war; the vast majority of their members never became involved in terrorism.

In brief, we can say that Ulster unionists divided by class and region in their response to political threat. The paramilitaries recruited primarily from the urban and secular working class. Rural and middle-class evangelicals expressed their opposition largely within conventional democratic politics. The first proposition needs to be qualified by two observations about the scale of support for violence. First, the vast majority even of urban working-class Protestants did not get involved in paramilitary organisations. Second, unlike a large part of the Catholic population that voted for Sinn Fein even when the IRA was active, working-class Protestant voters repeatedly declined to vote for the self-appointed defenders who claimed to murder on their behalf.

British Israelism and the dissidents

After the ceasefires of 1994, a number of small loyalist splinter groups were formed to continue the armed struggle: the Loyalist Volunteer Force (LVF), the Orange Volunteers (OV), and the Red Hand Defenders (RHD). A UVF leader memorably described the dissidents as 'a motley collection of scum-bags and Bible-bashers', and he is right. A few of the dissidents resented the cease-fires because they felt too much of principle had been conceded to republicans. Some simply wished to continue to murder. Others were ambitious men who felt they were under-valued in the UDA and UVF. Some were professional criminals (mostly drug dealers) who resented the half-hearted attempts of the paramilitary leaders to constrain their activities. But that point about Bible-bashers is intriguing. Although we are talking about a handful of people, they are worth pursuing for what they tell us about the kind of Protestant religion that *might* support violence.

Billy Wright, the Portadown UVF leader whose expulsion from the UVF started the breakaway, had been a born-again Christian. During a five-year absence from the organisation, he sometimes acted as a gospel preacher in the County Armagh area. Always a man for the grand gesture, the code word he gave the LVF for claiming its murderous acts in statements to the media was 'Covenant'. The man who led the Orange Volunteers in 1998–99, Clifford Peeples, was a keen but peripheral UVF man who later became a Pentecostal pastor. One of the OV's first actions was a synchronised arson attack on 11 Catholic churches, which Peeples defended on the grounds that they are the bastions of the Antichrist: 'We are defenders of the reformed faith. Our members are practising Protestant worshippers.'[37] A close colleague of Peeples was a former Paisley supporter, an evangelical Christian lay preacher, and a British Israelite. Although there is no evidence that he was involved in any crimes as a result of this association, the man who acted as the link between the LVF and the wider world was an Elim Pentecostal pastor. Four is not a large number but to have four evangelicals out of at most 200 dissidents, when you have none among 2,000 loyal UDA and UVF members, is suggestive.

What the four had in common was a hyper-ethnic unionism, tinged with British Israelism. This creed argues that the British race (exemplified now by Ulster Protestants because the rest of Britain has proved itself unreliable) is descended from one of the lost tribes of Israel, and hence is not just metaphorically but actually the Children of God. With local variations in just who is held to compose these lost tribes, British Israelism was popular in the heyday of the Empire, especially in places such as the USA, Canada, Australia and New Zealand where British settlers competed with the Irish and other Catholic peoples. Evangelical Protestantism has long been a major component of the ethnic identity of Ulster unionists, many of whom are tempted to think that, even if they are not quite God's chosen people, then they are still pretty special in his eyes. They suppose that God practises a form of ethnic favouritism.[38] Paisley and his supporters often speak of 'the Protestant people of Ulster' as if they were a people of whom God particularly approves but they do not confuse a nation and the people of God. For Protestants salvation is an individual burden. It cannot be inherited by being born into the right family or tribe or people. Ulster Protestants might typically be more Godly than the Italians, for example, but that does not mean that all Ulster Protestants will be saved or that salvation is an heritable property. When he preached at an Orange Lodge dedication service, Paisley would flatter his audience by reminding them of the Godly principles that the Order supposedly maintained, but he would also point out that those principles meant nothing unless each individual Orangeman got saved and lived a Godly life.

British Israelism offends most evangelicals because of its negative view of those who are not descended from the lost tribes of Israel. The Free Presbyterian minister who succeeded Paisley as Moderator of the Church concluded a lengthy critique of the Biblical interpretation behind British Israelism by saying:

> Some of the communications I have received have made me righteously indignant. How shocking it is to receive literature defending Sheldon Emery as a man of God. In one of his books the Negro is described as 'the beast of the field' and Christianity as being a religion ONLY FOR THE WHITE MAN.... We believe that the Bride of Christ is the Church made up of some out of *every tribe, tongue, people and nation*. We in the Free Presbyterian Church have no room for those who teach the blasphemy that Adam is the father of the white race only.[39]

British Israelism also offends Ulster evangelicals because its offers an unwarrantedly positive view of Ulster. Unlike Peeples, Wright and the unnamed former Paisleyite, Paisley subordinated the political fate of Northern Ireland to the will of God. Though he hoped they might be closely linked, they were not the same thing. Outsiders who see only Paisley's anti-Catholicism miss the point that the vast majority of his protests were directed at the Church of Ireland and the Irish Presbyterian Church. He also frequently denounced 'those who are Protestant in name only'. In politics he appealed to the Protestant electorate but he did not believe that they were God's chosen people. It was common to find FP ministers praying for Ulster but they also recognised that it might be God's will to 'test' the people of God by forcing them into a united Ireland. Some could even see some value in that; it would test their faith. As a senior minister put it in a sermon:

> The spiritual health of the church is not dictated by the political health of the nation. This is something we in Ulster need to learn. We have become

used to the cause of Christ being allied to the political cause of our Province, so that we have begun to think that the well-being of the Church of Christ is indissolubly linked with the political entity of Northern Ireland. That is not the case. ... God's Kingdom is a superior land unaffiliated to the kingdoms of men.... God's cause may flourish, irrespective of who sits upon the throne of government.[40]

To summarise, Protestantism played a major role in Ulster unionism by virtue of its place in the ethnic identity and political history of Ulster 'Protestants' (here using the term in the political sense). The major Protestant churches generally supported unionist political preferences. The importance of religion can be seen in the assistance that it gave Ian Paisley in building his political career. However, church leaders also consistently and rigorously campaigned against vigilante violence. Apart from his willingness to use them during the 1978 strike, even Paisley consistently opposed the UDA and UVF.

Conclusion

The Northern Ireland conflict is a religious conflict. The casual use of words is a nuisance but it is not an accident that the matched pair 'Catholic and Protestant' is often used as a synonym for 'nationalist and unionist' or 'republican and loyalist'. Religious affiliation is a major part of ethnic identity and religious culture has often legitimised competing political aspirations. However, we should be clear that religion is implicated primarily through the medium of ethnic identity. Small groups on each side may see jihad elements in the struggle: conservative Catholics seeing unionism as no more than you would expect from heretics and evangelical Protestants seeing the hidden hand of Rome behind the IRA. But for most people the specifically religious did not figure highly in its own right.

Religious organisations encouraged the conflict by legitimising the competing political agendas. However, church leaders also tried to blunt the severity of the competition and ensure that it was confined to the accepted means of liberal democracy by repeatedly and forcefully criticising terrorism and by doing so in cooperation with religious leaders from the other side of the divide. Even Ian Paisley, who denounced such ecumenical cooperation as unbiblical, consistently denounced vigilante violence as usurping the state's legitimate monopoly on coercion.

Quite what impact this had on the general public cannot be known with certainty. Someone who doubts the causal impact of religious ideas can reasonably suggest that the greatest contrast between Northern Ireland and, for example, Afghanistan in 2000 or Croatia in 1941, is not the peaceful intentions of religious leaders but the solidity of the state. For a brief period in the early 1970s it seemed that Ulster might collapse into anarchy but by the end of the 1970s most people were able to live relatively normal lives and most economic, legal and social institutions operated reasonably effectively. The Irish and British states were powerful enough and seen as legitimate by such a very large proportion of citizens that the Troubles never degenerated into the chaos that would have obliged religious leaders to give up their posture of supporting legality and instead become solely spokesmen for the interests of their people in a context of open warfare.

However, to suggest that it was only the stability of the political environment that kept religious leaders on the straight and narrow is to exaggerate the role of circumstances and to miss a small but important point that can be drawn in the Northern Ireland case: the paradoxical link between partisanship and personal piety. Being willing to use violence for political ends is a function of commitment to the cause. In ethnic and nationalist competition, it is excessive commitment to the ethnie or nation that allows group advantage to trump civility. Or to put it another way, in order to feel justified in killing and maiming 'them', we need to deny them the humanity we extend to our own people. Religion has a complex interaction with ethnic or national identity. It commonly legitimises it as the ethnie or nation flatters itself as being in some sense favoured by God. But in most religions the faith that makes us God's special favourites is a watered-down, conventional, and mundane version. The idea that a particular people enjoys a special position in the eyes of God can best be taken for granted (and it is important that it is taken for granted rather than consciously embraced) by those who do not have a deep personal interest in, and commitment to, the faith. Any serious thought about what God requires will expose the manifest failings of 'the people'. Hence we will often find the religious virtuosi either sceptical or openly critical of the profession of faith of their people. Paisley could talk of 'the Protestant people of Ulster' when campaigning for votes but when he preached from his pulpit, his understanding of the gospel forced him to criticise those whose religious profession was nominal. When we analyse various correlates of attitudes to paramilitary violence in a 1999 survey we find that frequency of church attendance is strongly correlated with a rejection of loyalist terror. Indeed, it is a better predictor than age or gender.[41] Within the ethnic category of 'Protestant', those who are most religiously 'Protestant' are those most opposed to the use of violence for political ends, even those political goals that they themselves share.

Frequency of church attendance has less impact on Catholic attitudes to political violence than it has on the views of Protestants. There are a number of possible explanations for this. It could be that church attendance is a better measure of personal piety for Protestants than for Catholics. It could be that, because Catholics are more alienated from the political status quo than Protestants and thus see a greater problem to be solved, similar values produce a different calculation as to what is justified to remedy the problem. But even if both of these are true, there is a central difference between the two traditions of Christianity that concerns the balance of the individual and the community. Evangelical Christianity is a thoroughly individualistic faith: religious merit cannot be transferred between individuals, the church is a bureaucratic convenience, and membership of a visible community makes no difference to one's salvation. Catholicism permits merit transfer, the Church mediates God and humankind, and the way to salvation is through the Church and the community. What this suggests is that personal piety may not have quite the same debilitating effect on communal identity for Catholics as it does for Protestants. That could explain why we do not find so the same strength of correlation between church attendance and negative views of paramilitary activity for Catholics as for Protestants.

In the absence of more detailed and pertinent survey data, the Protestant–Catholic comparison must remain tentative and suggestive. Nonetheless, as I have argued in this chapter, there is a Catholic version of the idea that religiosity has a constraining effect on the conflict in Northern Ireland: obedience to the Church. We can see the Catholic Church's critical attitude to republican terrorism and it seems reasonable to assume that the Church's teaching has played a part in restraining support for republicanism and in restraining republicans.

This chapter has tried to sketch an answer to the question 'What part has religion played in the Northern Ireland conflict?'. The answer is paradoxical: it has encouraged partisanship but it has also encouraged moderation.

4   Sectarianism in Scotland

Introduction

It may not always be, as Robert Burns put it, 'a giftie' to see ourselves as others see us but it is often salutary. From 1978 to 1991 I worked in Belfast and frequently visited family and friends in Scotland. From 1991 I reversed the direction: living in Scotland and travelling frequently to Northern Ireland to continue my research on Ulster unionist politics and loyalist paramilitaries. I spent the best part of 30 years personally and professionally comparing sectarianism in Scotland and Northern Ireland and long ago concluded that such conflict as did exist between Protestants and Catholics in Scotland was trivial compared to the deeply-embedded animosity, often exhibiting itself in murderous violence, that I found in Ulster. Hence I was taken aback when in around 2005 friends in Manchester – educated, well-informed people with an interest in religion and politics – told me that Scotland was almost as bad as Northern Ireland and cited as evidence newspaper reports of sectarian violence. Tracing back I found their impressions were based on two sources. One was a report from the Crown Office on statistics of religiously aggravated crimes. The other was a widely summarised compendium of apparently sectarian murders.

Since June 2003 it has been possible for a criminal offence to be 'aggravated' by religious prejudice. A mugger who shouts obscenities at his victim could be hit with a second charge if those obscenities included expressions of religious hatred. In 2004, the Crown Office and the Procurator Fiscal's Service released the results of their study of the first six months of the new system. The press mostly led their reports with a comparison of victims, as when the *Daily Telegraph* opened with: 'Catholics are twice as likely as Protestants to be the targets of sectarian abuse'.[1] Or they reported the Catholic Church's condemnation of the data: 'Church leaders yesterday condemned the scourge of sectarianism ...'[2] A quick glance at phrases such as 'Catholics target of most abuse' and 'Catholics are twice as likely to be victims of sectarianism' might well create the impression of gangs of religious bigots wandering the streets of Glasgow and Motherwell asking people their religion before assaulting them.[3] A detailed examination of the figures suggests something importantly different.

First, almost all of the original offences (92 per cent) were breaches of the peace and the aggravation was verbal. Add to that the facts almost half the accused were drunk (and we may speculate about the blood chemistry of others) and that one-third of those verbally abused were police officers. Second, and this point was missed by every report, we do not know the religion of victims. All we know is the content of the verbal abuse. This may seem like nit-picking until we follow the logic through to the end. As the perpetrators generally could not know the religion of the policeman or club bouncer they were insulting, we must assume that the insult was produced ritualistically and hence tells us about the identity of the abuser, not the abused. Two-thirds of the perpetrators expressed anti-Catholic sentiments and hence were probably Protestant and one-third voiced anti-Protestant sentiments and hence were probably Catholic. If the drunken hooligans of Glasgow divide two-thirds Protestant and one-third Catholic that is about par for the area. Incivility is evenly distributed.

We have good information about sectarian violence. A major survey in Glasgow in 2002 asked respondents if they had ever been victims of certain classes of crime and, if so, what they thought was the reason. Of 1,000 respondents, 147 had been physically attacked in the previous five years. Leaving aside the personal and the domestic, the most common reason for being attacked was 'area where you live', which was cited by 18 people. Only seven people, less than 1 per cent of the sample, cited 'religion'. Slightly more often cited were country of origin, gender and sexuality.[4]

The other source of my Manchester friends' bleak view of Scotland was a newspaper report of a claim by a spokesman for Nil By Mouth, a voluntary sector organisation that campaigns against sectarianism. Peter McClean told a committee of the Scottish Parliament: 'In 1999–2000 no racially motivated murders were recorded. However, Nil By Mouth has researched sectarian-related offences and has found eight murders during that time that had a clear sectarian element.'[5] Six months earlier he had given the same figure to the *Daily Record*: 'Our statistics for 1999–2000 show no racist murders but at least eight sectarian murders in Scotland.'[6] In 2002, the Church of Scotland's Church and Nation Committee claimed 'eleven Old Firm related murders since 1995'. When I asked Nil By Mouth and the Church of Scotland for their evidence I was referred to a report written by Elinor Kelly and Gregory Graham that listed 11 murders but for a longer time period: 1984 to 2002.

In most years there are just over 100 homicides in Scotland. On that base the proportion of homicides that were sectarian is 4 per cent according to Nil By Mouth, 1.6 per cent according to the Kirk, or 0.6 per cent by Kelly and Graham's list. Nil By Mouth seem to have taken the 1995–2000 part of Kelly and Graham's list and trebled the apparent incidence of sectarian murder by truncating its time period from six years to just two years. The Kirk had gone for the full 11 cases listed by Kelly and Graham but the shorter time period preferred by Nil By Mouth. And thus by error and repetition 11 sectarian murders in 18 years becomes – if Nil By Mouth is right – 68 such homicides.

But even Kelly and Graham's original list is almost certainly an exaggeration. When a colleague and I reexamined the list we came to the conclusion that only four of 11 cited cases seemed sectarian. In 1984, a young man died after falling under a train during a fight between Rangers and Celtic fans at Partick tube station. In 1989, a man was stabbed to death as a result of a fight between two neighbouring families who supported opposite sides of the Old Firm. In 1995, a young Celtic fan had his throat cut by Jason Campbell in Bridgeton. Campbell was a member of a well-known loyalist family: his father and uncle had served time for explosive offences connected with the paramilitary Ulster Volunteer Force. In May 1999, after the cup final, Thomas McFadden, a Celtic fan, was chased and murdered by two Rangers fans.

The sectarian character of the other murders is far from sure. For example, according to Kelly and Graham: 'John Ormiston …[a] Rangers fan died after being beaten up in West Lothian after an Old Firm game.' The details given in court suggest something rather different. Ormiston had been involved in a serious road accident that left him with a damaged spleen. He drank heavily and had a reputation for touching women inappropriately at his regular haunt: the Fa'side Inn in Wallyford, East Lothian. Justin Smith, 23, was in the pub on May 2 1999, when his girlfriend went to the bar to order drinks. She complained after Ormiston had grabbed hold of her. She stuck her elbow into him and shouted to her boyfriend: 'Get rid of this idiot'. Smith and Ormiston went outside, where Smith punched Ormiston on the body, knocked him to the ground, then punched and kicked him again. The victim apparently offered no resistance. Afterwards, the two men shook hands and Ormiston went back to the bar for another drink before making his way home. The next morning he told his uncle he was not going to work. The uncle left under the impression that Ormiston had a hangover. Later that day he returned to find his nephew dead. Although the fight occurred the same day as an Old Firm game, nothing in the evidence suggested that football or religion had anything to do with the incident.

Another dubious inclusion was the murder of George Reid in August 1999. Reid was killed by Patrick Nicol after Nicol's Rangers shirt was accidentally burned in a pub. Reid was an alcoholic of no fixed abode who spent his time begging and drinking. He often slept in a friend's flat in the block where Nicol lived. On 6 August 1999 Nicol bought a new Rangers football top which he wore that evening. He drank a large amount of alcohol during the afternoon and evening and in the later part of the evening he spent some time in the Falcon Bar, Stirling, where his new top was accidentally burned by a fellow customer. This upset Nicol who became aggressive. Some time after two o'clock the following morning Nicol met Reid. According to Nicol's recollection – not disputed by the Crown – there was some physical contact that Nicol construed as an unwelcome sexual overture. His reaction was rapid and violent. He repeatedly stabbed Reid with a large kitchen knife. As we can suppose that the drunk Nicol would have become as aggressive had it been a new Ralph Lauren shirt rather than a Rangers top that was damaged and as the trigger was an unwanted sexual advance, there is no reason to code this as sectarian.

If we set the toll of sectarian murders at four and divide it by the 1,800 or so homicides over 18 years, then only 0.3 per cent (that is, less than one-third of one per cent) of Scotland's homicides were sectarian and in every case the religious component implied by the term 'sectarian' was actually football fan allegiance. During the Troubles in Northern Ireland thousands of people were killed because of their religio-ethnic identity; in Scotland between 1984 and 2002 nobody was.

Competing visions

What I found most striking in reviewing years of Scottish reporting was the ease with which reporters and commentators accepted the dystopian image of Protestant–Catholic relations in Scotland. Repeatedly events were shoe-horned into the sectarian frame with little or no justification. To give just one example, in November 2004, the day after a Rangers–Celtic match the *Sunday Mail* ran a number of stories under the two-page headline 'Real Toll of Old Firm Mayhem'.[7] One page was taken up with an account of the burning down of a Catholic chapel in Stornoway. The clear implication was that the chapel was torched by a Rangers fan. A few days later the police announced that the fire had been caused by an electrical fault. No newspaper gave that announcement banner headline coverage. As we will see below, it is a regular feature of surveys that Scots respondents say that there is a great deal of sectarian violence or labour market discrimination but when asked if they have themselves suffered any, they demur: the classic outcome of perception being shaped by inaccurate stereotypes.

I have to plead guilty to accepting the dystopian view. When in the 1980s I first researched sectarianism in Scotland, I assumed that the Irish Catholics who settled in the second half of the nineteenth century had been the victims of systematic discrimination and I took my main task to be explaining why, in contrast to the situation in Ulster, the discriminatory system had gradually weakened and collapsed. It was only 20 years later, going over the same material for a second time, that I became aware of the extent to which the historical record relied on just one source: historian James Handley.[8] Worse, it depended on a careless reading of Handley, who was properly objective in his reporting both of the dire circumstances of many immigrants and the hostility towards them of some Scots. My carelessness was to forget that the same dreadful material conditions were enjoyed by a far greater number of native Scots and to assume that the problems of the migrants were caused by the anti-Irish and anti-Catholic sentiments that Handley reports.

In retrospect I can see that the dystopian history of the Irish in Scotland was heavily influenced by the circumstances of Northern Ireland. With the Ulster Troubles as our guide, it is easy to suppose that anti-Catholic bigotry was a powerful social force that kept Catholic migrants isolated, introverted, poor and politically impotent. However, there is a very different Catholic migrant experience that we could use to frame our understanding of Scotland. If we take the very successful rise of Irish Catholic migrants to the United States as our model, we might conclude that Catholics migrants to Scotland were poor because they brought their poverty with them and that they gradually worked their way out of poverty at much the same rate as did poor native Scots, of whom there was a very large number. The main obstacle to Catholic advance was not the prejudice of anti-Catholic Scots (which was largely ineffectual) but the self-reproducing nature of poverty, which caused families to send children out to work, at the earliest possible age, for the highest possible wage. The jobs that gave the best immediate return for untutored vigour were those that offered no long-term prospect of advancement. Scottish elites were reasonably accommodating (for example in the generous terms on which they funded Catholic schools). Far from being the ideological justification for organised discrimination, most anti-Catholic sentiment was the pathetic complaint of weak social groups unable to prevent changes that marginalised them.[9] Far from being excluded, Irish Catholics and their heirs quickly achieved considerable power through the trade unions, Labour party and local government. A century after the high point for Irish migration, Scots Catholics are much the same as everyone else. With the erosion of class differences, there has been significant integration of Catholics in Scottish society, signalled most importantly by the high degree of inter-marriage between young Scots Protestants and Catholics.

The evidence of sectarian discrimination

One might have imagined that something sufficiently important to persuade Jack McConnell, when he was Scotland's First Minister, to launch a crusade to eradicate it would have been so thoroughly investigated that its extent and nature was beyond doubt but there has been a dearth of good quality social science research.[10] Typical of what we do have is a study of discrimination in the workplace that inadvertently offers a fine example of the dystopian vision in action. Researchers interviewed 72 people in the west of Scotland – 39 Catholics and 33 Protestants – about their experience and knowledge of discrimination at work and found 'evidence of continuing experience of sectarian discrimination at work'.[11] Actually what they found were *claims* of actual discrimination. The authors wrote: 'seven out of a total of thirty-nine Catholics described personal experience of discrimination'[12] but the paper quotes from only three Catholics who made such claims and one of those referred to the experience of a relative.[13] Most of their respondents did not claim firm knowledge even of disparity, let alone discrimination. It is characteristic of many of the excerpts that they report hearsay: 'I was speaking to somebody ...'; 'I can remember my uncle James saying. ...'; 'I was told ... they had never employed a Catholic'; 'I suppose the rumours were just that ...'; 'there were certainly a number of years ago rumours that ...' and so on.[14] The obvious problem with this is that if discrimination is as common as the respondents, think why have they not suffered it?

Frustrated at the way so much of the discussion of sectarian in Scotland proceeded by anecdote and focused on football fan animosity, three colleagues and

I set out to examine all the available social scientific evidence of disadvantage and discrimination and published our conclusions as *Sectarianism in Modern Scotland*.[15] We were aided by three major sources that became available in 2001 and 2002: a module of religion questions in the 2001 Scottish Social Attitudes survey, a major survey funded by Glasgow City Council in 2002, and the 2001 Scottish census, which for the first time included questions about current religion and religion of upbringing.

Social statistics cannot show discrimination directly but, if it is the case that Catholics have been the victims of systematic discrimination, there should be persistent signs of disadvantage. Of course, not all disadvantage is a result of discrimination. Some disparities may well have explanations that have nothing to do with deliberate social exclusion. For example, some differences in employ-ment patterns may reflect differences in the culture and occupational background of teachers in Catholic and state sector schools. But the connection does work the other way round. If there is little sign of disadvantage, then unless one sup-poses Catholics are inherently superior, the discrimination claim falls.

The Scotland and Glasgow surveys show very similar results. In Scotland as a whole, Catholics were more likely than Protestants to work in lower-status semi-routine or routine jobs: for managerial and professional positions, the rela-tionship is precisely reversed. As Table 4.1 shows, the greatest differences in work status are found in the oldest age cohorts. Among those aged 55 and over, only 26 per cent of respondents raised as Catholics but 49 per cent of those raised in the Church of Scotland were in non-manual occupations (a difference of 23 points). Among younger respondents the difference was small (5 percent-age points) and statistically insignificant, confirming the impression derived from those for educational qualifications: what was once major disadvantage has been reduced markedly.[16]

National comparisons may distort the picture because Protestants and Cath-olics are not evenly distributed across the areas with the best and the worst pro-spects. For like-for-like comparison, we can look at Glasgow alone.

In Table 4.2 we see differences in occupational status that are related to reli-gious upbringing, but in a very similar fashion to the national data, they are

Table 4.1 Religion of upbringing by class and age, Scotland, 2001 (%)

Age cohort	Percentage of each group in a non-manual occupation				
	Roman Catholic	Church of Scotland	No religion	Other religion	All
18–34 years	58	63	45	65	58
35–54 years	47	58	45	62	55
55+ years	26	49	33	63	48

Source: Scottish Social Attitudes Survey (*n* = 1,597).

Note: Non-manual refers to 'Employers and managers', 'intermediate occupations', 'small employers and own account workers' in the National Statistics Socio-economic Classification, 2000.

Table 4.2 Religion of upbringing by class and age, Glasgow, 2002 (%)

		Roman Catholic	Church of Scotland	No religion	Other religion	All people in h'hold
18–34	Non-manual	41	46	49	56	48
	Manual	59	54	51	44	52
		100	100	100	100	100
	n =	*117*	*102*	*47*	*62*	*318*
35–54	Non-manual	31	38	32	50	36
	Manual	69	62	68	50	64
		100	100	100	100	100
	n =	*114*	*133*	*25*	*36*	*308*
55+	Non-manual	14	30	25	52	27
	Manual	86	70	75	48	73
		100	100	100	100	100
	n =	*108*	*292*	*12*	*27*	*376*

Source: NFO Social Research.

Note: The social grade of the chief income earner in the household was used to infer the social grade of the respondent. The non-manual socio-economic group comprises of social grades A, B and C1; the manual group comprises of social grades C2, D and E but, in addition, social grade E also includes those on state benefit or unemployed.

closely associated with age. The differences only reach statistical significance for the oldest age group, where 30 per cent of Church of Scotland identifiers and only 14 per cent of Catholics have non-manual profiles. Such differences in socio-economic status diminish through the middle-age group (where it is only 7 points) and are again small for the youngest age group: at 5 percentage points. These results come from sample surveys and it is always possible (though unlikely) that they are unrepresentative of the population as a whole. The great virtue of the 2001 national census is that it contains information about social class for the entire population.

The census data so far released are a little awkward to interpret for two reasons. There is some distortion for the youngest age group because the census treats social class as a household measure and attributes the class of the 'household reference person' (the person who completed the form; usually the main wage earner) to all members of the household. If, as our surveys suggest, there is upward mobility over the generations, this will be under-reported in the census. There is also some difficulty interpreting social class E, which, in addition to households where the reference person is in the lowest grades of employment, includes those where the reference person is long-term unemployed, living on state benefits, or over the age of 74 and living in rented housing. In Table 4.3, we present just the data for the middle age cohort, for Scotland as a whole, and for Glasgow City. This confirms the picture we derive from the 2001 Scottish Social Attitudes survey and the 2002 Glasgow City survey: differences in the

Table 4.3 Religion of upbringing by class in middle age cohort, Scotland and Glasgow, Census 2001 (%)

		Roman Catholic	Church of Scotland	No religion	Other religion	All
a) Scotland						
	AB	22	24	19	30	24
	C1	27	29	26	29	28
	C2	17	20	20	16	18
	D	21	19	24	16	19
	E	13	9	12	9	10
		100	101	101	100	99
b) Glasgow City						
	AB	16	17	18	23	18
	C1	23	25	25	27	25
	C2	15	15	13	13	14
	D	23	21	20	17	21
	E	24	22	24	21	22
		101	100	100	101	100

Source: GRO Scotland, Census, 2001

Note: The results are for 35–54-year-olds. Category AB includes managerial and professional occupations whilst E includes lowest-grade workers and those who are on state benefits or unemployed. Table A3.4 in the appendix provides more details. Percentages do not always total 100 because of rounding.

proportions of Catholics and Protestants in white-collar occupations are of the order of 5 percentage points or less for the middle age cohort. Taken together these three large-scale data sources paint a clear picture: religious differences in social class are largely restricted to older Scots.

One disadvantage of the sectarian trope is that it may blind us to more significant patterns. In many of our detailed multivariate analyses of the links between religious upbringing and education and social class, it is often the group of those who said they were raised with 'no religion' that fares worst. For example, Table 4.1 shows that, for the youngest age cohort, those raised in no religion are 13 points behind those raised as Roman Catholics for white-collar occupations: a greater difference than the separation between the other three groups. Curiously the pattern for Glasgow City is reversed. For the youngest age cohort, 49 per cent of those raised with no religion are in white-collar work, which places them ahead of those raised as Church of Scotland and Catholic. The Census data confirms both patterns: those raised in no religion are ahead of Catholics and Church of Scotland in Glasgow but behind both in Scotland as a whole.

Why this should be the case is not obvious but the finding is important. If we suppose the pattern reflects a social reality, then whatever explains it is unlikely to be discrimination. Even if we thought that people with power and influence wanted to penalise those not socialised in any religion, it is hard to see the mechanism that would allow it. One might guess the religion of a Protestant or

Catholic from name, residence or school but none of those would identify those raised in no religion. As we cannot imagine a mechanism for effective discrimination against the non-religious, we must conclude that the socio-economic fate of a significant number of Scots is being influenced by religious background (or, to be more precise, lack of it) in a way that does not involve discrimination. If that is so for one group, it may also be so for all groups.

If it is the case that Scotland is sectarian in any non-trivial sense, this should be visible not just in socio-economic differences but also in marks of segregation or social distance, in communal self-identity, and in differences in major choices such as political party support. I will consider each of these in turn.

In Northern Ireland, Protestants and Catholics live together only in a small number of upper-middle-class areas. While areas of Glasgow became somewhat Green or Orange following the immigration and settlement of both Irish Catholics and Ulster Protestants, no districts were dominated by one or the other. What are now thought of as Protestant strongholds such as Bridgeton were actually quite mixed, as were the Irish Catholic enclaves such as Garngad. By 1914, over 700,000 people were living in Glasgow's three central square miles, the densest concentration of population in Europe. Such lack of space was an obvious constraint on the creation of the rival ethnic ghettos that emerged in Liverpool and the Lancashire mill towns. Glasgow Corporation assumed control of working-class housing during the 1920s and for the next four decades cleared the slums, rebuilt the inner city, and constructed large peripheral housing schemes. The Catholic- and Labour-dominated council had no reason to separate Catholics and Protestants in the shift of population. In Belfast and Londonderry on the other hand, control over housing allocation was a key pillar of Unionist power; housing segregation maintained predictable electoral outcomes. The outbreak of the Troubles in the late 1960s sharpened segregation in Northern Ireland as many Catholic and Protestant families were forced to flee back into traditional strongholds of towns, villages or particular housing estates.

The 2001 Census allowed us to compare, for the first time, segregation in Glasgow and Belfast. Catholics make up 29 per cent of the population of Glasgow. In no council ward do they form a majority, although they come close in Toryglen (45 per cent) and Hutchesontown (43 per cent). The commonly held view that Garngad remains a very Catholic part of Glasgow is not supported by the data; for every Catholic living in the Royston ward (approximating to the old Garngad district) there are two non-Catholics. On the other hand, the supposedly Protestant strongholds of Bridgeton and Govan, are in fact, both 30 per cent Catholic. The area with the smallest proportion of Catholics (12 per cent) is Pollokshields East, which also has the largest ethnic minority population in Scotland: four in ten residents are Muslim. In short there is no obvious geographical pattern to Catholic residency in Glasgow.

In Belfast, 42 per cent of the population is Catholic. However, 11 council wards contain at least twice this figure, with five being at least 90 per cent Catholic. At the other extreme, Catholics form less than 3 per cent of the population in 13 wards. The highly Catholic wards are generally situated in the west of the city and the highly Protestant wards situated in the east. However, some hugely contrasting areas sit side by side in more central and northern parts of Belfast; both New Lodge (93 per cent Catholic) and Falls (86 per cent Catholic) are neighbours to Shankill (less than 1 per cent Catholic), while Ardoyne (86 per cent Catholic) borders Crumlin (less than 2 per cent Catholic). If Catholics were to be equally spread across Belfast, then 40 per cent of the Catholic population would need relocated. The corresponding figure for Glasgow is only 11 per cent. In the household survey of 2002, less than 7 per cent of Glaswegians felt that their religion had a bearing on where they could live and only 5 per cent said they would avoid a particular part of the city for the same reason. In brief, Belfast is segregated; Glasgow is not.

The extent to which two populations inter-marry is important both as a symptom and as a cause of integration. It is a symptom, because the willingness to marry someone of another race, nation, ethic group or religion shows the importance of those characteristics as against personal emotional attachment. Because we can only marry those we meet, inter-marriage also indicates the extent of mixing as equals. But it is also a cause of further integration. For bigots to maintain a culture or structure of discrimination they must be able to divide 'oor ain folk' from those they wish to deprive of opportunities. The more inter-marriage, the harder it is to discriminate and the more likely it is that religious or ethnic preferences will be over-ridden by other considerations. As populations mix, being a good uncle or brother-in-law competes with being a loyal Catholic or Protestant, and in stable affluent societies that are not divided by competing political agendas, family generally trumps loyalty to religio-ethnic group.

What do our two surveys tell us about inter-marriage? First, they tell us that the vast majority of Scots voice no objection to a relative marrying someone of a different religion. Across Scotland, only 3 per cent 'mind a great deal'; a further 7 per cent mind 'slightly'. Over two-thirds did not mind at all. There were no significant differences between the expressed views of Protestants and Catholics, irrespective of age. The same pattern was found in Glasgow, where only 3 per cent mind a great deal and over 80 per cent did not mind at all. Around a third of those in Glasgow who minded a great deal about mixed marriages were Muslim; a gross over-representation. Catholics in Glasgow express, marginally, more tolerant views than Protestants. In turn, Protestants in Glasgow express more tolerant views than both Catholics and Protestants in Scotland as a whole.

The sentiment expressed in answers to the hypothetical survey question is matched by action. Put simply, it was once the norm for Catholics to marry other Catholics. In our Scottish survey, 94 per cent of married Catholics aged 65–74 were married to a Catholic. The corresponding figure in the Glasgow study was 80 per cent. For Scotland as a whole the figure for those aged 55–64 was 86 per cent (69 per cent in Glasgow) and it gradually goes down for each age cohort until, for those aged 25–34, more than half of the Catholics are married to non-Catholics. For Glasgow, over 40 per cent of married Catholics have non-Catholic spouses. To put these figures in context, we can note that in Northern Ireland in 1991 only 2 per cent of marriages were religiously mixed and in the USA in 1999 only 3 per cent of marriages were racially mixed. The point is compelling and simple. Young Scots no longer regard religion (or more precisely religio-ethnic identity) as an important consideration in the most important personal decision they make. This relative indifference to religion also shows up in socialising patterns. In the Glasgow survey only 6 per cent said that religion was a factor in whom they could have as a friend and that response was much more common from Muslim respondents than from Catholics or Protestants.

Joseph Bradley has suggested that, although the main objective differences between the heirs to the Irish and other Scots have been largely eroded, there is still a degree of cultural exclusion that has caused Scots Catholics of Irish descent to discover a renewed or entirely new interest in 'Irishness' as a distinct cultural identity.[17]

Catholics of Irish decent in Scotland do have the opportunity to express a wholly or partial Irish identity through sporting, cultural or political organisations including the Celtic Football Club, the Gaelic Athletic Association, Ancient Order of Hibernians and, for the more radical, the James Connelly Society. By far the most popular outlet for the expression of Irish identity is the Celtic Football Club. In the Glasgow survey, three-quarters of Celtic supporters were Catholic. However, we must immediately qualify that by saying that almost half of those surveyed did not follow any football team.

But that football allegiance does not translate into a more abstract sense of identity. We certainly find no evidence that Scots Catholics think of themselves as Irish. The Glasgow survey allowed respondents to choose as many national or ethnic identities that they felt best represented them: 81 per cent of Catholics chose Scottish, 23 per cent chose British, and only 8 per cent chose Irish. And those 8 per cent may well have been Irish in the entirely conventional sense of being Irish people working in Glasgow. Bradley's claims fare no better with data from the all-Scotland survey. Catholics were more likely than Church of Scotland identifiers or people who claimed no religion to describe themselves as 'Scottish not British'. In both 1999 and 2001 Catholics were less likely than Church of Scotland identifiers to describe themselves as 'Equally Scottish and British', but in this they were no different from those people who claimed no religious identity. The surveys allowed respondents to claim another identity. It was thus open to those who felt Irish rather than Scottish or British to say that. They did not.

In an effort to provide the evidence to support their views, scholars such as Bradley and Mary Hickman encouraged those of Irish descent in Scotland and England to record their identity as 'Irish' in the 2001 census. Adverts were taken out in places such as the *Irish Post* (a London-based paper) and *Celtic View*. The campaign did not produce the desired effect. The number of people resident in Scotland at the time of the census who choose to describe themselves as Irish (40,000) was less than the number of people who had been born in Ireland (55,000). That is, they were not Scots Catholics reacting to their oppressive environment by thinking of themselves as Irish. They were simply Irish in the sense that the people who said they were Swedes were Swedish.

Even before the census, a convenient explanation for this failure of reality was being composed. It was asserted that 'people born in Scotland with Irish parents or grandparents frequently hide their roots because they fear hostility' and hence 'the "Irish" box will not be fully used by those who feel they have an Irish cultural background'. This seems implausible. When survey respondents are quite happy to declare their income, views about abortion, religious upbringing and attitudes to capital punishment, it is not likely that they become coy over ethnic identity.

Another place we might find evidence of Catholic alienation is in attitudes towards devolution. Some commentators supposed that Catholics were reluctant to support devolution during the 1970s campaigns because they feared that an autonomous Scotland would be a more unpleasantly Protestant country than one run from London. In the run-up to the referendum on the Scottish parliament, the late Cardinal Winning announced very publicly that Catholics had nothing to fear from a Scottish parliament. Whether he led or merely represented a change is not clear but the voting suggests no Catholic hostility: 62 per cent were in favour. Of those who did vote, Catholics were as likely as Protestants to vote for a Parliament, and also less likely than Protestants to have voted against.

It is typical of deeply divided societies that religio-ethnic groups pursue competing politics, either to further their own interests as a bloc or to promote the interests of members of the religio-ethnic bloc in another state. When the Irish first moved to Scotland in significant numbers they exhibited both patterns. Irish politics were repeated in a minor key in Scotland. There were branches of various Irish parties active in central Scotland but once the Irish problem was resolved with the formation of the Irish Free State in the early 1920s, the Irish in Scotland turned to local issues. Unlike the model of continental Europe, where Catholics formed sectional, often clergy-led, parties that were antithetical to the Left, Scotland's Catholics became involved through the trade unions in the organisations that became the Labour party. Once the Labour movement had conceded the main Catholic Church demand – control over its own schools – and once it became clear that Scottish labourism was neither communist nor particularly socialist, the Catholic Church dropped its opposition.

There has long been a strong ideological connection between Protestantism and unionism, meaning in this context support for the union of England and Scotland as the centre of the British Empire. That connection was strengthened when Gladstone's support for Irish home rule split the Liberal party and moved Liberal unionists into what became the Conservative and Unionist party. For the first part of the twentieth century religious and political identities tended to overlap: Catholics were pro-Labour and anti-Conservative and Protestants were more likely to vote Conservative. A simple way of expressing the connection is to say that significant numbers of Catholics and Protestants voted against what elsewhere would have been their class interests: many working-class Protestants voted Conservative and many middle-class Catholics voted Labour.

Does this pattern still hold? Catholics do have a distinctly strong preference for Labour; the 2001 survey showed them to be overwhelmingly Labour voters.

More importantly, they remained so when we controlled for social class: in the Scottish survey 50 per cent of middle-class Catholics respondents said they voted for Labour. They were less likely than Protestants to support the Scottish Nationalists, or come to that, the Liberal Democrats and were even more distinctive in their hostility to the Conservatives: almost none voted Conservative. Looked at from the other end, although current levels of support are low, Scottish Protestants remained much more likely than others to vote Conservative.

In these calculations, we have identified respondents simply by the religious label they selected. We repeated the analysis for only those who attended church regularly. Church-going Catholics were much more likely to vote Labour (65 percent) than nominal Catholics and nominal and church-going Protestants (35, 36 and 37 percent, respectively). And church-going Catholics are distinctive in their support for Labour irrespective of their class background. On the other side of the divide, it is middle-class church-going Protestants who are distinctive in their support for the Conservative party in Scotland (but still only 23 per cent).

This much continues the patterns of the past. However, a new pattern was revealed once we divided the sample into three age bands. There was a marked decline in Labour support among younger Catholics (from more than two in three of older Catholics to less than one in three). In addition, the class divides of the past seem also to have disappeared among young Scots: they are now only really evident among older non-Catholic Scots. Put simply, only for an older generation of Scots do traditional class and religious loyalties still matter; for a younger generation they do not. In the 2001 general election, the most popular choice of Scots under the age of 35, irrespective of class or religion, was to abstain.

If we consider only the choices of those who did vote, we find some continuity with the past: younger church-going Catholics do vote (three-quarters voted in 2001) and they vote Labour (two-thirds of those who voted chose Labour). On the other side of the divide, the Conservative party is more popular with younger church-going Protestants than with other younger Scots. Thus, religion and politics continue to be intertwined, but even so, the reach of religion has been so diminished in Scottish life, and also the political landscape and even what is understood to count as politics has so changed for a younger generation, that the same general conclusion can be drawn: for most younger Scots religion does not drive political preferences (and apparently, for many, the political process in Westminster does not matter anyway).

One might carelessly suppose that any sign of difference between Catholics and Protestants is evidence of a divided society. The matter is more complicated. When we compare Catholic and Protestant voting in Northern Ireland we see two radically separated populations pulling in competing directions. In Scottish politics, Catholic distinctiveness is not divisive. Catholics are unusual only in being more likely than other Scots to support the political party that most Scots support. Labour is the preferred option of all Scots who vote. It is also the preferred party of Protestant Scots taken as a bloc: almost half of those Protestants who voted chose Labour, more than twice the number who voted for the next most popular choice. The minority Catholic population is not un-Scottish; it is hyper-Scottish. It is not Catholics who are unusual: it is that very small number of traditional Scottish Protestants who vote Conservative.

It is worth adding that just as it did in US Democratic party politics, Catholic involvement in the Scottish Labour movement brought considerable rewards. Of 76 Glasgow City Labour councillors between 1922 and 1931, 21.1 per cent were Catholics: well in proportion to Catholic support for Labour.[18] By the mid-1980s over half of elected Labour members in Glasgow District Council were Catholic.[19] Although we cannot be absolutely sure, it is almost certainly the case that, during the lifetime of Strathclyde Regional Council (1975–95), every leader of the Labour party and every Lord Provost was a Catholic. A study of Labour councillors in Glasgow in the late 1980s showed that, out of 54 surveyed, half described their current religion as Catholic with several more have been brought up as Catholics.[20] We have no exhaustive list of the religion of MPs but my own estimate from the early 1990s was that 16 out of 22 Labour MPs in the industrial heartlands of west and central Scotland were Catholic. That is 73 per cent of MPs Catholic against 24 per cent of Labour voters who are Catholic: a massive over-representation.

To summarise all of the above, I am suggesting that the proximity of Northern Ireland and its superficial similarity to Scotland has encouraged the adoption and maintenance of a particular view of the history of Protestant–Catholic relations that is fundamentally misleading. A far more instructive model is provided by the Irish experience in the USA where a migrant population begins at the bottom of the heap because it lacks capital and scarce professional skills and gradually works its way up, becoming better integrated and less distinctive on the way.

Explanation

Why did Protestant–Catholic relations in Scotland turn out more like the American than the Ulster experience? In retrospect I have to confess to a second mistake. My initial acceptance of the dystopian view led me to an explanation of recent Scots history that, though not wrong in its essentials, created a misleading impression by its focus. In my early writings on sectarianism in Scotland I assumed that anti-Catholic sentiments were common but were rendered ineffectual by social–structural constraints. For example, I drew attention to the gradual replacement of the locally owned family firm by the national (and later multinational) joint stock company to explain the waning of nepotism. To construct an exaggerated example from the employment histories of relatives who worked in the Vale of Leven, the factory whose owner was the local Unionist MP, member of the Orange Order, JP and elder of the Church of Scotland might well allow the Orange foreman to ensure that his fellow Orangemen got jobs before Catholics. Once the factory was absorbed into a national or multi-national company, such particularistic and informal hiring practices were replaced by formal procedures that gave no particular favours to Orangemen. Using the observations about the centralised nature of UK politics laid out here in Chapter 7, I made a similar case with regard to political choices. As competition between Protestants and Catholics was a concern only for some parts of Scotland (and parts of the North West of England) and party politics and Westminster legislation were determined by national interests that paid scant attention to minority regional interests, the wishes of the bigots were over-ruled. In brief, I explained the relative absence of sectarianism in Scotland compared to Northern Ireland, and its demise, by the impotence of the Scots bigots.

On revisiting all the evidence 20 years later, I came to a rather different conclusion. Amidst the frequently reported examples of anti-Catholic sentiment (such as the Church of Scotland's late-1920s commitment to the racist view that the Irish were an inassimilable bloc with a variety of social characteristics damaging to the Scottish race) I started to notice that in every example of vocal anti-Catholicism, the bigots were a minority who lost the argument, usually because powerful elites behaved well. My structural approach ('the bigots could not effectively discriminate') implied that lots of Scots did want to behave badly; going over the same material for a second time, I realised that I should have stressed how often Scots with power and influence acted fairly. We can document the opposition of various artisan guilds to the Catholic Emancipation Act of 1829 but we should also note that significant bodies of Scots (evangelical Presbyterians for example) were in favour of emancipation. We can be shocked by the racist language of John White's 1920s campaign to mobilise the Kirk against the Irish but we should also note that leading politicians and the *Glasgow Herald* (then the house paper for Scotland's industrial bourgeoisie) very deliberately snubbed White's campaign. We can note that Protestants ran for election to school boards on anti-Catholic platforms but we should also note that once in power leading Unionists such as Sir Charles Cleland (who as Convenor of the Glasgow Education Authority worked hard to ensure a smooth accommodation of Catholic schools under the terms of the 1918 Education Act) behaved in an entirely even-handed manner.

The state's attitude to Catholic schools offers a salutary illustration of the way in which focus on the protests of such bigots as Alexander Ratcliffe with his 'Rome on the Rates' campaign can distract us from the more important story. Through the nineteenth century the government increasingly became involved in shaping and funding what was becoming a national system of education. The main difference between Church of Scotland schools and those provided by the Catholic Church and by dissenting Protestants was not the extent of direct grant-aid from the state. Despite vociferous anti-Catholic campaigns, grant-aid was given to Catholic as well as to Free Church schools. The main disadvantage was in what might be thought of as local rates. Parishes of the Church in Scotland were originally funded by 'teinds', a local land tax. During the eighteenth and nineteenth centuries, as new congregations were created, this source of revenue declined in relative importance and, of course, it was not available to the various dissenting Presbyterian churches. But it remained an advantage. For Scotland as a whole in 1864 direct state aid accounted for only 15 per cent of the funding for schools, and the churches raised another 10 per cent. The majority of funding came from rates (21 per cent), fees (33 per cent) and subscriptions and gifts (20 per cent). It was that 21 per cent in rates which made the great difference between Church of Scotland schools and the rest. And of course the reliance on fees and gifts meant that schools reflected the prosperity (or otherwise) of the families and neighbourhoods that provided their pupils.

In his survey, Handley concludes: 'In the quarter of a century that had elapsed from the enactment of 1847 the state had dealt with the managers and teachers of Catholic schools in a spirit of fairness.'[21] But the need was great. The Argyll Commission of the late 1860s reported that only one-third of Catholic children in Glasgow attended a school of any kind. Attendance itself was irregular because pupils were kept off school for casual labour and most left school at the earliest opportunity anyway. The schools offered very little. As Gallagher notes, 'Catholic education was very rudimentary, school buildings were of inferior standard, and the meagre resources at hand were barely able to provide the three "R's" and religious instruction to a minority of children.'[22]

The 1872 Education Act was the state's response to the failure of a church-based system to serve the needs of a modern industrial urban country whose population was divided between four major churches. A popularly elected school board was to be established in every parish and burgh. It would have the power to manage those schools transferred to it. It would also be able to create new schools, to levy rates to pay for the erection and maintenance of those schools, and to enforce attendance of all children aged between five and thirteen. Religious education was not compulsory but was left to the new boards. However, it was clearly specified that parents could withdraw their children from any religious education of which they disapproved and to make that easy, such religious education as did take place should occur at the start or the end of the day. With hindsight we can see this as the start of a secular system but the Presbyterian churches handed over their schools willingly because they simply took it for granted that the popularity of Presbyterianism would be reflected in the composition of local school boards, which in turn would preserve the ethos of the schools. They never anticipated that the local sentiment would eventually become thoroughly secular.

Callum Brown talks of 'the exclusion of Catholic schools from the state system',[23] but the word 'exclusion' places the decision to stay out of the 1872 settlement in the wrong quarter entirely. Civil servants were anxious to incorporate Catholic schools but the Catholic Church rejected the terms under which schools could remain denominational: they would have to separate religious instruction from secular teaching. According to James Treble, 'board [that is, state] schools were seen as either an instrument for advancing the interests of the Church of Scotland or, at worst, as a force promoting apathy and leading ultimately to the possibility of secularism dominating National Education'.[24]

State support for Catholic schools did not end in 1872. Lay Catholics argued successfully that their schools should continue to be supported from parliamentary grants and local rates; after all, the community was having to contribute to the education of non-Catholic children via the rates that they paid. However, while boards could borrow money on easy terms, the Catholic Church had to rely on its own resources; aid for the maintenance of Catholic schools was awarded only after they had been built and equipped. The consequence of rejecting the 1872 settlement was that Catholic schools failed to improve at the rate of state schools. In 1886 when 71 per cent of female staff employed by the Boards had been educated in a training college, the comparable figure for Catholic schools was only 41 per cent.[25] By the end of the First World War, it was becoming clear that the gap in efficiency between Catholic and non-denominational schools was widening, with less than 3 per cent of the Catholic school population receiving secondary education and a shortage of well-qualified teachers.[26] The financial burden was so heavy that the Catholic school system could no longer survive without participating in the public sphere and securing the benefits of local education rates.

Catholic schools joined the state system under the terms of Section 18 of the 1918 Education (Scotland) Act. They were transferred on the understanding that certain safeguards were met: the church had the right to veto teaching appointments, religious instruction was to carry on to the same degree as before, and Catholic clergymen were to be allowed full access to the schools to oversee the continuation of such mandatory instruction. The schools were actually transferred in 1928, after a 'loan' spell that gave the Catholic authorities the opportunity to see that their demands were being met. The burden for financing and maintaining the schools was removed and, as Tom Gallagher notes, 'in no other predominantly Protestant country did Catholics enjoy such latitude in the educational sphere'.[27]

Although it is important to distinguish analytically motives and intentions from the opportunities to act on such preferences, the two fields obviously interact, so that the opportunity to act successfully on one's preferences reinforces them while long-term failure to get anywhere will eventually cause all but the most obstinate to change their preferences. My mistake in explaining the failure of sectarianism in Scotland was to put such stress on the social–structural constraints that prevented Scots bigotry being effective that I created a misleading impression as to just how much of such bigotry there was, especially among those with the power to make vital decisions in such fields as education. The constraints argument was not wrong and I have repeated it in the introductory chapters and will return to it in Chapter 7 but I should have made it clearer that, irrespective of the powerful obstacles to its effective expression, anti-Catholicism was always a marginal force.

Having placed that correction on the record I can now recap the social–structural constraints argument. The native Scots and Irish immigrants had competing economic interests: employers used migrants to weaken the power of organised labour, for example. They also possessed rival religious identities. That these two sources of animosity did not create and sustain an Ulster-style division is partly explained by structural features of both populations. By the time of significant Irish migration, native Scots were themselves religiously divided in a way that prevented religion becoming and remaining a major issue:

the most religiously anti-Catholic Scots were primarily located in the highlands and islands and the urban lowland Scots who competed economically with the migrants were the least religious.

Second, Irish Catholic migrants posed little 'objective' threat to Scots political interests. Orangemen tried to persuade Scots Protestants that Catholic loyalty to Rome endangered British interests and that the Catholic lack of civic virtues threatened the character of Scottish public life, but they failed miserably in this project and that failure is largely explained by the fact that once the status of Ireland had been settled (temporarily as it turned out) in 1926 the Catholic minority in Scotland had no distinctive ambition. It was not trying to shift national frontiers nor was it trying to deprive Scotland of its independence (that had been done centuries earlier). Apart from the Church's education demands, which had been conceded in 1918, there was no Catholic agenda that prevented working-class Protestants and Catholics pursuing their common interests through the trade unions and the Labour party.

Third, the lack of regional autonomy and the power of the Westminster parliament ensured that any distinctive Scots interests were subsumed within those of the national parties. The point can be illustrated by returning to John White's Kirk campaign to repatriate the Irish. In 1928 the churchmen finally won an opportunity to present their case to the Conservative government: a delegation was granted less than an hour with William Joynson-Hicks, the Home Secretary, and Scottish Secretary Sir John Gilmour (who, as a member of the Grand Lodge of the Orange Institution might have been expected to be sympathetic). The delegates were to receive a rude shock. Gilmour told the petitioners that, even if it was the problem they asserted, which he doubted, migration from the Irish Free State could not be prevented because it was not a foreign country: it was part of the British Empire! Gilmour's successor was no more sympathetic. William Adamson, an evangelical Baptist, became Secretary of State for Scotland in the Labour government. When, in May 1930, White led another delegation, Adamson dismissed his schemes out of hand. We do not know where the private sympathies of Gilmour and Adamson lay but we do know that both men acted in accord with the national agendas of their respective parties.

Finally, we need to appreciate the relationship between secularisation and religiously defined conflict. For reasons explained at length elsewhere, modernisation generally undermines religion.[28] As documented in Chapter 1, the twentieth century saw a steady decline in all indices of religious involvement. We know that serious conflict between populations defined by religion can retard secularisation: witness the popularity of the Catholic Church in Poland and Ireland when it served as the only effective form of opposition to respectively Soviet-inspired communist and British domination. That rates of church involvement in Scotland are very close to those for England shows how little religious conflict endures in Scotland and allows further secularisation. The vast majority of young people have no commitment to Protestantism or Catholicism and their willingness to marry with no consideration for their partner's religion will ensure that their children are even less likely to acquire and sustain a religious identity.

Football's distorting prism

It may seem perverse to leave until the very end the task of defining the chapter's subject matter but I wanted to show the reality before presenting a formal characterisation. Traditionally sectarianism in the Scottish context has meant an inappropriate dislike of Protestants or Catholics (depending on one's own identity) and an inappropriate regard for religious affiliation. Quite what is inappropriate depends on context and changes with time. There is now far less understanding of the differences between the Protestant and Catholic strands of Christianity but I do not suppose that many of us would expect a Calvinist Presbyterian to like the Church of Rome or a cardinal to pretend that he regards the Free Church as a valid expression of God's will. I do suppose that most of us would expect competing Christian bodies to play nicely in public and to keep their disdain for each other to gatherings of their 'homies'. One of the characteristics of the religiously diverse modern liberal democracy is that it expects religious differences to be confined to the family, the home and the leisure sphere. So we may chose our spouses with regard to their religion but not our co-workers. It is that assumption which defines 'the inappropriate regard' aspect of sectarianism. A Vale of Leven cooperage that hires only Orangemen is acting in a sectarian manner. Although it need not form part of the definition, most discussions of sectarianism, like those of racism, sexism, ageism and other forms of discrimination, suppose that individual improper acts form part of a wider culture of shared discriminatory attitudes that is in turn sustained by a social structure characterised by an unequal distribution of rewards, rights and privileges. When commentators describe Scotland as a sectarian society they mean (1) that sectarian acts are sufficiently common; (2) that such acts are in some sense approved of by sufficient (or sufficiently powerful) Scots for them to be accepted; and (3) that both the commissioning of such acts and their consequences in reward and deprivation are sufficiently embedded in the institutions of Scottish life for the proposition that Scotland is a sectarian society to be more accurate than the proposition that Scotland is a vegan society.

The assertion that sectarianism is significant and institutionalised justifies the otherwise disproportionate attention given to football. 1955 was a watershed year for two major Scottish institutions. In the general election that year, the Conservative and Unionist party won 50.1 per cent of the vote. It was also the point when the communicant membership of the Church of Scotland started its long and steady slide.[29] The ideal Rangers fan of the post-war era was a skilled worker, a Conservative and Unionist voter, a member of the Orange Order, and a church-attending Protestant Christian. While most Rangers fans fell well short of this ideal – many voted Labour and many more rarely attended church – the image was an effective one because it mirrored the image of the opposition. The ideal Celtic fan was unskilled or semi-skilled working-class, a confirmed Labour voter, a Mass-attending Roman Catholic, perhaps a member of the Ancient Order of Hibernians, with strong Irish roots. When the Ulster Troubles came along in the 1970s, the Irish dimension gained a new lease of life. Rangers fans tended to support the Ulster unionist cause and the fans who travelled from Ulster were a small but vocal presence. A very small number pretended to support loyalist paramilitary organisations and a tiny number actually did. Again Celtic fans were the mirror image: many supported Irish nationalism, a few became Republicans, and a tiny few supported the IRA. So Old Firm games became a venue for the symbolic demonstration of important social, religious and political divisions.

Half a century later, all of those props of Rangers and Celtic identity have collapsed. The manual working class has all but disappeared, as have most of the residential areas that its various fractions inhabited. Whatever being British meant in 1955 it means a lot less now. The combination of ceding power to the European Union and devolving power to Edinburgh, Cardiff and Belfast means that there is a lot less of Britain to be British about. Most Scots are still (somewhat grudgingly) in favour of the Union but unionism as a philosophy is hardly popular with Scottish Conservatives, and the Scottish Conservatives are hardly popular with the Scottish electorate.

The power and influence of the Orange Order has always been exaggerated: at its peak the Order had less than 2 per cent of adult male Protestants in west-central Scotland in membership. [30] The growing popularity of Scottish nationalism has given a new salience to the Order's unionism but the 12,000 Orangemen and women who marched in Edinburgh in March 2007 to celebrate the Act of Union is still a tiny minority of Scots and it now recruits from a base far narrower than that which supports Glasgow Rangers. In the 1920s the Order still had great men (such as Sir John Gilmour) in its ranks. It now has no elite support and no Church of Scotland minister is visible in its ranks.

Even the Ulster part of a popular Protestant identity has gone. All Ulster unionist parties actively support the devolution settlement. The most popular, the Democratic Unionist party, is in government with Sinn Fein. And the loyalist paramilitary organisations have disarmed and disbanded. It is hard to imagine that the views of Northern Ireland held by most Rangers fans (insofar as they hold any) differ at all from the Scottish consensus, which is to be glad not to have to think about the place again.

The elements that form the ideal Celtic fan of the 1950s have changed in much the same way. Despite the majority of lowland Catholics being educated in Catholic schools, the Catholic Church has followed the Protestant churches in precipitous decline. Between 1994 and 2002, Catholic Mass attendance fell by 20 per cent. Catholics are no longer concentrated in small distinct areas. Apart from the state funding of Catholic schools there is no distinct Catholic political agenda, and even that support has declined in recent decades, with recent surveys showing only a minority of Scots Catholics in favour of a separate school system. As we saw above, even Irishness has gone.

In 1955 Old Firm rivalry could be taken to stand for something else. Now it signifies nothing but itself: a competition between two teams that is more bitter than most because no other teams in their league pose any serious threat to their domination. Liverpool fans can share their animus around the fans of Arsenal,

Chelsea, Tottenham and Manchester United. The Old Firm have only each other to hate. The vast majority of fans of Rangers and of Celtic do not actually care about religion, about ethnic origins, about the Troubles in Northern Ireland, or about the constitutional future of the British Isles. They only pretend to care in order to maintain an identity that offends the other side and in order to have an excuse to offend the other side.

What are at stake are not actual shared social identities built on real differences but pantomime costumes. The fans of both teams wear false noses. Each lot pretends to find the noses of the other ugly and grotesque while claiming to be deeply hurt by the cruel remarks that those scumbags have made about our noses. That a very small number of Old Firm fans are also violent drunken hooligans is deplorable but it does not make them a symptom of a deeply divided society. Most Scots are not football fans. Most football fans do not support the Old Firm. And most Old Firm fans are law-abiding men whose 'sectarianism' is confined to the ritual abuse of opposing fans.

The above evidence should persuade any impartial reader that sectarianism is no longer a serious social force. That the Irish Catholic migrants have successfully integrated into Scottish society shows that it was not much of a force in 1900 or 1930. Had Scotland been deeply bifurcated in 1969 the Ulster Troubles would have resonated seriously in Scottish life. They did not. What is now casually called sectarianism is not the tip of an iceberg of systematic prejudice and discrimination. It is all the iceberg there is.

5   Protestantism and democracy?

Introduction

This chapter has a number of purposes. It assesses the contribution of the Reformed strand of Christianity to the rise of liberal democracy. Insofar as it is persuasive, it illustrates the possibility of treating religion as a cause of political phenomena. And as far as space constraints allow, it draws attention to some complexities of causation that are often overlooked in the rather ritualistic arguments over the role of religion in politics.

It is common for contemporary scholars to suppose religions so flexible, malleable, and variegated as to be capable of producing and justifying any form of social organisation, any social action and any set of social mores. Fred Halliday, a noted political scientist and Islamic specialist, quoted favourably a scholar saying of Islam that it is so broad that:

> it is possible to catch almost any fish one wants. It is, like all the great religions, a reservoir of values, symbols and ideas from which it is possible to derive a contemporary politics and social code: the answer as to why this or that interpretation was put upon Islam resides therefore, not in the religion and its texts itself, but in the contemporary needs of those articulating Islamic politics.[1]

Bruce Lawrence takes a similar line when he writes that religion's 'pervasiveness as a general condition was matched only by its malleability as a contextual variant open to limitless interpretation'.[2]

I am happy to go a long way with both writers. The great religions do indeed contain such a variety of ideas that many different outcomes can be justified as the will of God or Allah. Lawrence is right that context matters a great deal. Nonetheless I wish to argue that there are certain 'socio-logics'. There is orderliness to the world. Although there is a wide variety of possible combinations of cultures, economies and polities, some are rare and certain combinations are not found because they are impossible. It is not an accident that there are no feudal democracies; the principles of feudal economy and of democratic polity are incompatible. To return to the fish and sea analogy, it may well be the case that similar fish can be found in many seas and many seas support a variety of fish. Nonetheless, there are systematic variations in the kind of fish found in warm and in cold waters, in salt and in fresh waters, in shallow and in deep waters.

A number of preliminary asides may clarify my approach. First, I am not an 'orientalist' who deserves Edward Said's censure for using sweeping generalisations about differences between religions as a basis for invidious comparisons of Christianity and Islam.[3]

Second, I do not subscribe to Samuel Huntington's comparative treatment of civilisations (clashing or otherwise). As is clear in my longer treatment of these themes, some of the features of religions which I believe to have political consequences cut across the civilisations that some hold to clash.[4] Although by no means unique, my approach is essentially different in that it supposes the crucial differences either to be abstract and or to form part of the deep, rather than surface, structure of each faith. For example, whether or not a religion mandates a particular way of public life seems of much greater importance than the specific content of what it mandates or prohibits.

Third, as Max Weber argued in his classic essay on the Protestant Ethic, the major consequences of religious innovations are unintended and inadvertent.[5] My approach, like Weber's, cannot be dismissed as unsociological idealism, because its causal connections are generally ironic. They result from socio-psychological and socio-structural obstacles and imperatives causing ideas to be developed in ways quite other than those intended by the people who promoted the innovations.

Fourth, nothing in my approach requires that major religions be utterly unalike. To point to the many similarities in the major religions as an objection against citing differences as causes of subsequent major political differences is a red herring because there is no reason why small differences cannot cause big differences.

Fifth, nothing in my approach requires that major religions be unchanging. Brevity requires me to use terms such as 'Protestantism' with few qualifying adjectives; this does not mean that I am unaware of differences within Reformed Christianity. To talk of a 'Protestant ethic', as Weber does, is not to suggest that all Protestants, throughout Christendom and over four centuries, are the same. It only requires that he has correctly identified the beliefs and values of certain Protestants and that he is basically correct in supposing those beliefs and values to differ from those of adherents to other religions in comparable circumstances. Far more could be said on these points but their significance should be clearer once I elaborate my argument.

Spokesmen for the Loyal Orange Institution and other Protestant organisations believe that their forefathers were responsible for a variety of social virtues and social institutions that either constitute or promote liberal democracy: personal autonomy, freedom of choice, literacy, diligence, temperance, loyalty, democratic accountability, egalitarianism, and the overlapping ties of voluntary association we now call 'civil society'. Hence Popery is not just the wrong religion; it is a social evil. As a former Presbyterian clergyman and Ulster Unionist MP put it:

The seeds of democracy were sown in the Reformation. The liberties of Europe began with the growth of new nations. William of Orange stood with his family motto, 'Je maintendrai' appended to the slogan 'the Protestant Religion and Liberties of England'.[6]

Most academics will not relish taking lessons in political theory from Orangemen but there is enough in the historical record to make such a claim worth considering. British political history was shaped by conflicts between despotic Catholic monarchs and a Protestant parliament. Protestant nations were generally in the vanguard of the rise of parliamentary democracy. And there is much in the twentieth-century history of Europe to suggest some non-accidental connection between religion and democracy. There are four major Christian traditions in Europe. There are the two communal religions of Orthodoxy and Catholicism, the individualist religion of thoroughly Reformed Protestantism and, somewhere between them, Lutheranism, which promoted most of the theological principles of the Reformation but constrained them within the ecclesiastical frame of the pre-Reformation church and moderated the political radicalism with a quiescent attitude to the state. With varying degrees of willingness, most of the countries of twentieth-century Europe have enjoyed a dictatorship of either the Right or the Left. If we take the fascist regimes first we find that almost all were Catholic: Italy, Spain, Portugal, Slovakia, Croatia, Austria and Lithuania. Germany was two-thirds Catholic. And there were three Lutheran examples: the Quisling regime in Norway, and the rather moderately right-wing dictatorships in Estonia and Latvia. The Communist regimes were mostly Orthodox (the Soviet Union, Bulgaria) and Catholic (Poland, Lithuania, Czechoslovakia), Lutheran (Latvia, Estonia and East Germany) or, as in the case of Yugoslavia, a mixture of Orthodox, Catholic and Muslim. Given the very large numbers of countries that have had totalitarian or authoritarian regimes in the twentieth century, it might be easier to compile the list the other way round and ask what was the religion of those societies that avoided dictatorship. Holland, the United Kingdom and its white colonies, Switzerland, and the USA were predominantly Reformed Protestant. Sweden and Finland were Lutheran.

We could draw further examples from a very different setting: Latin America. In the twentieth century oppressive regimes of the Right were Catholic and there is a strong connection between the spread of evangelicalism and Pentecostalism and democratisation.[7]

The matching is nowhere near perfect but there is enough of an apparent pattern for us to understand how Protestants can believe that their religion confers some sort of resistance to authoritarianism.

The impartial observer could retort that, even in the twentieth century, militant Protestantism has produced its own authoritarian movements. In 1930s Scotland, the Scottish Protestant League in Glasgow and Protestant Action in Edinburgh won local council seats on an anti-Irish and anti-Catholic platform.[8] In the USA, the Ku Klux Klan and various other nativist movements presented a similarly curtailed notion of freedoms and rights: democracy was to be restricted to white Anglo-Saxon Protestant males.[9] And the two contemporary examples of Protestants in power – Northern Ireland from 1921 to 1972 and apartheid South Africa – hardly offer models of liberal democracy. Below I will suggest that the eventual failure of these movements and regimes strengthens the claim for a causal connection between reformed religion and democracy because all were partly undermined by their own democratic rhetoric. However we can acknowledge them here simply as evidence that social reality is vastly more complex than the partisans would wish.

To state my conclusion before I elaborate the grounds for arriving at it, my general response to the Orange claim is to accept that there is a strong and non-accidental relationship between the rise of Protestantism and the rise of democracy but to add that the strongest links between Reformed Christianity and democracy are *unintended consequences*. The shift from feudal monarchy to egalitarian democracy was not a result of actions intended to produce that effect. Instead it was the ironic (and often deeply regretted) by-product of actions promoted for quite different reasons. The Reformation contributed to the evolution of democracy but its supporters can hardly take the credit.

I would like to work through a number of possible causal connections between Protestantism and what might commonly be regarded as necessary conditions for, or features of, liberal democracy.

Individualism and lay activism

The Reformation did not invent the autonomous individual; it was itself a response in the religious realm to changes in social relations that had seen many organic communities undermined. But it did give a powerful boost to two notions fundamental to liberal democracy: that people are more than their social roles and that, despite their social roles, people are much of a muchness.

The Reformation raised up the individual by ending the possibility of the transfer of religious merit from the more to the less Godly. If the good could not pass on merit to the less good by performing religious acts on their behalf then each individual had to stand on his or her own feet before God. This assertion of the freestanding individual gave very little place to rights. It was an individualism primarily of responsibilities. But by ending the system in which religious officials could placate God on behalf of the community and by making every one of us severally (rather than jointly) responsible for our salvational fate, the Reformers created a powerful cat that would eventually escape the theocratic bag.

At the same time, by removing the special role of the clergy as intermediaries between God and his creation, the Reformers laid the foundations for egalitarianism. Initially this assertion of equality was confined to that small part of life concerned with entry to the next kingdom but it did mean that an important potential was created, which subsequent economic and political changes would allow to be fulfilled. As we will see in Chapter 6, they also gave a new impetus to lay activism. Medieval Christianity tended to mirror the feudal structure in expecting and allowing little of the common people; the Reformers demanded an active laity, mindful and diligent. Lay participation without the mediation of the clergy created a model in the sphere of religion for what later became the ethos of modern democracy.

Factionalism and schism

One of the most significant inadvertent consequences of the Reformation was cultural diversity. In insisting that everyone could discern the will of God through the reading of his Holy Word, the Reformers shifted the basis of religion from an authoritarian and hierarchical epistemology (in which the truth was available only to a very small number of people) to an essentially democratic one. They did not, of course, endorse the ultimately liberal and relativistic view that what everyone believed was equally true. The long-term consequence of that was barely appreciated by the Reformers because, being theists who believed in one God, one Holy Spirit and one Holy Word, they assumed that the false and dangerous cohesion previously maintained by the hierarchical church would be replaced by a true and liberating cohesion that came naturally from responding to the Creator. They were wrong. The human default position is not consensus. Removing the theologically justified coercion of the hierarchical church and permitting open access to the salvational truth allowed many competing visions to arise as different social groups developed the dominant religious tradition in ways that better suited their material and cultural interests.

Although many of the Reformers were highly authoritarian and attempted to impose their particular vision on others (Calvin's Geneva and Knox's Edinburgh were not after all tolerant democracies) such impositions lacked core theological justification, were short-lived, and did little to retard the proliferation of competing convictions.

Furthermore, the theocracy version of Calvinism was only one (and the least popular) strand of Reformed thinking about the role of social order. There were at least two powerful alternatives that militated against theocracy. Christianity began by asserting the separation of church and state: Christ said that we should render 'unto Caesar the things which are Caeser's and unto God the things that are God's'.[10] That sentiment was reinforced by Christianity's three centuries in the political wilderness before it moved into the seat of Roman imperial power. That combination of belief and history is quite different to the experience of Islam, which did not at its foundation advocate a division between the spiritual and material world, and which did not have to because it achieved political power immediately. Of course, when they could, many Christian church leaders attempted to impose their faith upon the world, but the older tradition of pietistic retreat to the catacombs remained a powerful resource that could be called upon when necessary. It returned with the Reformation, which 'postulating two "kingdoms" insisted upon the total difference between the spiritual order and the temporal or secular world of physical beings and object'.[11] The Lutheran strand easily accepted the two kingdoms and permitted the secular to dominate. The Calvinists tried to maintain a compact of mutual support between the civil magistrate (or the state, as we would now call it) and the church. For brief periods the preachers ruled their burghs. On the other side, a strong pietist tradition argued that undue entanglement with the temporal world contaminated the righteous.

That position is common in Latin American Pentecostalism, where pietistic retreat is seen as an effective way of avoiding the corruption of 'big man' politics. It remains influential in American fundamentalism. When television evangelists such as Jerry Falwell and Pat Robertson led the Christian Right in the 1980s and 1990s, a section of fundamentalism associated with Bob Jones University argued that their movement was positively dangerous because it would mislead the unregenerate into thinking that social reform was an effective alternative to personal conversion: the Catholic sin of thinking good works bought salvation. Indeed the pietist case can be taken to the extreme of arguing that a bad society might actually be a better environment for preaching the need for personal redemption than a good one because dire circumstances are more likely to bring the soul under 'conviction of sin'.

One cause of Protestantism's increased factionalism was deliberate, though again, the consequences were not at the time foreseen: the insistence on lay activism. The replacement of a largely passive liturgical mode of religion by one that required every individual to become personally committed to propagating the new faith inevitably increased the tendency to schism by increasing the number of people who felt they had, not just a right, but a responsibility, to decide what was the true religion.

Factionalism led inadvertently to toleration and eventually to religious liberty. It is important for my argument to appreciate how reluctant the early Protestant sects were to accept the implications of their voluntarism. What persuades me that we have a genuine causal connection is precisely that people were led by the logic of their own arguments and by the consequences of their actions to do things *they did not want to do*. Only after they recognised the inevitable did they rummage around in their ideology to provide a new interpretation that legitimated the initially undesired outcome. I will illustrate the point with the example of the fragmentation of the Christian Church in Scotland.[12] The first two major schisms were thoroughly committed to theocratic rule. The Covenanters (later called the Reformed Presbyterians) refused to accept the seventeenth-century settlement of the relationship between church and state, not because they were opposed to the idea of the state coercing conformity, but because they had not been given sufficient weight in determining just what was to be imposed.

The second major wave of splits, which gave rise to the Seceders, was also theocratic. The Erskines and their followers broke away from the Church of Scotland in 1733 because they objected to the heritors (the Scottish equivalent of patrons) imposing insufficiently Godly ministers on congregations. They had no problem at all with the imposition of ministers of whom they approved. It was only with the third split (that of Thomas Gillespie in 1751 whose followers styled themselves the Relief Presbytery) that we find a movement opposed on principle to the state support for the church. Gillespie had trained with the English Congregationalists before entering the ministry of the Church of Scotland and had acquired something of their liberal spirit.

It is a mark of the times that this third split was the least popular of the three and grew markedly more slowly than the Secession. The fourth and largest split – the 1843 Disruption, which led to the formation of the Free Church of Scotland – was, like the first two, rooted in the intolerant idea that the state should support the true religion. However it is significant that there had by then been an important change in what it was thought proper for the state to do to ensure the correct religion. In the seventeenth century it was acceptable for the state to use armed troops to force the people into the parish church and the dissident Covenanters objected only to losing, not to the principle of coercion. By the middle of the nineteenth century, what the theocrats thought it was proper to do to support the correct religion was limited to social pressure, public taxation, and preferential access to such means of socialisation as the national school system. Contrast that with the current constitution of the Islamic Republic of Pakistan that mandates the death penalty for apostasy. For all that softening, there was little recognition that people had a right to choose their religion and considerable opposition to the idea of secular provision of social services.

The irony of Protestantism is that it was its own impossible combination of an open epistemology and an insistence that there was only one truth that created pluralism. By reducing theological support for human coercion while at the same time insisting that there could be only one way to God, the Reformers encouraged a proliferation of competing groups. We can see the result in the changing attitudes to toleration displayed by the various Scottish sects. Gradually each sect came to appreciate that it had failed in its mission and that it would remain a minority. Not surprisingly, it then began to appreciate the virtues of toleration. Simultaneously the state was also coming to accept that, in a context of increasing religious diversity, social harmony required the state to become increasingly tolerant and finally neutral in matters of religion. And each sect gradually reduced the claims that it made for its unique access to the saving truth, and came to see itself as one denomination among others.

This is, of course, a simplifying summary but a good case can be made for saying that one of the greatest impacts of the Reformation on the relationship between church and state was the line that ran from factionalism and schism to increasing diversity to increasing toleration to a finally neutral state. In different countries the accommodation developed in different ways. In Britain, there was a gradual fudge, in which the state churches were allowed to retain nominal privileges but were gradually stripped of their real powers. In the early twentieth century, their funding base in public taxation was commuted to a lump sum. Thereafter, they were on their own. In the American colonies the need to devise a new political structure from scratch hastened the process and made it explicit. Although nine of the thirteen founding colonies had state churches, many of those were challenged by internal diversity and taken together there could be no state church because the colonies had different religions established. In order to make one out of many, that one had to be religiously neutral (or at least very ill-defined) and that requirement was made explicit in the founding documents of the USA. In Australia, the British began by establishing the Church of

England and then responded to the reality of sectarian diversity by briefly supporting a number of churches. The 1836 New South Wales Church Act added the Catholic, Presbyterian and Methodist churches to those financially supported by the state but in 1862 the state shifted to the US position of supporting none.

Metaphor and privatisation

It is worth noting one feature of Christianity that marks it off from Islam, Judaism, Hinduism and Buddhism: its stress on doctrine as distinct from ritual or way of life. Christianity (especially in its Protestant version) is a religion of orthodoxy rather than orthopraxy and this has profound social consequences. A religion that mandates a particular way of life (and in Islam that is quite specific because its founding text contains detailed instructions for the good life) tends to be theocratic. If there is only one God and God requires that we fast during Ramadan, it is difficult for adherents to suppose that they must observe Ramadan while their neighbours do not. Muslims, when they can, impose their faith on the entire society.

All faiths have what we might call a 'bolstering interest' in imposing themselves on others; acquiring social power for our ideas is useful in reassuring us that we are right. But Christians do not have a strong theological imperative to impose on others because there is very little that their faith mandates as a way of life. To understand why that is the case we need to go back to the foundation of Christianity. As we can see in the construction of its sacred text, Christianity begins by taking the religion of the Jews and treating it *metaphorically*. The promises that God makes to the Jews in the Old Testament were taken as a metaphor for the real promises that God made to the Christians. Similarly the specific requirements set on the Jews (circumcision, dietary laws and the rest) are reinterpreted as either meaning something else or as belonging only to a particular historical dispensation. Although the Catholic Church reintroduced ways of life in its mode of treating faith as a communal and organic matter, the Protestant Reformation swept much of that away and reduced the Christian faith to a series of beliefs and attitudes. Holding the right beliefs did not require much of the surrounding world. The point can be seen clearly if we consider the visibility of the consequences of piety. A pious Hindu, Jew or Muslim is highly visible; an evangelical Christian can be almost invisible.

To repeat, I am not denying that Christians are sometimes tempted by theocracy. I am merely saying that Christianity (and especially its Protestant strand) has less need than other major religions to govern the social and political worlds. More easily than most religions, Protestantism can become privatised.

Economic development and egalitarianism

If we accept that the seed of egalitarianism was inherent in the Reformation, what delayed its germination for 300 years? The following simplified account, which concentrates on the functional prerequisites of economic development, seems plausible.[13]

Economic modernisation brought with it an increased division of labour, increased social mobility, and an increase in the extent to which life became divided into distinct spheres, each with its own values. The simple hierarchies of the feudal world, with their relatively few opportunities for social mobility, were replaced by a larger (and ever-increasing) number of task-specific hierarchies. The feudal lord could not recognise that his serf and his lieutenant were similar beings because to have granted that degree of likeness would have threatened the feudal order. But with the proliferation of task-specific hierarchies, it became possible to see people in terms of a variety of roles, judged on a number of specific status scales. Thus the mill owner could dominate his workers during the day and yet sit alongside them and even listen to one of them preach in a Methodist chapel. Of course power based in one world could be deployed in another. In the Vale of Leven, an industrial area north of Glasgow, in the early twentieth century, it was still common to find the factory owner who was also the major landlord, the local Member of Parliament, the senior elder of the Church of Scotland congregation, a leading Freemason, a magistrate, a major figure in the Orange Order and patron of almost every voluntary association. But unlike the medieval serf, the worker who resented his employer's power could change churches, change jobs, move house or leave the county. Although the local magnate could hope that his standing in one sphere would entitle him to high status in another, he could not impose himself. And that degree of concentration of power was already rare and died out shortly after the 1914–18 war, undermined by the extension of the franchise broadening the electorate and the limited liability joint stock company displacing the locally-based family firm.

In the circumstances of economic modernisation it becomes possible to distinguish between the roles people played and their essential selves. It thus becomes possible, at least in theory, to accord to all humanity a common worth, while maintaining specific status differences in specific fields. It took a long time and much social conflict before that basic egalitarianism was translated into a language of civil liberties and human rights but gradually the privileges of the rich were extended to all men and then to rich women and to all women and then to children.

If it is the case that economic modernisation and increased prosperity were crucial to the rise of democracy in the West, then it is also likely, if we accept Max Weber's argument for a causal but unintended connection between the Protestant ethic (a psychology created by a combination of popularised Reformation innovations) and the spirit of capitalism, that Protestantism played a part in that particular equation.

If we now return to the point about diversity we can see why egalitarianism is central to the story. In most societies, the response to diversity is to crush it. Enduring supra-national units as the German Holy Roman Empire, the extended Hapsburg kingdoms or the Ottoman empire usually found ways of incorporating religions and nations relatively peacefully. But by and large, when two competing religions came into contact, one attempted to impose itself upon the other. Egalitarianism is an important part of the equation because it explains why

Western societies gave up trying to impose conformity. The egalitarian impulse of modernisation meant that, at the political level, the costs of coercing religious conformity were no longer acceptable: the state was no longer willing to pay the price of social conflict. Instead it became neutral on the competing claims of various religious bodies. In the seventeenth century, Treaty of Westphalia states accepted the need to tolerate neighbours of different religious hue. Two centuries later they came to the same recognition with regard to variations within their own citizenry.

So in addition to the minority loser's route to toleration sketched above with the example of the Scottish sects, we have a majority route. Gradually the modern state reduces its support for the dominant religion and the state church comes to see itself as one denomination among others.

One of the difficulties in trying to evaluate possible causal connections is that social practices that originated in one place for one reason can become attractive for quite different reasons and hence relatively autonomous. Thus it may be that the Puritans had a particular Protestant ethic that made them unusually susceptible to attitudes conducive to capitalism but once their work practices were patently paying off, it was quite possible for those practices to become divorced from their original attitudinal base and be adopted by Catholics. The same can be said for toleration. By the second half of the nineteenth century the different routes to toleration found in France (with its cataclysmic revolution), Britain (with its peaceful evolution) and the USA (able to construct a constitution from scratch) were coalescing to form the general idea that modern democracies did not prescribe or proscribe religion. If we take the example of Norway in the second half of the nineteenth century we find some pressure for increased religious liberty coming from dissenters but the schisms from the Lutheran church (and even the reforming movements within the church) were far less powerful than they had been in Britain. But dissenting self-interest was powerfully augmented by political reformers, who argued on philosophical grounds that religious liberty should be a fundamental plank of democratisation.

The Catholic Church was extremely reluctant to accept this idea and as late as the 1960s one can find Vatican officials arguing that error should not be tolerated but in most European countries the fatal flirtation with fascism was enough to persuade Catholics to endorse democracy. After 1945, European Christian Democrat parties, although officered and voted for by pious Catholics, allowed the 'Democrat' part of their identity to constrain the 'Christian' part.

Social democracy

The above mention of the French Revolution reminds us that Protestantism was not the only source of progressive and radical political ideas. However, there is a crucial religious difference in the environment for the playing out of such ideas. There is a very clear contrast in the development of working-class politics in reformed countries and Catholic countries (with the Lutheran states of northern Europe lying somewhere in between) that can be traced back to the eighteenth

century. Because Protestantism allowed the creation of religious diversity, movements of political dissent *did not have to be anti-clerical*. The close ties of the
Catholic Church to the *Ancien Régime* meant that the radical forces in France, in
rejecting the feudal order, also rejected the Church. But because the culture was
Catholic, it did not readily allow new classes to develop their own form of the
dominant religion. In contrast, the Protestantism of Britain allowed political
rebels to shape their own dissenting religion. External force could be used to
suppress the dissenters but there was nothing in the core ideology of Protestantism that prevented them making the psychological break from any particular
form of Protestant church. Thus in France political dissent became anti-clerical
while in Britain it often led to religious innovation.

This difference carried through to the nineteenth and early twentieth centuries. In Britain, the Labour movement did not oppose religion per se (but only
particular privileges of its particular forms). In Catholic countries there was a
clear division between a rural, conservative and clerical bloc and an equally
powerful organic anti-clerical bloc. Hence it is in those European countries that
remained Catholic (Spain, Portugal, France and Italy) that we also find the most
powerful communist parties. In the Scandinavian countries, there was initially a
split along the Catholic lines with the left-wing parties being anti-clerical and the
state churches profoundly opposed to labour movements. In 1917 the Finnish
parliament took advantage of Russia's weakness to declare independence. But
the Finns then split. In January 1918 the Left, or Reds, staged a coup, the Whites
retaliated and in the ensuing civil war some 30,000 people died. The Lutheran
Church by and large supported the Whites and lost considerable support among
the working class. However, over the inter-war years and during the struggles of
the Second World War, the Finns gradually developed a strong shared sense of
national identity and the Lutheran Church came to occupy an important role as
the carrier of a culture and a history that marked Finland off from its ever-
threatening Russian neighbour. In all the Nordic countries, the Lutheran churches
were able to switch from a strong association with the political right to back the
cause of social democracy so successfully that, despite the thorough secularisation of beliefs, there remains widespread popular support for the Churches as
carriers and symbols of national identity. In contrast, the Catholic Church in
Spain and Portugal found it very hard to shed its historical associations with
right-wing dictatorships.

To summarise, the inherently fissiparous nature of Protestantism prevents it
becoming intractably associated with any particular ideological position. There
is thus a case for saying that it permitted emergent class conflict to be less
polarised than was the case in Catholic countries.[14]

Civil society and social inclusion

There is a further sense in which Protestantism has contributed to modern
democracy and that is in pioneering a particularly effective combination of
individualism and community spirit. The Protestant sects constructed themselves

as egalitarian self-supporting voluntary associations.[15] Although every individual was responsible for his or her own fate, the Saints had an obligation to support each other through this vale of tears. In some sects and at times, that support could be thoroughly oppressive and even unforgiving. The English Quakers of the eighteenth century would expel a bankrupt from fellowship even if he were not the author of his misfortunes. But more often there were strong injunctions to mutual support and charity that did a great deal to blunt the harshness of modern industrial life. As Martin has argued in his explanation of the popularity of Pentecostalism in Latin America, evangelical Protestantism offered a functionally adaptive combination of a new persona suited to urban industrial capitalism (the self-reliant striving autonomous individual) and a supportive community of like-minded peers.[16]

To the extent that Protestantism thrived, the old organic feudal community of subservience, descent and fate was displaced by a series of overlapping voluntary democratic associations: the sect's business meeting, the conventicle, the self-organising prayer group.[17] Protestant sects and denominations themselves formed an important part of the network of civil society, but more than that they provided the organisational template for savings banks, workers' educational societies, friendly societies, trade unions, and pressure groups. They also provided millions of ordinary people with training in public speaking, in committee management, and in small group leadership. And they provided the persona – the autonomous and self-reliant but caring individual – that could operate the new lay institutions. This was recognised by a mid-nineteenth century historian of the Secession Churches:

> They insisted on the right of popular election in its full and scriptural extent – that every member of the congregation, of whatever sex or social status, should enjoy the right of choice. Called upon in this way to perform a most important duty, the people have been trained to interest themselves in their own affairs, and in attending to their own interest have acquired that habit of exercising individual judgement, which stands closely connected with the continuance of ecclesiastical and civil liberty.[18]

An important part of interesting themselves in their own affairs was learning to read and write. There are short connections and long links between Protestantism and literacy. The short connection concerns the religious need. If people were to be individually responsible for their own salvation, and if that depended more on correct belief than on correct ritual performance, then they had to have access to the means of saving grace. Hearing sermons was useful, as was learning the catechism, but reading the Bible was essential and 'the stress on scripturalism is conducive to high levels of literacy'.[19] Protestants translated the scriptures into the vernacular languages and taught people reading and writing. In many Protestant lands, the state positively encouraged the people at least to read. There was some reluctance to teach writing. Hannah More, in her Mendip schools, refused to do so.[20] If the common people could read, they could be fed a diet of conservative and improving tracts. If they could write, they might write their own not-so-conservative pamphlets. But even with that reservation, Protestantism encouraged literacy. Post-Reformation Sweden required it. In the seventeenth century full membership of the Church was open only to those who could read.

A longer route concerns the more general connection between literacy and economic development. As part of his larger project of explaining the rise and role of nationalism, Gellner makes the case that a shared literate culture was a functional pre-requisite for economic modernisation. Any country serious about lifting itself out of feudally organised agriculture had to have an effective communication across the economy, between people of all stations and not just the nobility and their clerks.

We need to be cautious of claiming literacy as an especially Protestant characteristic. Religion had been associated with language long before the Reformation. In the tenth century two Greek priests, brothers Cyril and Methodius, were sent to Moravia to teach Christianity to the common people in the vernacular. They translated the liturgy and some of the Bible into Slavonic and invented a new alphabet with which to write their translations. We might also note that as a response to the Reformation the Catholic Church authorities in a number of countries promoted reading as a new means to instruct the common people *against* the heresies of the Huguenots and other Protestants.

Nonetheless, with those two qualifications, we can accept the causal connection between the Reformation and the spread of literacy. Cyril and Methodius had the rather limited interest of providing the material for the Church to operate. What distinguished the Protestant interest was its intensity (it was *very* important for people to learn to read) and its democratic reach (it was very important for *all* the people to learn to read). The contrast with Islam is strong. The Muslims of the Ottoman Empire opposed printing because they saw the mechanical reproduction of the sacred text as a threat to traditional methods of teaching Islam. Foreigners in Istanbul had printing presses but the only one used by Muslims was forced to close in 1730 when pietists wrecked the presses. Muslims in India embraced printing only in the nineteenth century and then only because they feared the threat of Christian missionaries. The Koran was translated into Urdu to make it available to the masses but even then there was a Catholic Church-like fear of democratic interpretation. Those who advocated printing also insisted 'do not read any book without consulting a scholar'.[21]

Irony

The sense in which new ideas, when embodied in actual social changes, can then constrain actors, is perhaps made clearer by adding a few more illustrations of people being subverted by the consequences of their own actions or ideas. Various Scottish anti-Catholic movements of the 1930s foundered for reasons that can be similarly traced back to their own nature. Both the Scottish Protestant League and Protestant Action found their ability to act as political parties undermined by their members' inability to agree or to accept direction. Their activists were so committed to the idea of freedom of conscience that they constantly squabbled and voted against each other. They also found that the voting public expected ideological consistency. They built their attack on the state support for Catholic schools on the principle of equity: it was unfair for Catholic teachers to have equal access to jobs in state schools and yet have protected access to jobs in Catholic schools. To the extent that this argument from equity was accepted, it made their other platforms (such as the repatriation of immigrants from Ireland and preferential hiring of Protestants) vulnerable to the charge of hypocrisy.[22]

Activists of the Christian Right in the United States have similarly found themselves constrained by the secular embodiment of principles that their forebears promoted. Using the same term 'fundamentalist' to describe US organisations such as the Moral Majority and Christian Coalition and Muslim groups such as Islamic Jihad and Hezbollah disguises the important difference that the former have confined their campaigns to essentially democratic means.[23] Even if they really sought to impose a theocracy on the American people, Falwell and Robertson have had to promote that goal with secular language. To their 'home boys', they can denounce divorce and homosexuality as contrary to the will of God but to the electorate they have had to argue that such practices are socially harmful. To their church audiences they can argue against evolution on the grounds that the Bible says God made the Earth in seven days but in their campaigns to influence school biology classes and textbooks they have had to show that 'creation science' is as plausible an explanation of the facts as is evolution. In so doing, they accept rules of engagement that ensure they will lose. And because they are by and large democrats, they accept the fact that they have lost their campaign to turn America back to God and instead campaign for conservative Christians to be treated as a legitimate cultural minority.[24]

The fate of Ulster Unionists can be mentioned in this context. For 50 years they defended their domination of Northern Ireland on the grounds that they represented a majority of its citizens. As the population balance shifted and Catholics became an ever-larger part of the electorate, some Unionists openly espoused a different argument: that Ulster Protestants were an ethnic grouping that had a right to self-determination irrespective of electoral arithmetic. But as we saw in Chapter 3, even the supporters of Ian Paisley accepted that they must confine their politics to democratic means. A narrow majority of Ulster unionists have endorsed the new power-sharing politics. Most of the rest do not like it but are unwilling to break the law to oppose the new arrangements.

The cynic could easily say that in all these cases theocrats have simply accepted their impotence. The reason the Scottish Protestant League, the Moral Majority, or Ian Paisley's Democratic Unionist party have confined themselves largely to democratic politics is that, in a secular culture, they lacked the power to do otherwise. It is *realpolitik* that prevents them acting like Hezbollah. My response is the case I have made above: the reality to which these groups have had to accommodate is in large part an unintended consequence of the very principles that inspire them.

Secularisation

I have left until last the most obvious connection between Protestantism and the rise of liberal democracy. Supporters of various Islamist political movements often point out that those movements are considerably more democratic than the regimes that they aim to displace. It is certainly true that the government in Iran is elected by an almost universal franchise. However, Islamic democracies differ from the Western European model in allowing Islam to act as a trump card. Only those candidates approved by religious leaders may stand in Iranian elections; laws passed by the parliament have to be approved by the ayatollahs. The laws privilege Muslims over non-Muslims. The core principle of liberal democracy is that each citizen's vote counts the same; for that to be the case rights must be distributed irrespective of religious rectitude. Put bluntly, religion taken seriously is incompatible with democracy. Either the will of God or the will of the people is sovereign.

Essential to the liberal democratic character of Western European polities is the fact that they are secular. Either few people are seriously religious or the seriously religious accept that religious imperatives should be confined to the home, the family and the voluntary sector.

Many of the strands of this argument have been mentioned above and are elaborated at great length elsewhere and brevity prevents me repeating the case here.[25] I will merely assert that Protestantism, by encouraging individualism and creating religious diversity, undermined the organic and communal basis for religion. As Martin puts it: 'the logic of Protestantism is clearly in favour of voluntary principle, to a degree that eventually makes it sociologically unrealistic'.[26]

Conclusion

This rather condensed discussion has considered various claims for the proposition that Protestantism was responsible for democracy. My conclusion is that Protestantism has been causally implicated in the development of democratic polities and civil liberties and that in many particulars the causal connection is the unintended consequence.

To return to the point raised in the introduction: what does this tell us about religious belief systems as *causes*? My conclusion is rather banal. It is worth asserting only because a decade of postmodernism has rather confused the nature of sociological explanation (when it has not denied outright the possibility). My model might be called the Robert Burns theory of social change (after his line: 'the best-laid plans of mice and men gang aft aglay'). Beliefs and values shape motives. Motives produce actions. Because people do not have perfect knowledge and complete control, the consequences of their actions are often not what were intended. The new circumstances are interpreted in the light of shared beliefs and may cause them to be modified. That produces new motives and new actions, and so it goes. The scope and ambiguity of religious belief systems always permits a range of interpretations of God's will, and social circumstances obviously play a large part in explaining why some people prefer one interpretation to another. But this is not the same as saying that religious beliefs are either without consequences or that their consequences are limited to making those who use God as rhetorical justification for base actions feel better about themselves. Religion makes a difference and this essay has given one example of the profound difference it can make.

6   Methodism and socialism

Introduction

Philip Snowden, Labour Chancellor in the 1930s coalition government, wrote in his autobiography, 'the early socialist movement in Great Britain ... derived its inspiration far more from the Sermon on the Mount than from the teaching of the Economists'.[1] Morgan Phillips, general secretary of the Labour party in the 1950s, seems to have been the man who first introduced the alliteration into the general point when he wrote: 'socialism in Britain owed more to Methodism than Marx'.[2] As a quick web search reveals, this quote is attributed variously to Harold Wilson, Dennis Healey, Tony Benn and others beside. It is an observation that is true twice. Whether said with a sneer or with a chuckle, the aphorism, like the historical claim it makes, exemplifies the contrast between British pragmatism and continental philosophising. It is the equivalent in the sphere of ideas of the virtue of honest roast beef over fancy French cuisine. It is also a reference to a classic argument in British social history; begun by the French historian Elie Halévy and continued by Edward Thompson, Gertrude Himmelfarb, and Eric Hobsbawm among others.

Halévy's argument that Methodism (and evangelical religion generally) had a pacifying effect on the English working class and thus explains the absence of our equivalent of the French Revolution is best known from his six-volume *History of the English People in the Nineteenth Century* but it was first aired in an earlier essay 'On the birth of Methodism in England'.[3] Halévy's case was that the spread of Wesleyan Methodism, attractive as a response to the despair created by economic crisis,

> bent the popular impulses of 1739 to the form which most favored the respect for and maintenance of existing institutions.... A force capable of expending itself in displays of violence or popular upheavals assumes, under the influence of a century and a half of Methodism, the form least capable of unsettling a social order founded upon inequality of rank and wealth.[4]

Subsequent argument added a more positive complement to the theme of evangelical religion as a diversion of revolutionary potential into safe channels.

Chapel culture not only helped poor people reconcile them to their hard life but also offered positive adjustments. Their Puritanism harboured scarce resources; their self-reliance, diligence and probity ensured that they got the best jobs; and the chapel offered training in skills that would allow them to better themselves.[5]

The despair version became a popular explanation for the appeal of evangelical religion, especially in the shape of Primitive Methodism (which had broken away from the more bourgeois Wesleyan strand around 1810). George Parkinson concludes his account of the founding of the chapel in Lambton as follows:

> The chapel thus created was the centre of almost all extra-domestic life ... and gradually all that made for good living, high character, and even the elements of education, found its home and sphere in the little sanctuary. The work was maintained at the cost of many sacrifices and much self-denial by the poorly-paid pitmen, who found in the Methodist services their consolation amidst hardships and hope for better things to come.[6]

Jim Bullock's account of a West Yorkshire pit community notes:

> Bowers Row was an isolated community in which a chapel was really needed. It was not only the isolation, it was also the fact that the collieries were going through a very difficult period – there were strikes and lockouts and real poverty was apparent in the village. The homes were bare and offered no physical comforts to men and women who were already weary and anxious. They felt that all the rest of society were against them, but religion came and religion saved them.[7]

Like all the best big ideas, Halévy 's thesis is probably too sweeping and, as Thompson suggested, needs to be fixed to more specific times and places. One place to which it has been applied with apparent success is the Durham coalfields. Durham miners have conventionally been regarded as atypically religious. Both professional histories and family reminiscences stress the importance of chapel culture in coalmining villages. That Methodism was a force is clear from the 1851 Census: County Durham had almost twice as many Methodist chapels as Anglican churches: 351 to 169.[8] However there is an alternative history of the north-east collier: 'there is certainly a good deal of evidence ... that the miner liked nothing better than a drink'.[9] Interestingly, the popularity of Methodism and alcohol are explained by the same cause. Some miners reacted to their grim working and living conditions by placing their hope in the next life; others: 'found a means of escape from harsh reality in the beer parlours'.[10] What makes the Durham miner an interesting subject for study is that Primitive Methodism made a major contribution to the creation of the main miners' union – the Durham Miners' Association (or DMA) – and to local Labour politics.

This chapter will first demonstrate the importance of the 'Prims', as they were generally known both to the DMA and the Labour movement more widely. It will then consider the extent to which three distinct Durham mining communities were influenced by Methodism. Finally, it will explain the rapid secularisation of the mining communities.

The political preachers

Many contemporaries took for granted the influence of Methodism. A doctor who had worked among north-east miners for 15 years attributed the improvement of their moral condition to religion: 'the ruffian is considered as much a ruffian in a colliery village as he could be anywhere. Much of this is due to Methodism'.[11] W. M. Patterson's partisan history of Primitive Methodism in the North East introduces his account of the east coast villages with the triumphant sub-heading 'Capturing new collieries'.[12] Timothy Eden's history of County Durham credits Methodism with the development of the mining unions: 'But Mr Wesley had shown a light in the darkness of the pit and his successors, the Primitive Methodists, taught the people how to lift up their hearts and their heads and to band together for defence.'[13] A decade later, Henry Pelling wrote: 'the strength of Primitive Methodism among the Northumberland and Durham miners of the mid-nineteenth century is a well-known fact.'[14] And it was routinely claimed for much later periods. When novelist and former pitman Sid Chaplin addressed Durham University's Sociology Department seminar in 1971, he mentioned the communal toilets: 'I dare say these pit villages were Primitive Methodist villages. They were very religious communities and I suppose a lot of praying and sermon composing also went on in the netty.' He added: 'the whole life of the village revolved around the chapel.'[15]

One of the most persuasive grounds of supposing Methodism to have been influential among the working class of County Durham was the remarkable consistency of a Methodist background in the biographies of the early leaders of the DMA.

William Crawford was born in 1833. The son of a collier, he was 'set on' alongside his father at the Cowpen pit, Blyth, but was allowed to return to school after a serious accident cut short his labouring career. An active Primitive Methodist lay preacher, 'and a hard-working man in connexion with all the various social and political reform associations, which had for their object the welfare of miners in Northumberland', he was chosen as one of the first secretaries of the newly-formed Northumberland Miners' Association and at the age of 30 became its general secretary.[16] When the Durham miners formed their own association, Crawford was first offered a job as an agent and then in quick succession elected president and appointed general secretary, a job he held until his death in 1890. He added another important role when he was elected to the House of Commons in the 1885 general election as a Liberal. He was quite clear that he owed his success: 'socially and spiritually, largely to Primitive Methodism'.[17]

Crawford's successor was William Patterson. Forced by the death of his parents into an early start to a life of labour, he began work as a quarryman at the age of 11 and a year later moved to Heworth colliery, where he eventually became a hewer. He was also a prodigy in the Methodist New Connexion; at the age of 16 he was an active and popular local preacher. He was the founding secretary of the union lodge at Heworth and one of the founders of the DMA. Patterson was also an elected local councillor, an elected member of the Durham School Board, and an energetic promoter of the Mechanics Institute and other enterprises for the education of working men. On his death at the early age of 49 he was succeeded as general secretary of the DMA by John Wilson.

Like Patterson, Wilson was orphaned by the age of 12, started work in a quarry and quickly shifted to collieries, where he first worked as a 'pony putter': the driver of a pony pulling a wagon of coal. After a brief career at sea and a spell working in coalmines in Pittsburgh, Wilson returned to Durham to work at Haswell colliery. He was converted at a Prim meeting, gave up drinking, studied hard in Sunday school and became a local preacher:

> As a Trade Unionist he was outstanding. Accepting office in 1875, he went to the Midlands three years later as a pioneer of Trade Unionism among the miners of North Staffordshire, Warwickshire, and Leicestershire. William Brown, a religious enthusiast, accompanied him, and regularly opened their meetings with gospel songs and public prayer. Many of the gatherings were held on Methodist premises.[18]

In 1882 he was appointed treasurer of the DMA and he succeeded Patterson as general secretary in 1896. Like Crawford, he was also a local councillor and chaired the county council for three years. He was elected to parliament as a Liberal for the Houghton-le-Spring Division of Durham at the same election as gave Crawford the mid-Durham seat. He lost his seat in 1886 but returned to parliament by winning the by-election caused by Crawford's death and held the seat for 25 years.[19] The eulogist at Wilson's funeral had no doubt about the importance of his religious background:

> he would never have been the man he was, he could never have achieved the work he did, had it not been for his religion.... Upon his conversion he had the good fortune to unite himself with a Church that provided him with ample opportunities for service. In its pulpits he was trained in the art of public speech, and in its quarterly meetings he received the first initiation into the principles of democratic government, and no man was more ready to acknowledge his obligations. He was never the man to conceal his Church connexions, and throughout his career ... he remained a loyal adherent to its doctrines, a devoted servant to the cause and a generous supporter of its funds.[20]

Many others could be added to this list. John Johnston, financial secretary of the DMA and elected MP for Gateshead in 1904 was a Primitive Methodist local preacher as was William House, a DMA president and local councillor. Thomas Cann, who followed Wilson as general secretary, was a Prim Sunday school teacher and local preacher, as was the man who succeeded him: W. P. Richardson. James Robson, who followed House as president, was a New Connexion Methodist.

The most celebrated of Durham's Methodist miners' leaders was Peter Lee, who achieved such prominence that the North East's first new town was named after him. He was born in 1864 in the pit village of Trimdon Grange and started work at Littletown colliery at the age of ten. After a decade of working in local pits he went to the United States for a year. On this return he took up mining again at Wingate. Nine years later he migrated to South Africa and spent a year working in the gold mines before returning to Durham. At the age of 33 he was converted and became a committed Primitive Methodist. In 1902 he was elected as checkweighman[21] at Wheatley Hill colliery; the following year he was elected chairman of the parish council, which was the start of a long career promoting municipal socialism in local government. Five years later he was elected to the Rural District Council and two years after that, to Durham County Council. When the Labour party won a majority of seats in 1919, Lee was elected chairman, a position he held with only a short break in opposition until his death in 1935. His career in local government was matched by his rise through the Durham Miners' Association, from local branch representative to full-time agent to chairman of the DMA in 1930 and president of the Miners' Federation of Great Britain in 1933.

The problem with the 'Great Men' approach to the impact of Methodism is that is entirely possible that the reason for their popularity was secular. What explains the success of Crawford, Wilson, Lee and others may not be their faith as such but its attendant civic virtues: confidence in public speaking, honesty, literacy, and administrative experience. In order to assess the Methodist penetration of the Durham mining areas, we need to examine directly the evidence of chapel affiliations. In order to see the effects of change over time and to compare different sorts of mining, I have taken three areas of County Durham at three time periods to represent different sorts of mining and miners: Upper Teesdale 1851–1921; the Deerness Valley 1891–1931; and the Peterlee area 1911–71. The three areas are located west to east and miners moved between them: when lead mining ceased in Teesdale, the miners moved to the shallow pits of the Deerness Valley and then when those pits became uneconomic, they moved to the deep mines of the east coast.

Methodism among Durham miners

Although there are technical issues in the collection and interpretation of church data, it is possible to assess and compare the penetration of the Durham mining area by Methodism. Membership totals can be calculated from the records of the various Methodist chapels. The three strands of Methodism – Wesleyan, Primitive and New Connexion – had a clear notion of membership: members are those who profess the faith and join a society, initially for a trial period of a year. Each 'society' kept meticulous records and reported membership every quarter to the circuit – the group of chapels around which preachers moved – and to the district: a unit usually the size of a county. Many reporting schedules survive. Membership figures were also often mentioned in the minutes of chapel trustee meetings. Circuits produced quarterly 'preaching plans' which listed who would preach at which chapel when and most circuit plans had a membership total next to each chapel. Where data for particular years are missing these can usually be reasonably estimated from extant data.

One final important technical point: the data reported below do not directly concern miners. We have only environmental information. We can calculate what proportion of an area's population had what degree of involvement. However, all religious statistics for mining populations have the same weakness. Such information remains valid because, for the three case studies, miners formed a very large proportion of the population of those areas at those times. It is just possible that the people who belonged to the New Brancepeth Primitive chapel in 1911 included everyone in those settlements except the miners and their families, but such sources as the occupations listed for chapel trustees and detailed chapel histories tell us otherwise. Many Durham chapels were entirely dependent on the colliery for the livelihood of their members. The quarterly reporting schedules used by the Primitive Methodist circuits demanded explanations of any decline in membership. The superintendent of the Thornley circuit wrote in 1896:

> our circuit is still suffering much from the total stoppages of the Thornley, Wheatley Hill and Ludworth collieries. We have taken from the roll books the unusual larger number of 319 names for the year; many who were members with us at the time when the collieries stopped have had no employment since and in consequence have ceased to meet with us.

The 1906 return noted that '100 members have removed from circuit during the year because of colliery closures'.[22] With the chapels in the mining areas so clearly dependent on the mines it seems reasonable to take their total membership and attendance figures as describing the religiosity of the miners.

In a perfect world we would have reliable data for membership of, or involvement in, all the churches, sects and denominations represented in our three cases study areas. Unfortunately the data is thin and only sporadically available. In Upper Teesdale, there were three Baptist chapels in the early nineteenth century that lost members to the Methodists and there was a handful of Catholics. There was a larger Catholic presence in the Deerness and East Coast pit villages. Two major landowners in the Deerness area were Catholic and the large seminary at Ushaw Moor meant the regular provision of religious offices, which in turn attracted Catholics. Moore estimates Catholic density as about one-third at the end of the nineteenth century and one-quarter in the 1930s, but that is nominal affiliation.[23] Based on relatively weak sources such as estimates of population born in Ireland, we could estimate the Catholic population of the East Coast area as around 10 per cent.[24] We have no idea what proportion of those people were in any sense religiously observant. However, we do have reliable data on the Church of England.

Until the 1919 Enabling Act created the category of elector, the Church of England had no notion of membership. It regarded all parishioners who did not openly dissent as members. However, there is something comparable in the notion of a communicant. Frequency of communion varied considerably between churches and over time. In the nineteenth century many celebrated communion less than once a month; by the end of our period, at least weekly communion was standard. However, communion has always been celebrated at Easter and communicating then was a minimal requirement. In the period under review, incumbents maintained a register of services in commercially printed pro-forma books that included columns for attendance and communicants at each service. Although very few incumbents completed the attendance column, all recorded communicant numbers, especially at Easter, and these were reported to the diocese and collated. Typically Easter communicants were considerably more numerous than the communicants on any other Sunday. For example, in Castle Eden on Easter Sunday 1921, 98 people took communion; almost ten times the average for other Sundays. Hence it is a much weaker measure of attachment than Methodist membership but nonetheless it gives some indication of what proportion of the population regarded themselves as Anglican rather than something else and it can thus serve two useful purposes.[25] First, it provides another measure of total religiosity and thus can allow us to distinguish what part of the decline of Methodism is due to the general secularisation of society and what is due to Methodism's own loss of relative presence. Second, it provides something of a test of the commonly made claim that part of the appeal of Methodism to the Durham miners was its role as a form of displaced politics. There is certainly plenty of evidence in the historical record that miners resented the Church of England's political conservatism and, as the vituperative comments on Methodism made by many Anglican incumbents in their visitation returns show, the dislike was reciprocated. Hensley Henson, who was Bishop of Durham from 1920 to 1939, alienated many by his repeated criticisms of the DMA. With that background in mind, Anglican Easter communicant figures can cast additional light on the supposed Methodism of the Durham miners.

Upper Teesdale

The first Methodist chapel in Upper Teesdale was built in Newbiggin in 1759, but growth was initially slow. In 1800 Newbiggin had 34 members, Middleton had nine, and Eggleston had six: a total of 49 Methodists. Eggleston grew sufficiently to open a chapel in 1828. The second half of the nineteenth century saw considerable consolidation. In 1860 the Primitive and Wesleyan Methodists of Harwood erected a shared chapel. In 1868, the Bowlees Primitive Methodist chapel, seating 530 people, was opened. Two chapels were erected in Forest. The Primitives, who had previously shared a Baptist chapel, built on the north side of the road in 1881; the Wesleyans built on the south side in 1867. Both Primitive and Wesleyan societies in Middleton, the main town of the upper dale, prospered enough to replace their previous chapels with impressive new buildings in 1870.

The growth of evangelical dissent was aided significantly by people who shared the evangelical ethos of the Methodists. The London Lead Mining Company (LLC), a Quaker firm, took its first leases at Newbiggin in 1753, gradually bought up others, and in 1823 bought a large estate in Middleton on which it built an impressive headquarters for its manager and cottages for its workforce. The LLC set the standard for progressive paternalism. However arduous the work of lead extraction and difficult the circumstances in which it was done, those conditions were far better under the LLC than previously or elsewhere. It provided good housing for its workers: 'shops' near the mines where workers who also farmed further down the dale could bunk during the week and cottages in Nenthead and Middleton. It provided gardens for its cottagers and smallholdings in the dale so that workers could grow their own food. In response to periodic grain shortages, it established a Corn Association that imported grain in bulk and sold it to the miners at cost price. It freed its workers from unscrupulous moneylenders by providing credit and advances on wages in times of unusual hardship. When falls in the price of lead made the workings temporarily unprofitable, it employed men on non-mining tasks such as repairing buildings and stone-walling the dale rather than laying them off. And, to the great credit of the Company's owners and managers, it did not confine its benefits to its workers but made the various services available to all the residents of the dale.

The Company also invested heavily in education. It built and endowed schools and lending libraries. It supported the building of chapels (and in Nenthead, an Anglican church) and it gave Bibles to be distributed as Sunday School prizes.[26] With the carrot came the paternalist's stick. The Company's workers were banned from pubs, threatened with dismissal for drunkenness and fined for swearing. Any worker who fathered an illegitimate child was required to provide financial support or face dismissal. All the young people in the Company's employ were required to attend Sunday School until they could pass basic literacy and Bible knowledge tests. The children who attended the Company schools were required to attend church or chapel every Sunday: 'steady persons are stationed by the Company's agents at the door of every place of public worship, from whom the pupils of the Sunday schools received tickets on entrance'.[27]

The high point of chapel construction also marked the start of the dale's decline. Cheap imported lead made the mines increasingly unprofitable. In the last decades of the nineteenth century, the Company ran down its operations and sold what remained in 1905. As we can see from Table 6.1, in 1881, when Methodism in the dale peaked, 28 per cent of the population aged 15 and older was in membership. By then Anglicans were well served. The parish churches at Middleton and Eggleston, and a small chapel of ease at Harwood, had been augmented by St Jude-the-Less in Forest, which was built by the Duke of Cleveland in 1844. However, the Church was considerably less popular than the chapels. In 1881 only 15 people at Forest took communion on Easter Sunday. In total, Anglicans measured in this way numbered only one-seventh of the Methodists at the start of the period and one-tenth when lead mining was at its height.

Table 6.1 Methodist Members (MM) and Anglican Easter Communicants (EC) as % of adult population, 1851–1971

	Upper Teesdale		Deerness Valley		East Coast	
	MM	EC	MM	EC	MM	EC
1851	14	2				
1861	20	3				
1871	26	2				
1881	28	2				
1891	25	3	12	6		
1901	24	6	11	9		
1911	22	6	9	11	4	4
1921	21	7	9	10	4	6
1931			8	12	3	6
1941					3	6
1951					3	5
1961					3	4
1971					2	4

Deerness Valley

Between 1801 and 1901 County Durham's population increased from 150,000 to almost two million; growth that was largely due to coal. By 1913 165,807 people were employed in coalmining. This rose to a peak of 170,181 in 1923 and, despite the steady closure of worked-out pits, remained above 100,000 until 1957. Labour was drawn in from all over the country but one major source was Upper Teesdale: as Hunt notes, 'the normal destination' for redundant lead miners was 'the coal area of the north-east'.[28]

The Deerness Valley, the site of a major study of Methodism by Robert Moore, lies a few miles west of Durham City.[28] There had been drift mining in the 1850s but the coming of the railway in 1857 encouraged the opening of new pits and villages. The New Brancepeth pit was opened in 1858, Waterhouses in 1859, Esh in 1866, and Hamsteels and Cornsay two years later. By 1896 almost 7,000 men and boys were working in the Deerness pits and many more were employed in brickmaking and coking. Pit employment peaked between 1919 (for East Hedley Hope, which then employed 550 men) and 1923 (for Ushaw Moor, with 750 men).

Most societies were founded shortly after the houses around the pithead were constructed. Typically they met first in colliery offices or the schoolroom (which had usually been built by the pit owners), and were then given a site and building materials. Owners also helped with start-up costs. In 1883 Bearpark Colliery subscribed £200 of the £500 costs of the Bearpark Wesleyan chapel and the following year gave the same sum toward the Primitive chapel.[29] Like the LLC, Pease and Partners was a non-sectarian Quaker promoter of evangelical religion. It gave two houses (and labour and materials) to the Esh Primitives to convert to a chapel in 1875 and loaned a colliery building to the Wesleyans. Arthur Pease laid the foundation stone for the Waterhouses Wesleyan chapel (for which Lord Boyne had given the land, as he did for the Primitives). The sites and bricks for Ushaw Moor Wesleyan chapel were given by Pease and Partners in 1900. Coal owners also often gave free coal or coke for heating. Bearpark Colliery company supplied all three Methodist chapels until the industry was nationalised. Joseph Love, who owned Cornsay Colliery, was a self-made man and New Connexion lay preacher, who gave most of his considerable wealth to fund chapel-building. At Cornsay he gave the land and materials for the chapel, paid its running costs, and provided the colliery trap for visiting preachers. Of the local pit owners, only J. B. Johnson of Hamsteels colliery seems to have been niggardly. He insisted that his domestic servants (even the Methodists) attend the parish church but his firm, Johnson and Reay, gave the land and £100 for the erection of the Primitive chapel at Quebec in 1876, while Reay and his son each gave a further £52 each; in total the company and its owners covered more than half the costs of the chapel.

As in Upper Teesdale, paternalistic influence was exercised at close quarters in the Valley by various managers and officials of the collieries who were themselves committed Christians. For example, among the first trustees of the New Brancepeth Wesleyan chapel were the manager of the brick works and the colliery manager.[30]

In the wider Deerness area there were 27 chapels: total membership is displayed below in Table 6.1. When Methodism was most popular, shortly after the pits became fully operational, 12 per cent of adults were Methodist members and that proportion fell steadily thereafter. An 1859 guide to Teesdale wrote: 'the miners are, for the most part, sober and industrious; there appears to be something in their metalliferous employment which makes them, as a class, more respectable than coal-miners'.[32] If by 'respectable' the author means 'Methodist', he was right. Despite considerable support from the colliery owners, Methodism was much less popular in the colliery villages than in Upper Teesdale. The 12 per cent of the adult population in membership of the chapels in 1891 was well above the English average but was much lower than the Teesdale figure and by the 1930s the Methodist core was less than 10 per cent. It is interesting to note that the Church of England was much more popular in the Deerness Valley than in Upper Teesdale. Taking communion in the Church of England on Easter Sunday is a much weaker test of allegiance than being a member of a Methodist chapel but it is a mark of allegiance nonetheless and it rose steadily from 6.2 per cent in 1891 to 12 per cent in 1931, overtaking Methodist membership in 1911.

East Coast

The narrow seam mines of the west Durham villages became uneconomic when the oil and gas reduced demand. The coal in East Durham lay deeper but in thicker bands. There was a false start in its exploitation. The first deep pit in the region was sunk at Hetton in 1821 and by 1832 it was part of the largest mine in England. New pits at Thornley, Wheatley Hill, South Wingate, Hutton Henry and Shotton created settlements that became ghost towns when the ventures failed. Wheatley Hill failed twice before the end of the century. South Wingate closed in 1857. Castle Eden Colliery closed in 1893, Haswell in 1876, and Hutton Henry a year later. Shotton opened in 1840 and closed in 1877. The second phase began with the Horden Coal Company reopening Shotton in 1900. New technology and greater investment saw the creation of a cluster of super-pits at Horden, Easington and Blackhall. By 1967 the east coast pits were producing almost three times as much coal as those of west Durham.[33]

The population of Easington Rural District grew from almost 22,000 in 1851 to 76,000 in 1911 and 88,000 in 1931, and that growth was almost entirely due to the deep pits. The parish of Monk Hesleden, which contained one of the first deep pits, grew from 1,495 in 1851 to 7,298 in 1931. Shotton parish grew tenfold over the same period. The far-sighted clerk of Easington Rural District Council promoted the creation of a new town over the piece-meal building of new housing. Although, when the Peterlee Development Corporation was created in March 1948, it was England's first new town, the result was a disappointment. Many miners preferred poor but free housing in the old settlements to new but relatively expensive houses in Peterlee, the Corporation had trouble attracting industrial factories to provide alternative work, and the older villages resisted attempts to reduce their housing stock in favour of the new town. Nonetheless, by 1971, half of the population of my study area – the parishes of Easington, Monk Hesleden, Castle Eden, Horden, Shotton and Peterlee – was in Peterlee.

This area has been chosen to be large enough to have sufficient chapels and churches for us to suppose that local peculiarities are swamped by the generality. It has also been chosen to be typical of post-war Durham mining.

Methodist membership grew from 1911 to 1941 but it grew more slowly than the adult population. Most significantly, its peak penetration of 4 per cent in 1911 is well below the Deerness peak of 12 per cent and the Upper Teesdale peak of 28 per cent. To set the Methodist figures for the East Coast in context, we can note that those who took communion at Easter in the parish churches were as numerous as the Methodists in 1911 and more numerous thereafter.[34]

Community impact

The presentation thus far has under-represented the impact of Methodism because it has not allowed for the penumbra of 'adherents'. Sporadic references in minute books make it clear that chapel attendance was higher than membership but the only directly relevant extant data for individual chapels comes from the schedules for the Primitive Methodist circuit between 1899 and 1911, which asked for 'attendance at the Chief services'. Some reports seem implausibly high. In 1899 Bowlees chapel, for example, reported 48 members but an attendance of 200. That precisely the same attendance figures are reported by each of the six Upper Teesdale chapels for 1899, 1901 and 1911, and that those figures are always multiples of 50 when membership changes almost annually, suggests three possible explanations: carelessness, ignorance or dishonesty. The first is possible, though serious effort seems to have been put into completing other parts of the schedules. The second is unlikely. Other columns on the same page ask for the chapel's seating capacity and the stewards or minister should have had little difficulty recalling how full the chapel was and making the appropriate calculation. Dishonesty also seems unlikely. Although we might suppose that chapel stewards or superintendant ministers had an interest in inflating measures of their popularity, we know that declining membership was accurately reported.

There is a further reason for not rejecting such reports too quickly. The Primitive Methodist Connexion collated a national figure for adherents. Between 1881 and 1931, the ratio of adherents to members declined steadily year by year from 3.19 to 2.37. Unless we suppose a extraordinary degree of cheating and collusion, the regularity of the change suggests some underlying reality is being reported in such data.[35] This leaves us assuming that the attendance reports were in some way accurate and puzzling to work out just how. Let us suppose that 45 of the 48 members of the Bowless chapel attend both morning and evening morning service; that is 90 attendances. Adding in the Sunday school children for one service takes us to about 120. That still leaves 80 attendances unaccounted for and as the proportion of adherents that attended both services is likely to be less than that of members, the total of non-member adherents attending must have been between 60 and 80. This fits with the national figures but still seems high. In the absence of any other information, perhaps the best we can do is say that when the chapels were at their most popular, they were regularly attended by twice as many people as were members.

The penumbra for the Deerness chapels may have been larger. For the period 1891–1906 I found 13 reports in the schedules for the Waterhouses Primitive Methodist circuit that list 'attendance at the Chief services'. The degree of variation in the number of adherents claimed by similar chapels in one small area hardly inspires confidence. Hedley Hill in 1901 claimed 300 attendees, though it had only 30 members. Esh Winning had 50 members but 300 attendees. Moore notes that the Esh Wesleyan chapel in 1921 reported 74 members and 150 'hearers'.[36] It is possible to construct an explanation. In a semi-urban area with a much larger and shifting population, one might well have a greater proportion of people who regularly attended chapels but resisted the social pressure to take up full membership and attend the non-Sunday meetings.

The claimed adherents-to-members ratio was even higher for the East Coast pit villages. For example, for five date points between 1881 and 1906 the Shotton Colliery Primitive Methodist chapel reported the following figures for members and total attendances: 33/110, 40/100, 50/150, 39/250 and 73/250: on average an attendance four times that of the membership was being claimed. Again we may be sceptical of the precise figures without doubting the key point that far more people had some involvement with the chapels than were members.

That changed in the middle of the twentieth century. We cannot be sure exactly when because, with the merger of the various strands of Methodism in 1932, the Primitive adherents data series comes to an end. Thereafter the records have only sporadic data for attendance, collected on the basis of criteria that frequently change. However we can be confident that by the 1960s total attendance was less than membership. For example, the two chapels in Sacriston in 1964 had 200 members but typical Sunday attendance was only 100–120 people.[37] In 1974 Blackhall with 203 members reported attendances of 40 at the morning service and 76 in the evening. Peterlee Memorial, with 208 members, reported 76 at a morning service and 34 in the evening. On average attendances reported for six chapels were just over half the membership.

Adding some consideration of the penumbra of regular attendees casts the decline of Methodism in starker relief. It shows that in Upper Teesdale at the start of our period Methodism was considerably more popular than the membership data suggests; it also shows that in the East Coast at the end of our period, it was even less popular. That is, the gradient of decline was considerably steeply than it appeared when we considered only membership figures. As membership fell, the penumbra of loosely attached Methodists fell faster. Somewhere between 1930 and 1960 the two indices of attendance and membership crossed over so that instead of the chapels having a reach greater than their membership, by the 1970s not even the members attended every week. In the nineteenth century, Methodist membership was a privilege, withheld while a potential member was 'on trial', and withdrawn for poor attendance. As Methodism declined its officials became ever more reluctant to exclude. Members became gradually less committed but many were reluctant to cut their ties; they kept their names on the rolls but attended only rarely.

The complete disappearance of Methodism from the coalfields is demonstrated by a detailed study of a segment of East Coast miners who migrated. When it became clear that most mines in the north of England were uneconomic, the National Coal Board set up a transfer scheme to encourage miners to move south. In 1971, Gareth Evans surveyed a sample of Durham miners who had moved to Cannock Chase in Staffordshire in the 1960s.[38] Evans says of his sample: 'apart from being the product of a decline in the economic fortunes of a specific region, they shared certain other characteristics, such as a close identification with their area of origin, a history of militancy in union affairs, and an interest in social club life'.[39] Evans is aware of the obvious omission from that list and asks directly about it: 'the churches and particularly the chapels were remembered as playing an important part in the life of the community, although their importance began to diminish from the early 1930s.' He also notes: 'For men the centre of their social activities tended to be the pub or the club.'[40] Membership of a social club was common: 86 per cent of miners and 61 per cent of their wives belonged. Not one respondent belonged to a church or chapel and his detailed questioning led Evans to conclude that none had attended a church or chapel except for a funeral, wedding or christening.

Explaining Methodist decline

The comparison of our three case studies is complicated by the passage of time. As we see very clearly from Figure 6.1 (which graphs and extends the data in

Table 6.1) there is general decline from the 1880s. The lines for Anglican Easter communicants in Deerness and the East Coast villages are the only exception and their initial growth represents not an increase in the number of religious people but the Church of England's lag in providing worship outlets to service the demand we can assume already existed. Once Anglican provision is in place, all six lines show decline. In that sense, our three case study areas display the general secularisation of British society. But we can also add some local detail.

That Methodism was far more successful in Upper Teesdale than in either of the coalmining areas fits with what we know of its appeal to different classes and class fractions. The lead miners of Upper Teesdale were not industrialised workers. They were more like self-employed artisans, working autonomously in small teams that signed individual contracts with the mine operators. Part of their livelihoods was derived from family-based subsistence agriculture. And they were residentially dispersed rather than concentrated. The basic structural requirements for the growth of a secular class consciousness was largely missing and their material lives fitted well with the image of self-reliance promoted by their evangelical faith.

In Upper Teesdale the religious message of the chapels was reinforced by their unrivalled roles as centres of such social life as there was and by the efforts of the schools and by leisure facilities such as the lending library organised by the Harwood chapel (and funded by the LLC) and the 'British Workman' reading room in Eggleston.[41] In Deerness and, even more so in the East Coast villages, increasing prosperity and easier travel gave young people access to new secular forms of leisure. The cinema and the theatre would not attract core members but they competed for the attention of peripheral adherents. The

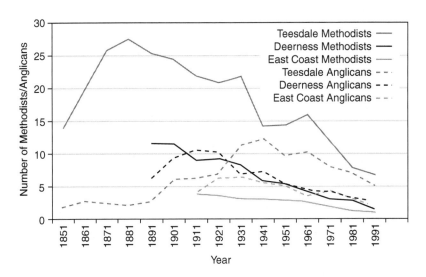

Figure 6.1 Methodist Members and Anglican Easter Communicants in Upper Teesdale, Deerness and Easington, 1851–1991.

chapels offered a very wide range of social activities: choir-singing, brass bands, celebration teas, illustrated lectures on secular topics, and holiday outings. But these were consumed largely by core members and their families. As the DMA became more powerful and as miners became more prosperous, secular institutions were created that not only served important social and economic functions but also provided opportunities for energy-absorbing social involvement. The Cooperative movement was extremely successful in the coalmining villages. The introduction in 1920 of a levy on all coal output, with the funds being used for miners' welfare, lead not only to pithead baths but also to the creation of expansive Miners' Welfare Institutes which competed with the most outgoing chapels in the range of activities they provided.[42] And most colliery villages supported at least one miners' drinking club (which in Methodist eyes compounded the original offence of drinking by permitting gambling). This alternative secular milieu of union lodge, drinking club, Cooperative store, and institute was growing in the Deerness Valley in the period under review: it was flourishing in the East Coast pit villages. As well as providing a social alternative to chapel culture, it created its own training and career paths for activists and thus reduced reliance on the chapel leadership. When the Labour movement was new, potential leaders could only have acquired credentials, status and experience from outside the movement. Once it had created its own secular structures, they became self-reproducing.

In both the Deerness and East Coast cases, Methodism was most popular at the start of the mining period and then declined. In part that may just reflect the general secularisation of the culture but the fact that support for the Church of England actually grew also suggests that far from being especially fertile fields, coalmining communities were difficult environments for Methodism. One obvious explanation is that the pit villages developed their own secular identity based on a series of inter-linked institutions that provided an alternative to chapel culture. In his response to a question in the 1892 visitation return, the Anglican incumbent of Brandon, the Reverend Joseph Lawson, wrote: 'Primitive Methodism is the "Miner's Union" seen in its Religious Aspect. Just as the Cooperation Stores is the "Miner's Union" in its Commercial Aspect.'[43] Lawson was perceptive in seeing the functional equivalence that would eventually render the chapel version redundant.

An important part of the process of the secular replacing the religious was the politicisation of the trade union movement and the attendant shift of loyalties from the Liberal to the Labour party. Initially the ambitions of Crawford and Wilson for their members were compatible with the Liberal party ethos, but in the early decades of the twentieth century the climate changed markedly. In 1901 the Taff Vale Railway Company sued the Amalgamated Society of Railway Servants for losses incurred during a strike and, in a ruling that exposed unions to being sued every time their members were in dispute, the union was fined £23,000. The Liberal government secured the passage of the 1906 Trades Disputes Act, which removed trade union liability for damage by strike action, but the Taff Vale case was a considerable stimulus to those who argued that the interests of working men would best be served by a Labour party. In 1909, the Miners' Federation of Great Britain (which had been formed in 1888 as a national coordinating body for the various county unions) joined the Labour party. While the other MPs sponsored by miners took the Labour whip in Parliament, Durham's John Wilson remained a Liberal. The shift from the Liberal to the Labour party was not a clean break. In 1911 when the DMA drew up its list of parliamentary candidates, all were members of the ILP and all were Methodists. But it was a break nonetheless. When Wilson chaired the County Council, he did so as a Liberal. Peter Lee and his successors were all Labour men.[44]

There were two related changes in values. The Liberal and Methodist perspectives coincided in being highly individualistic. Support for the working man rested on the view that oppressive conditions offended against the dignity of the individual and constrained his advancement. Salvation was a cure for poverty, in that it reconciled the poor to their circumstances and it offered this-worldly improvement. But neither advantage was easy to advertise when the audience was desperate. Hence improvement was a necessary condition for winning souls. Mutual trust between workers and owners (and an acceptance of the market) were the way forward. The Labour view was far more communal and far more political. Working people as a class had a right to a fair share of wealth irrespective of markets and were right to use their collective power to gain it.

The second value change was in the weight given to democratic principles. As Beynon and Austrin argue in great detail, the Methodist chapels were more democratic than the Church of England but that democracy was always constrained by the trumping status of religious truth.[45] The local preacher was not a representative of his audience but a prophet called to challenge their sins and bring them to the stool of repentance. In practice this encouraged successful chapel leaders to develop a highly authoritarian style, which can be seen both at the very top in the character of Jabez Bunting who, for two decades from the 1830s, dominated Wesleyan Methodism and at the very bottom, in the almost comic assertiveness of Jim Bullock's father, who sought to rule his large family as a despot.[46] A Derbyshire critic wrote:

> [Methodist] leaders are to be found in Co-operative societies or Hospital Committees, among Chapel trustees, and Deacons, in Teetotal societies … and a variety of other places. No-one can do anything but themselves. If they could rule, earth would be a paradise and, because they cannot injustice and misery are the consequences…. The moment the collier begins to think for himself their power is gone for ever'.[47]

In the early days of the DMA, when its agents often operated as lone promoters of the union and were actively resisted by colliery owners, the persona of the Old Testament prophet (with a little Daniel in the Lion's Den) suited well. In complex negotiations with large numbers of colliery owners and managers over details of disputes, the Primitive Methodist agents could use their claim to moral virtue as a bargaining device and as a shield for deflecting criticism from disgruntled members. Once the DMA's presence in the industry was reinforced by its control over the local Labour party, the benign despot style of leadership became anachronistic.

It is important not to replace the romantic myth of the Methodist miner with the equally exaggerated and sentimental myth of the socialist miner but, as the strength of its death-throes resistance to Thatcherism in 1984 proved, the world of the collier was a collectivist world. Band together in the union, pool resources in the Cooperative, drink together in the club, and use the power of the union and the party to improve conditions for everyone together. This was a solidaristic vision, which did not sit at all well with either the individualism or the other-worldly orientation of evangelical religion.

There is an additional change that may have been influential. One of the characteristics of modernisation that weakened the power of traditional religion was the gradual sense of growing mastery over fate that technology provided.[48] That we know far more about the material world and have far greater control over it than had our medieval ancestors does not prevent us being religious but it reduces the sense that we are in thrall to some ineffable higher power and it reduces the range of events for which religion provides the best (or only) response. Although it is difficult to demonstrate the causal connection, it is widely accepted that some of the appeal of evangelical religion lay in its ability to provide a psychologically satisfying response to the all-too-frequent incidence of fatalities in coalmining. In the nineteenth century mining was extremely hazardous and very few pit families were not affected by untimely death. In the absence of good attitude surveys we can only speculate, but it may be that the emotional draw of the chapels was reduced by the radical improvement in mine safety. The annual fatalities rate fell from a peak in 1877 of 2.63 deaths per thousand people employed in the industry to 0.55 in 1953 and 0.1 in 1983.[49] Death was never very far away. At Easington colliery in May 1951 the picks of a coal-cutting machine operating on a retreating longwall face struck pyrites and the sparks ignited firedamp and caused an explosion that spread through 16,000 yards of roadway and caused the deaths of 81 people. Two men of the rescue team also died. Nonetheless, untimely death and the opportunity it presented for religious activity was far less common towards the end of our period under review than at the start.

The final blow to Methodism among the miners came from an unintended consequence of values promoted within the chapels. One of Moore's respondents, raised in Waterhouses in the 1880s and returned to the Deerness Valley in the 1950s as a Methodist minister, stated that 'social climbing was the curse of Methodism'. He recalled that no leading Methodist had sons who went down the pit. Writing in the 1970s Moore confirmed this: 'Interviews with all the contemporary Methodists showed that over 80% of the men over 60 had worked in the pits. … Not one of the younger Methodists had ever worked in the pits.'[50] It is arguably the case that every dissenting movement has seen its children achieve a higher social status. Puritan sects that encourage literacy, diligence and temperance have always equipped their children to make the most of whatever opportunities for upward mobility existed. What was unusual about the 1950s was the unprecedented opportunities offered by a fundamental change in the class structure. Post-war Britain saw a marked shift from manual to white-collar work as the welfare state created new jobs in teaching, local government, the health service and the social services and the children of the chapels were unusually well placed to take advantage of that change.

Conclusion

County Durham was chosen as a site to explore the relationship between Methodism and the Labour movement not because it was typical but because first sight suggests an unusually strong bond. Methodism was far more popular in Durham than in England as a whole and very few unions could have matched the DMA for the consistency with which its early officials were drawn from Methodist chapels. Yet close examination shows that claims made for Methodist impact on mining communities were greatly exaggerated. It is certainly true that the lead miners of Upper Teesdale, with over a quarter of the population in full membership and a similar proportion regularly attending the chapels, were enthusiasts for evangelical religion but the same can hardly be said for the colliers of the Deerness Valley 40 years later. And by the time the centre of mining had moved to the Peterlee area, the impact of Methodism was slight. Despite Bishop Henson's reputation, more people took Easter communion in the parish churches than were members of the chapels. That the vast majority of miners did not share the faith of the men they elected to union and party office suggests that the major contribution of Methodism to the Labour movement lay not in its religious heart but in the secondary social consequences of its beliefs and values. Methodism encouraged in its members secular virtues and skills that made them strong candidates for leadership. Ironically those same virtues and skills allowed later generations of Methodists to avoid the mining industry altogether.

7 Opportunity structures and culture wars

Introduction

American sociologist James Davidson Hunter popularised the use of the phrase 'culture wars' to describe the attempts of contemporary US conservative Christians to turn the socio-moral clock back to the comforting certitudes of the Eisenhower era but, as with so many things, a good case can be made for saying that the British did it first but the Americans did it better. This chapter will compare two UK moral crusades of the 1970s – the National Viewers and Listener's Association (NVALA) and the Nationwide Festival of Light (NFOL) – with the US Christian Right, the most recent manifestations of which can be dated from the formation of the Moral Majority in 1978. The primary purpose of the contrast is to show how differences in the environments in which the British and American moral crusades operated shaped their tactics and settled their respective fates.

Moral crusades in Britain

Mary Whitehouse was an art teacher in the English Midlands who, on returning to work in 1963 after a long absence raising children, found herself profoundly disturbed by the moral values and attitudes of her school charges.[1] She came to see a direct connection between her pupils' moral outlook on life and the content of the television programmes they watched. Whitehouse recounts that she was distressed 'by their divergence from Christian standards'. When the children defended their views by referring to material they had seen on television, Whitehouse concluded that a generation was being lost to a 'sub-Christian concept of living' by the influence of the new media. Rather naively, she complained to a senior official of the BBC, to her local MP, to the Bishop of Hereford and to the Minister of Health and expected change. Particularly she expected that her criticisms of the BBC's moral pollution would figure in parliamentary debate on the renewal of its charter and that 'the Corporation would then be obliged to mend its ways'.

When her individual complaints made no difference, she determined to launch a public protest movement. In 1963, Whitehouse and an Anglican vicar founded the Clean Up TV Campaign. Its manifesto asserted faith in a Christian way of life and objected to the culture of 'doubt, disbelief and dirt ... promiscuity, infidelity and drinking' that the BBC was apparently promoting. In May 1964, she outlined her views on television standards in a Birmingham public meeting: 'if violence is shown as normal on the television screen it will help to create a violent society'.[2] The Clean UP TV manifesto was used as the basis for a petition to the Governors of the BBC that attracted half a million signatures. The following year, the National Viewers' and Listeners' Association was formed.

The NVALA was an expression of cultural defence in the face of changing values: it promoted 'the virtues of fidelity in marriage and chastity before marriage; respect for authority, patriotism, hostility to drugs and alcohol, and opposition to "foul language", homosexuality, pornography and abortion'.[3] In the style of asymmetric arithmetic common to such movements, the tiny NVALA claimed to represent the majority while dismissing the obvious majority who favoured liberality and permissiveness as the dupes of communists without and pornographers within the country. Although its supporters had the full spectrum of conservative complaints, the NVALA concentrated very narrowly on the mass media and in particular on television which, over the period that Whitehouse had been away from school-teaching, had gone from rarity to ubiquity.

The NVALA's tactics were limited. Local groups boycotted cinemas occasionally. A few failed attempts were made to persuade the Director of Public Prosecutions to start proceedings against cultural products of which it disapproved. But its main activity was the production of critical press statements, accompanied periodically by petitions and public rallies to show that its criticisms had popular support. The primary target for rebuke was the BBC. In part this was deserved. The BBC had staff who saw their public service remit as justifying the flouting of convention and the testing of boundaries of taste. Instead of presenting the nation with an idealised middle class view of itself, it offered political satire and a realistic portrayal of the lives of the poor and the working class. The Wednesday Play slot, which first aired 'Up the Junction' (described by Whitehouse as 'promiscuity as normal',[4] and 'Cathy Come Home' was a particularly frequent NVALA target. But the main reasons the BBC came in for more flak than the commercial TV broadcasters were remit and tradition. The BBC was the national broadcaster, paid out of a national licence fee and regulated by parliament: the ITV companies could give the people what they wanted but the BBC should be giving the country what was good for it. Imagining such a remit was made easy by the fact that for the first two decades of its life, John Reith, the head of the BBC between 1922 and 1938, had held precisely that view of its purpose.

Whitehouse quickly became a joke figure. In response to her criticisms of his 'kitchen sink' sitcom, the playwright Johnny Speight wrote an episode of *Till Death Us Do Part* in which his aggressive working-class Tory Alf Garnett satirised her opinions by agreeing with them wholeheartedly. Later the camp homosexual comedian Julian Clary began his career as performing under the title *The Mary Whitehouse Experience*. But the prominence accorded her views did cause some concerns. In his diaries, Michael Palin noted his fears that the Monty Python film *Life of Brian* – a comedy paralleling if not exactly parodying the life of Christ – might be banned.[5] In 1977, while the film was in production, Whitehouse achieved her greatest success with a successful private prosecution of *Gay News* for publishing a poem about a Roman centurion's homoerotic feelings towards the crucified Christ. This was rather close to home for the Monty Python team: Graham Chapman had helped launch *Gay News* and was a noted gay rights activist. To pre-empt a similar prosecution, it was decided to open *Life of Brian* first in America, where there would be more vociferous criticism but where the constitutional guarantees of freedom of speech and religious choice would protect it from an outright ban. In the end, Palin's concerns proved groundless. Attempts to have the British Board of Film Censors refuse *Life of Brian* a certificate failed and the film went on to be a great commercial success.

Judging the NVALA's record is a little difficult because it claimed the credit for legislation such as the 1978 Protection of Children Act and the 1981 Indecent Displays Act, which were also supported by more powerful bodies on the left of politics and by influential feminists. In those projects that were uniquely its platform (such as the restoration of theatre censorship), the NVALA signally failed, and its campaigns did nothing at all to arrest or reverse such trends as the rise in divorce or abortion rates or the growing acceptance of homosexuality. The failure of its campaign to end moral pollution on TV is obvious and can be illustrated with the example of swearing. In the 1960s, Whitehouse objected to the frequent use of the word 'bloody' by Alf Garnett in *Till Death Us Do Part*. Now, the 1994 film *Four Weddings and a Funeral*, which opens with the character played by Hugh Grant repeatedly saying 'fuck' because his alarm clock has failed to wake him in time for a wedding, is regarded as a 'national treasure' family movie.

There is something very British about Mary Whitehouse's long career. Over her 30 years as president of the NVALA she became increasingly domesticated as 'a good turn'. The programme makers she repeatedly criticised regularly invited her on to television and radio programmes. She became something of a darling to university debating societies. Her conservative mores were applauded by Margaret Thatcher's Conservative government at the same time as the private behaviour of many senior Conservative politicians proved that they did not personally share her Christian principles of chastity and fidelity. In 1980 she was awarded a CBE but the liberal economics of the Thatcher governments fatally undermined the structural requirements of her moral crusade by encouraging increased competition in an ever freer mass media market. One could argue that it was the state's job to regulate the public's exposure to sexual imagery or one could say that Rupert Murdoch was free to print bare-breasted women on the *Sun*'s Page Three. Although Thatcher tried to combine moral conservatism with liberal economics, even she could not have it both ways.

The second of the UK's moral crusades, the National Festival of Light (NFOL), was founded in 1971 by Peter Hill, a young evangelical Christian recently returned to Britain after a number of years evangelising in India.[6] Like

Whitehouse he was struck by what seemed like a marked decline in public morality. His initial aim was to organise a massive public parade that would dramatise the Christian majority's abhorrence for decadence and promiscuity. Whitehouse's NVALA helped with contacts, as did an array of evangelical Christian groups. NFOL initially had four aims:

> to alert and inform Christians and others like-minded to the dangers of moral pollution; to translate into action the concern that hundreds of thousands feel about the moral pollution in our nation today; to register the support of people of goodwill for Christian morals in such a way that the national leadership is influenced; and to witness to the Good News about Jesus Christ.[7]

In September 1971, a crowd of some 30,000 rallied in London to hear Mary Whitehouse, Malcolm Muggeridge and a variety of right-wing MPs and Lords denounce the lack of opposition to the moral pollution that 'presented a threat to mental health, family life, and the dignity of man'. The crowd then marched to Hyde Park for an evangelistic rally entertained by Cliff Richards and a variety of gospel groups.

Instead of disbanding the organisation once his aim had been achieved, Hill kept the NFOL alive and shifted its direction to concentrate on evangelism. Its main activity in 1973 was helping the Billy Graham organisation plan and run their crusade in London. From 1974 onwards it worked as a legislative 'think tank', collecting and collating evidence on the malign influence of the media, which it presented to such influential groups as church leaders, members of parliament, government ministers and media officials. Whatever the value of such lobbying, it is clear from its last great public rally that this direction did not excite the grass roots. In preparation for a major gathering in Trafalgar Square in September 1976, Roy Wallis and Richard Bland prepared a survey questionnaire, which I and other Stirling University students distributed at the rally. One of the survey questions asked:

> Many Christians feel that, in order to reverse the moral decline of Britain, pressure for more effective legislation on moral issues and more active evangelism are both needed. If you had to put a priority on one rather than the other for immediate action, which would you place first?

Remarkably 84.3 per cent of those who responded to the survey put evangelism first. Only 13.9 put legislation first.[8]

In summary, the tactics used by the NVALA and the NFOL seem both narrow and timid. They devoted most of their effort to talking to the 'establishment'. They collected evidence to support their arguments and presented it to church leaders, ministers, media officials and parliamentary committees. Although they periodically sought to produce crowds to dramatise their claims to represent a silent majority, those crowds were attracted not by the legislative campaigns but by the evangelistic imperatives of 'making a Christian witness'. For good reasons that I will explore shortly, there was no concerted attempt to mobilise power by, for example, bringing pressure to bear on election candidates. In contrast to the vigour and optimism on the US Christian Right, the UK moral crusaders seemed reconciled to defeat. In the write-in sections of the 1976 survey we find such sentiments as: 'It is worth while in my eyes if only, say, just one single person was brought to the Lord', 'even if only a few become believers it will be worth it', 'At least Christians will have made their opinion known which is better than failing to say anything' and, perhaps saddest of all, 'some seed has been sown which must have results somewhere sometime'.[9]

The US Christian Right

> Moral Majority Inc. is made up of millions of Americans, including ministers, priests and rabbis, who are deeply concerned about the moral decline of our nation, and who are sick and tired of the way many amoral and secular humanists and other liberals are destroying the traditional family and moral values on which our nation was built.[10]

The formation of the Moral Majority by televangelist Jerry Falwell in 1978 can serve as the opening salvo of what were later termed 'the culture wars'. Any division of history into periods simplifies and caricatures, but the mobilisation of conservative Christians around organisations fronted by television preachers does seem sufficiently novel to justify the title 'New Christian Right'. Where conservative Christian pressure groups of the 1950s and 1960s were concerned primarily with communism and race relations, this wave campaigned on socio-moral issues and on the social honour accorded to conservative Christian culture.[11] As 30 years have passed since Falwell's initiative the 'new' can be dropped, but the Christian Right (hereafter CR) continues.

There is neither space nor need for a full explanation of the rise of the CR. It is enough to note that, as with most of such movements, there was a combination of push and pull factors: causes for concern and causes for hope. The concern was the increasing secularity of American public life and the threat to conservative Christian mores from feminism, from the gay rights movement, and from liberalism generally. The longstanding conservative Christian response to the world changing in unattractive ways is pietistic retreat. The saints concentrate on building alternative institutions and as much as possible ignore what they do not like. However the federal government had already demonstrated its willingness to impose liberal values on conservative areas in its promotion of civil rights. The interventions of the central state certainly challenged the pietism option. But the mobilisation of conservative Christians also owed a great deal to a new awareness of their power. Although few Southern fundamentalists would have thanked him for this at the time, Lyndon Johnson's forced desegregation of the South removed a major obstacle to the South's full participation in American public life: it was no longer the pariah. It was also becoming economically more powerful as the decline of manufacturing in the rust belt weakened the Northern cities and the climate attracted wealthy migrants and new hi-tech industries southwards. And there was a parallel shift in the 'economy' of American religion. The liberal and mainstream churches were declining and the conservative denominations, particularly the Southern Baptists, were growing. In one particular field – the use of new electronic media – that growth was spectacular. The stars of the radio days had been mainstream clerics such as Norman Vincent Peale, the author of *The Power of Positive Thinking*, but it was the evangelicals, fundamentalists and Pentecostalists on the sectarian wing of Protestantism who were using television to build massive audiences and networks of financial support.

In short, the late 1970s saw the negative and the positive combine to create the right climate for mass mobilisation. On the downside liberal social changes were threatening the culture of conservative Protestants. On the upside, the parts of the USA where such conservatives were strong were becoming increasing affluent, powerful and self-confident. In the 1950s northern liberals could ridicule fundamentalists as sweating rednecks in bri-nylon shirts. By the 1970s, fundamentalists – at least those with their own prime time TV shows – were wealthy men with manicured fingernails and expensive suits who had long ago lost their inferiority complexes.

The Moral Majority and related organisations such as Christian Voice and the Religious Roundtable worked on a number of fronts. One involved the general sensitising of conservative Protestants to political issues and to their need to get involved. America was portrayed as a country in decline because it had turned its back on the religious values that had made it great. The politicising was carried out through Falwell's *Old Time Gospel Hour*, through campaign rallies, and through mailings to individuals who in some way or another had expressed support for conservative issues. Equally important were the meetings arranged for conservative Protestant pastors who were given the same general message, but who were also asked to preach on the subject from their pulpits and to arrange voter registration drives. This latter part of the campaign was crucial. The pietistic retreat tendency of many Bible Belt conservatives had to be overcome.[12]

In the late 1970s, the CR seems to have mobilised whole constituencies that had previously ignored the political process. It was also very successful in turning religious and moral issues into campaign topics. In the 1978 mid-term elections, liberal candidates were targeted with negative advertising. If someone had voted for abortion, for equal rights for women, or against prayer in schools, then their transgressions were made known to the voters. In broadcasts, handouts and rally speeches, liberals were depicted as being anti-religion, anti-family, anti-America, and anti-God.

The 1980 presidential election of Ronald Reagan was claimed by the CR as its work. A longstanding standard bearer of the Right, Reagan was happy to adopt the rhetoric of the Christian Right, though he was not known for his personal piety. In what was to become something of a recurring pattern, secular conservatives played to 'the Reverends' but actually delivered very little. Reagan's success created a major problem for the CR. Its leaders banged on about moral decline, threats to the family, and the erosion of the values that had made America great, and distinguished between the President (who was a good man) and Congress (which was a bad thing), but such analysis sounded rather unconvincing with a conservative in the White House for eight years. During the Reagan years, CR leaders found it increasingly hard to raise funds. In 1987, faced with a major hole in his income, Falwell folded the Moral Majority and retired from electioneering.

Falwell's place was taken by Pat Robertson, a Pentecostal minister who had made two major innovations in religious broadcasting. In styling itself as a current affairs programme, his *700 Club* had been a major departure from the traditional televangelism formats of the church service or the revival crusade. He had also departed from precedent in that, rather than just buying time on existing channels to air his show, he had created his own Christian Broadcasting Network (CBN). Robertson had initially been cool towards the CR but when he did finally commit himself, instead of seeking only to influence candidate selection, platforms and voting patterns, he decided to run for president.

Robertson's 1988 campaign for the Republican Party nomination established what was to become a common experience for the CR. In contests such as low turnout primary elections, where the enthusiasm of zealots was an asset, the CR could win. But such victories tended to backfire: the more CR candidates and their positions were publicised, the more those who did not like them were also mobilised. The CR tried to broaden its appeal by presenting its stars and its agenda in secular terms. Abortion was criticised on the ground that it offended the rights of the unborn child, divorce on the grounds that it was socially dysfunctional. Pat Robertson presented himself as a successful businessman whose business just happened to be Christian TV. The religious inspiration for the movement was kept for the church audiences. Unfortunately liberal groups such as People for the American Way proved adept at ensuring that the most sectarian and least attractive faces of fundamentalism were brought to the electorate's attention and many middle-of-the-road voters were repelled. The more people considered his candidacy, the more anti-Robertson feeling outstripped pro-Robertson sentiment. Robertson spent more money than any other candidate and failed to win a single primary. Even those who should have been most sympathetic had their doubts. Contrary to the assumptions of some commentators who counted the number of born-again Christians or the membership of conservative denominations and assumed that Robertson had those votes in the bag, a good proportion of fundamentalists were unhappy with such overt mixing of religion and politics. In one poll, self-identified conservative Protestants, by a margin of 42 to 25 per cent, said that Robertson's status as a former clergyman made them less rather than more likely to support him.[13] Many preferred a secular politician who had some of the correct positions to a born-again televangelist who had them all. In a poll that was confirmed by the voting patterns in the southern states primaries, southern fundamentalists and evangelicals divided 44 per cent for George Bush, 30 per cent for Bob Dole, and only 14 per cent for Robertson.[14]

Over the next decade, CR pressure groups formed and disbanded with great rapidity but also with growing success in elections for school boards and state legislatures. Gradually the Reverends became a powerful force in many branches of the Republican Party. Playing the same role as the labour unions did in the Democratic party, local CR groups were able to provide thousands of willing volunteers and a great deal of money. While party bosses might despair of the zealots' influence, they came to depend on them. So when the 2008 presidential Republican nomination went to John McCain, a wealthy liberal with the wrong position on abortion, the ticket had to be balanced with a candidate acceptable to the CR. Sarah Palin was needed to 'mobilise the base' as the jargon had it.

The Christian Right agenda

What does the Christian Right want? Most generally, it wants its religion and its religiously inspired social mores given pride of place in the operations of the state. It wishes to reverse the increasingly secular interpretations of the constitutional requirement for a separation of church and state that have seen nativity scenes banned from government premises and public prayer banned in state schools. For example, it supported Judge Roy Moore, the Chief Justice of the Supreme Court of Alabama, who insisted on displaying in his court an engraving of the Ten Commandments on an imposing wooden podium. His refusal to obey a federal court instruction to remove the monument eventually led to him being sacked in 2003 by a unanimous decision of the Court of Judiciary. The monument was removed to a separate room where the Commandments could be read by any Christian with a poor memory.[15]

The CR is in favour of the 'traditional family'. It disapproves of divorce, of mothers of young children working outside the home, and of challenges to the authority of the male head of the household.[16] It particularly disapproves of homosexuals because gay couples break the traditional bond between love, sex, childbirth and child-rearing. It is, naturally, opposed to hedonism generally. It is fervently anti-abortion: the one issue that unites conservative Protestants and Catholics. It is opposed to the teaching of Darwinian evolution in schools; more generally it is in favour of strong parental controls over what children are taught.

In addition to the above, the CR shares the wider conservative constituency's desire for a strong defence programme, an assertive foreign policy, unrestricted right to gun ownership, lower taxation, a curb on unions, the removal of restrictive business legislation, a reduction of welfare spending, and a general reduction in the power of central government. This last point is important because, despite the Moral Majority's self-aggrandising title, most conservative Christians appreciate that they are unlikely to ever form a majority in Congress; hence their interests are best served by localism.

Because it is central to this book's general concern with the impact of secularisation on religiously inspired politics, it is important to stress that, despite the

CR's considerable success in establishing itself as a force within the Republican party, it has failed to make any significant advance on its agenda (as distinct from those items which its shares with secular conservatives). In areas where they remain strong, fundamentalists have been able to exert some influence on aspects of education such as the content of school textbooks, but local victories have usually been overturned in the centripetal nature of political power. They win state elections but lose federal ones. They win primaries but lose general elections. They win seats in the House of Representatives but lose them in the Senate (where the electorate is much bigger). As many CR concerns involve either the separation of church and state or basic human rights, legislative victories in lower courts are frequently reversed in the appeals process.

The cause of gay rights has advanced considerably since the Moral Majority was founded. In most states, major employers now extend spousal rights to same-sex partners. The Supreme Court's sweeping judgement that the state has no right to legislate on private adult sex has rendered obsolete remaining prohibitions on homosexual activity. In 2010, Congress, with the support of the military, granted gays the right to serve openly in the armed forces. Despite considerable hedging of its management, abortion is still legal. For all their conservative majority, the Rehnquist Supreme Court (1986–2005) and the Roberts Court (from 2005) made no major changes to previous decisions on the separation of church and state.

In short, while the mobilisation of conservative Christians has managed to polarise opinion about socio-moral issues, they have not won the culture wars. And there is one obvious reason for that. Although the various US legislatures and courts are not a perfect representation of popular opinion, they are not oblivious to it and the simple fact is that the CR has failed to win over a majority of Americans. The Reverends may represent a growing proportion of US churchgoers but churchgoing is markedly less popular now than it was in 1978.

Motives and opportunities

As we have seen, there is much in the rhetoric of the US Christian Right that is similar to the concerns of those who supported the NVALA and the NFOL but the latter confined its lobbying efforts to almost invariably unsuccessful attempts to persuade government officials to take up their causes. They did not enter the political process directly either by running in elections or by targeting politicians whose positions were particularly offensive to conservative Christians sensibilities. And as the survey of the 1976 NFOL rally participants showed, the UK moral crusades failed to persuade their supporters that legislative coercion was as much a priority as evangelism.

There is an obvious explanation for the very different careers of the UK and US Christian Right organisations. Even in 1970 the UK was considerably more secular than the USA. As we noted in the two introductory chapters, the contrast between the gradual evolution of church–state relations in the UK and the clean-cut constitutionalism of the US situation leaves the UK looking the more religious polity but the crucial under-pinning of numbers was very different. The USA has proportionately far more Christians, and conservative Christians at that, than does the UK.

However, there is a less obvious but equally important explanation. In political mobilisation as in crime, motive is not everything; we need also to consider opportunity. Even if the concerns of the US Christian Right had been as widely shared in the UK, any resulting social movement would have had to follow quite different tactics. There are crucial structural features of the American context which encourage the activities of the Christian Right and which are missing in Britain. The major differences between the UK and US political systems can be summarised as follows. The UK's polity is more centralised, its public administration is paternalistic, its mass media is less open, and it is dominated by tightly disciplined political parties. I will elaborate these observations as matters stood in the late twentieth century and then consider recent changes.

Government

With the exception of Northern Ireland, which enjoyed devolved government from 1926 to 1972, the UK's government was, in contrast to that of the USA and even many European states, national and centralised, at least until Scottish and Welsh devolution in 1997. The Westminster parliament (and, despite the appearance of a bi-cameral legislature, that meant the House of Commons) ruled the country. Local government was weak, its ability to raise or spend taxes constrained by Westminster. In the 1980s, when the Conservative government got fed up with the Labour-controlled Greater London Council, it simply disbanded it. The American federal system has certainly become more centralised (for example with limits on the freedom of individual states to limit the franchise and gerrymander boundaries), but state legislatures still have considerable power. Each state has its own executive, its own court structure and its own bureaucracy, and major changes in legislation – constitutional amendments, for example – have to be ratified by the separate states.

The unusual status of Northern Ireland has caused Westminster governments to be unusually sensitive to socio-moral concerns in the province. For example, the legalisation of abortion did not apply to Northern Ireland and only defeat at the European Court of Human Rights caused the decriminalisation of homosexuality to be extended to the province in 1982. But the government has not hesitated to impose a metropolitan agenda on the British peripheries. For example, trading on Sunday was allowed in the 1980s, against the wishes of Scottish and Welsh Sabbatarians, because the South East of England wanted it. Until devolution, the power of Westminster was such that British parties tended to put national before regional interests. In the 1980s, Margaret Thatcher forced the Scots to drop the 'and Unionist' part of the title and stand simply as 'Conservatives'.

The greater openness of the US polity provides many opportunities for minorities to enter the electoral process. Baptist fundamentalists cannot hope to pack

Congress with true believers but fundamentalists in North Carolina can realistically hope to dominate the North Carolina state legislature.

Even within the US federal government there is greater openness because the administration and legislature are separate and are chosen in different ways and on different timetables. In the UK administration and legislature are combined so as to concentrate power in the leaders of the ruling party. The party in power has a near-monopoly of the right to introduce legislation. Each session permits space for two or three private members bills but the individuals who, through a lucky draw, win the right to table such legislation know that the government can kill it at birth and so generally chose some broad and popular subject such as the control of gangs of migrant workers. In contrast members of the Senate and House of Representatives can introduce bills and even those that have little or no chance of passing both houses and of winning the President's approval can have considerable value as a way of politicising some issue. By forcing liberals to vote against some pet CR bill, conservatives can create a voting record for use in electioneering.

Administration

British public administration has long been elitist and paternalistic; a tendency which was reinforced during the Conservative governments of 1979–87 when large areas of public life were removed from the control of elected local authorities and given to 'quangos' staffed by loyal Conservatives. The judiciary is staffed by appointment. In contrast, the American system elects: it is not uncommon for voters to chose half a dozen state officers apart from the governor, to elect state commissioners and judges, state treasurer and state attorney as well as their mayor, their councillors, the members of their local school board, their city court judges, their tax collectors and many more.[17] Ironically, there seems to be an inverse relationship between the number of elections and the interest taken in them. With many types of elections having low turnouts, there is ample opportunity for any highly motivated and well-organised minority to become an electoral force. To date, the elitist and paternalistic nature of British administration has been seen as a problem only by the Left. It is true that, for example, most British judges are conservative. Nonetheless, the fact that they are appointed rather than elected is equally an obstacle to the radical Right. The Society for the Protection of the Unborn Child has no more power than the Rail, Maritime and Transport Union to elect a judge to its liking.

We might add here that the smallness of the United Kingdom acts as a brake on localism, independent of the causal effect it has by encouraging centralisation. In a small country, the sense of national, as opposed to sectional, interest is more pressing. Administrators are more directly confronted by national issues and their professional mobility means that their reference groups are more likely to be national than local. In the end Judge Roy Moore's attempts to imply state support for the Ten Commandments were over-ruled by the federal judiciary but he could persist as long as he did because he knew that, whatever New Yorkers thought, his stand was popular with many Texans. It is hard to imagine the judges of Devon, Cornwall or Cumbria having such a sense of local interest.

Mass media

It is significant that while Mary Whitehouse saw television as the problem, the US Christian Right has seen it as the solution. Of course, American fundamentalists are as hostile to most of the programmes on the main networks as the NVALA was to the BBC's Wednesday plays but the mobilisation of conservative Protestants in the US has rested heavily on the CR's use of radio and television. Falwell was chosen by professional right-wing lobbyists to lead the Moral Majority because his syndicated gospel show (and the fund-raising mailing lists it generated) provided a ready-made market for conservative politics. Pat Robertson's Christian Broadcasting Network provided the launch pad for his presidential ambitions and for his Christian Coalition pressure group. James Dobson, one of American's most influential evangelicals, aired his conservative views in a daily programme *Focus on the Family*, broadcast on some 60 television stations and thousands of radio stations.

In the 1970s Britain had just three television channels, two of them run by the BBC. Although the BBC and ITV did something by way of regional broadcasting, the vast majority of their output was national (and it is a very small nation). More than national, it was London-centric. In contrast, American television, although dominated by a few major networks, has a much higher proportion of regional product. A similar contrast holds for radio.

In addition to being centralised, British broadcasting was closed. No one could buy time to air a programme. Even the ITV companies, which carried paid advertising, were restricted in the amount of such material they could air and in its content. Ideological advertisements were forbidden and the heavy hand of paternalism controlled what counted as acceptable output. As can be seen from the success of right-wing 'shock jocks' and Fox News, the American broadcasting system is nearly unfettered laissez-faire. The regulatory Federal Communications Commission has little power, less even than the UK's Independent Broadcasting Authority or Broadcasting Standards Council. And if there was a problem buying airtime, one could simply start one's own station. Pat Robertson did just that; his Christian Broadcasting Network put out, in addition to the expected religious services, a fundamentalist soap opera and a 'born again' chat show.

As with other points of contrast, the relative smallness of the UK constrains localism independently of the structures and regulatory frameworks. In line with their free-market principles, the Conservatives granted large numbers of licences for local commercial radio stations in the late 1980s. The smallness of the market meant that very few could succeed by presenting a distinct cultural product. Many ran into financial difficulties and were bought up by two large national companies.

The differences between the two systems became most stark at election time. American broadcasting was open to all candidates for as long as they could afford and candidates could say the most appalling things about their opponents. In Britain, time was allocated, free of charge, to the major parties in proportion to their support.[18] Individual candidates could not raise funds to buy time on local radio stations to insult their opponents.

Party systems

The most significant difference between the opportunity structures of British and American politics is the strength of the parties. The United Kingdom and the United States are superficially similar in having traditionally had two-party systems with third parties failing to have any major sustained impact. But the number of parties is where the similarities end. In Britain, candidates are chosen and endorsed by the party. Local party branches select candidates but they may chose only from a list approved by the party's national office. Furthermore, both Conservative and Labour parties have devised mechanisms for imposing national leadership favourites on local branches. For example, the Labour party has a rule that allows the centre to impose a candidate if the candidature becomes vacant too close to an election for the usual procedures of local selection to operate. Hence if the party leadership wishes to increase the proportion of cosmopolitan young women among its candidates, it quietly encourages an MP who intends to retire to delay the announcement until sufficiently close to the election date that the imposition rules come into force. The national party gets its favourite in position and the compliant retiree is rewarded with a seat in the House of Lords or some lucrative government appointment.

Because the British electorate appreciates that the legislative agenda is determined by the government and not individual MPs, it votes party and not person. Very occasionally some local dispute will become sufficient of a cause célèbre for an independent candidate to win (as was the case when the threatened closure of part of the local hospital allowed Richard Taylor to win the Wyre Forest seat in the 2001 general election), but generally elections are determined by electoral demography and the national popularity of the major parties. Once elected to parliament, British politicians are controlled by the party. The governing party obviously has a vast array of rewards for loyal members but even the opposition has considerable scope to reward its loyal members with preferment and to punish mavericks.

In contrast, the USA's Republican and Democratic parties are much more open. Candidates are chosen not by party managers but by the electorate in a primary election. In some states, candidates need not even have been a member of the party before their nomination to contest a primary. Hence the local voters determine who carries the standard for the Democrats or Republicans at any particular election, rather than the national party managers. In the 2010 mid-term elections a number of incumbent Republicans found themselves challenged by and losing to outsiders who mobilised frustration with 'Washington politics'.

Even though Republican Party managers knew that the primary election successes of a number of right-wing conservatives supported by the Tea Party movement would cause them to lose seats that they would have won with more moderate candidates, they were powerless to prevent zealots choosing Christine O'Donnell to contest the Senate race in Delaware.

As a result of the vast sums spent on television advertising, US elections are bizarrely expensive. In 2010 Meg Whitman spent $144 million in failing to win the governorship of California. The parties will spend on behalf of candidates in some seats in the general election but individuals have to raise their own fortunes at the primary stage and many will spend far more money than they get from the party. The general weakness of the American party system is exaggerated by the role of pressure groups. The precise details of campaign finance law regularly change as Congress half-heartedly attempts to limit the power of special interests, but it remains the case that many candidates will owe more to the pressure groups that promoted them for their ideological positions than they will to the party in whose name they stand.

Conclusion

All of the above can be summarised in a simple observation. In a very large number of ways, aspects of the structure of American public life create opportunities for interest groups to use electoral politics that are denied their British counterparts. As I suggested in pointing out that, for all its apparent influence on the Republican party, the CR has achieved little or nothing of its agenda, the final outcome of particular battles in the culture wars may not be that different in the USA than in the UK. Since the last quarter of the twentieth century, both societies have become increasingly secular, increasingly respectful of religious and cultural diversity, increasingly sensitive to gender issues and increasingly tolerant of homosexuality. In the USA those changes have been vigorously contested by conservative Christians; in the UK they have been attended largely by grumbling from the sidelines. The purpose of this chapter has been to draw attention to the role of structures in creating differential opportunities and hence differential encouragement to political mobilisation.

There have been two significant changes to British politics since I first tried to explain why the UK had a Mary Whitehouse but no Pat Robertson: devolution and PR voting. Despite the Union of the Crowns in 1603 and the Union of the Parliaments in 1707, Scotland continued to enjoy a degree of independence from London by virtue of maintaining its separate education, legal and religious systems but that devolution was administrative and paternalistic.[19] With the restoration of the Scottish Parliament, the creation of a Welsh Assembly and an assembly for London, and the reestablishment of the Stormont parliament in Northern Ireland, the UK now has a range of democratically elected regional bodies. And we also now have directly elected mayors in London and a number of other English cities. This has not only weakened the stranglehold of Westminster; it also loosened the grip of the national leadership on their parties. As the first prime minister to operate the new regime, Tony Blair spectacularly failed to understand what he had created. He tried to prevent the London Labour party from nominating Ken Livingstone for mayor. Livingstone stood as an independent, won, and was retrospectively accepted as the Labour man. Blair imposed a close friend Alun Michael as leader of Labour party in Wales. He was defeated in a vote of no confidence and was replaced by Rhodri Morgan, the man Blair had tried so hard to block.

The other great change was the introduction of proportional representation voting systems. Northern Ireland had long used a single-transferable vote (or STV) system for Stormont elections because a first-part-the-post (FPTP) system would have delivered a grossly disproportionate number of seats to unionists. Since 1999, elections for the Scottish Parliament, Welsh Assembly and London Assembly have used the hybrid additional member system. This uses FPTP to elect the majority of representatives and then uses the disparity between votes cast and members elected to allocate additional 'top up' members to the parties that have polled well but failed to win a due proportion of seats. Also, European elections in Britain are now conducted using multi-member constituencies and a regional party list system.

Neither of those changes increases the number of evangelical Christians in the population or alters the balance of socio-moral liberals and conservatives but together they do represent new opportunities for UK moral crusade organisations. In the next chapter we will see what advantage they took of those opportunities.

8   Christian parties

Introduction

In the nineteenth century and the first half of the twentieth century, the main attempts to use religion to mobilise British electors concerned ethnic identity and the old Reformation divide. The two fields overlapped in the attempts of the Scottish Protestant League and Protestant Action to present Irish Catholic immigrants and their British-born descendents as a threat to the Protestant basis of British identity. Anti-Catholicism failed to survive the secularisation of British culture. When the political conflict in Northern Ireland erupted into violence in the early 1970s, tiny numbers of militant Protestants in Britain tried to promote the idea that Irish republicanism was proof of the continued threat of Popery to British democracy but far more popular was the 'pox on both their houses' reading of the Ulster conflict. Insofar as most Britons had any response to the Troubles, it was to conclude that all religion taken too seriously is a threat. Ian Paisley tried to stimulate protests against the visit of Pope John Paul in 1982 but he and his supporters from Northern Ireland formed almost the entirety of what turned out to be trivial protests.

Although we can find faint echoes of the old identity politics in the way that conservative Catholics and Protestants focus on different grievances, contemporary Christian political ambitions concern not who we are but what we do: a series of related socio-moral issues. From the 1970s on, there were a number of electoral interventions by anti-abortionists. Since the turn of the century a broader agenda of complaint, which includes campaigns against gay rights, has been politicised and it has been augmented by concerns about what its opponents call 'Islamic aggression'.

This chapter will document the various British attempts to mirror the success of the US Christian Right. British political parties remain sufficiently robust that there has been no serious attempt to replicate the success of American conservative Christians in establishing effective caucuses within the Republican Party by taking over parts of the Tory party. Instead British moral crusaders have founded their own parties. I will present brief histories of these interventions, detail the social and cultural background of Britain's culture warriors, describe the parties' platforms, document their electoral performance, and consider what that tells us about the relationship between religion and politics in the UK.

Abortion and its opponents

Abortion is an age-old solution to the problem of unwanted pregnancy. What stimulated its legalisation was the desire not to make it more popular but to make it safer. Wealthy women could always find skilled surgeons to break the law for a price. Poor women could only afford unskilled and unhygienic backstreet abortionists whose incompetence usually threatened the health and sometimes threatened the lives of their clients. Abortion in Britain was legalised by the Abortion Act of 1967, which permitted abortion up to 24 weeks gestation and made it available on the National Health Service. The legislation was introduced by Liberal MP David Steel as a private member's bill but was strongly supported by the reforming Labour Home Secretary Roy Jenkins. Because in Northern Ireland the strong opposition of the Catholic Church was augmented by the opposition of the Protestant churches and leading unionist politicians such as the Reverend Ian Paisley, the reach of the act was limited to England, Wales and Scotland.[1] Although abortion was never as contentious in Britain as in the USA, it was occasionally opposed through the electoral process. As the Labour MP for Preston South from 1964 to 1970, Peter Mahon had stymied Steel's first attempt to introduce an abortion reform bill. When, having lost his Preston seat, Mahon was not selected by the local Labour party for a vacant Liverpool seat in 1971, he stood as an 'Independent Labour and Anti-Abortion' candidate. He polled a decent 10 per cent of the vote but then the Liverpool Scotland constituency did have the largest concentration of Catholics of any English seat, Mahon's father had been a long-serving local councillor, and his brother was the MP for the neighbouring constituency. It is hard to imagine the issue gaining as much support anywhere else at that time.

The relative unpopularity of abortion as an election issue is clear from later and better organised interventions. In 1997 Josephine Quintavalle and her son Bruno founded the Pro-Life Alliance (PLA), which contested 56 seats in that year's general election and attracted 19,355 votes: an average of 345 votes per constituency. In only five seats in England and Wales did the PLA gain more than 1.0 per cent of the votes: Billericay in Essex, Leyton and Wanstead in Greater London, Solihull and Manchester Withington in the North West, and Doncaster Central in south Yorkshire. With its higher proportion of Catholic voters, Scotland offered a more fertile environment. The PLA contested nine seats, all in the greater Glasgow area. There it averaged 1.5 per cent of the vote and in three seats it gained more than 2 per cent.

But the PLA failed to maintain its candidates or its presence. Two years later it contested the first elections to the Scottish Parliament, which for the reasons outlined in the previous chapter, should have produced an improved performance. The additional-member form of PR used in that election allowed each voter two votes: one for a candidate in the first-past-the-post part of the election and the other for a party that would be used to calculate a compensating top-up. Voters who in previous elections would be reluctant to waste a vote on a minority party could be encouraged to split the ticket and vote, say, Labour with the first vote and Pro-Life Alliance with the second. But rather than improving on its previous performance, the PLA vote went down. It may well be that Scots voters were too excited by the prospect of the restoration of the parliament after a gap of 292 years to be interested in apparently fringe issues. On the other hand, considerable effort was put into explaining how the new voting system allowed people to vote for two different parties. The PLA fielded no candidates in the Highlands and Islands, north-east Scotland and South of Scotland; regions with few Catholics. In the Lothians it won 0.3 per cent and in Mid-Scotland and Fife 0.2 per cent. In the three regions with the highest Catholic concentration (Central, West of Scotland and Glasgow), it scored respectively 0.8, 1.0 and 0.8 per cent of the vote.[2]

At the 2001 general election it fielded 37 candidates; this time averaging only 255 votes per seat. Thirty of the candidates polled less than 1 per cent of the vote; 26 came last in their races. The PLA did not contest the next general election and when it entered the 2004 European elections it had so much trouble recruiting candidates that seven of the 22 standing in England contested more than one region. The PLA disbanded in December 2004.

It is difficult to describe that history as anything other than failure and the electoral performance can be simply traced back to a failure to win the argument. Although advances in the survival rates of premature babies have caused some people to consider if the time period in which abortion is permitted should be shortened, opinion polls have consistently shown little appetite for a return to back-street abortions. For example, in 2005 over 70 per cent of Britons believed that abortion should be always or mostly legal and less than a quarter thought it should be always or mostly illegal.[3] In the British Social Attitudes survey of 2008, 'over three-quarters believe that abortion is wrong only "sometimes" or "not at all" if there is a high risk that the baby will have a birth defect'. When respondents are divided by a variety of measures of religious belief and behaviour, we find that 86 per cent of the unreligious approve of abortion for good reasons but we also find that more than two-thirds of the religious sample take the same view.[4]

Christian democracy

A more significant electoral intervention came from two parties that presented themselves not as single-issue movements but as part of the well-established continental tradition of Christian Democracy. In 1990 a small cross-party group of Christian MPs formed the non-party Movement for Christian Democracy.[5] A decade later some members of that group formed the Christian People's Alliance (CPA). The CPA described itself as embodying the following fine-sounding principles: Active Compassion, Respect for Life, Social Justice, Wise Stewardship, Empowerment and Reconciliation. It also said: 'the CPA is a party rooted in the historic Christian faith that seeks to demonstrate the love of God through political service. Our faith and principles are drawn from the Bible, especially the life and teaching of Jesus Christ, as well as from Christian political insights through the centuries.'[6] Initially the CPA had a surprisingly liberal agenda or, perhaps more accurately, its platform was sufficiently complex and nuanced that it was hard to place. Under the leadership of Ram Gidoomal, an Indian multi-millionaire businessman, one of the CPA's main items on its 'build reconciliation and seek justice' agenda was action to regularise the status of refugees and make it easier for them to find work legally.[7]

In May 2002, the CPA fielded 69 candidates in local government elections (mostly in London but with a few in Ipswich and Gloucester) and won one seat in the East London district of Newham.[8] Gidoomal ran for mayor of London twice. In 2000 he gained 2.4 per cent of the vote, coming behind the three main parties but ahead of the Green party candidate. In 2004 his vote was exactly the same but this time he came behind the United Kingdom Independence party (UKIP), Respect (a party led by former Labour MP George Galloway and supported largely by Asian voters), the Greens and the British National party (BNP). In between, the CPA gained two further local council seats in Newham. The CPA also fielded candidates in the Scottish parliamentary elections where they competed with the Christian Party (CP).

This second intervention was the work of the rather exotic George Hargreaves: a Black British Londoner who had had some success as a pop-song writer with the gay dance classic 'So Macho' before becoming a Pentecostal clergyman. His interest in a political career predated the CPA. In 1997 he had stood as the Referendum party candidate for Walthamstow. Although a founder member of the CPA, Hargreaves left to mount his own election campaigns, initially under the title of Operation Christian Voice (OCV) and later the Christian Party (with its Scottish and Welsh variants). In contrast to those of the CPA, Hargreaves's interventions were based on the most controversial (and thus publicity-gaining) parts of a conservative Christian agenda. OCV stood in every region (except Northern Ireland) in the 2004 European parliamentary election on an anti-abortion platform. When contesting the Scottish parliament elections three years later, Hargreaves concentrated on gay rights: he was against them. In that election, the CPA (with 15 candidates) and CP (with 76) competed, sometimes rather bitterly. Teresa Smith, leader of the CPA, said about the Scottish Christian Party: 'I can't stress enough that we have nothing in common with these people.'[9] With a change in leadership in the CPA, the two parties formed an alliance and thereafter contested elections on a common platform.

Key to these novel forays into electioneering was finance. It is relatively cheap to contest a British election. To stand a candidate must deposit £500, which is returned if he or she gains more than 5 per cent of the vote. Still, to lose 100 deposits requires £50,000 before any money is spent on backroom facilities or candidate promotion. In 2009, the CP raised £273,937 and in the run-up to the 2010 general election, it raised a further £160,000. Although the CPA and CP presented themselves as populist movements, very little of their money came from ordinary members. Between 2002 and 2008, the CPA was given £365,000 by P. H Giles & Co. Ltd of Altrincham, Cheshire and Peter Giles then gave £9,000 in 2008–10. The Christian Party was primarily bankrolled by City of

London money. Philip Richards, a hedge fund star who gave his bonuses to Christian causes, donated at least £200,000.[10] In 2010 it was given £100,000 by Visile Frank Timis, a wealthy Romanian–Australian businessman.[11]

What do Christians want?

The CPA believed that:

> Christianity gives a vision for the whole of politics – through principles, policies, peacemaking, economic policy and ethics. The Bible as God's revelation and Jesus' words and life are our central guide. We see the death and resurrection of Jesus as the central human event, bringing peace with God, and renewed life. We want to live within God's love and forgiveness, rather than remain within the old patterns of human failure in life and politics.

The party aimed to use the 'talents of Christians in different callings' to bring the grace of the Gospel to bear upon the religious, spiritual, moral and social problems in society.[12] As the inability of Christians to agree routinely demonstrates, the problem with that ambition is that the Gospel does not automatically generate positions on the issues of its day, let alone those of our day. As noted, the CPA's initial attitudes to refugees (and thus in the public mind, to immigrants and foreigners, those hate figures for the British Right) were tolerant. It advocated 'reconciliation among nations, races, religions, classes, gender and communities'[13] and made that rhetoric real by permitting non-Christians to join and even giving them important public roles. More predictably it was also anti-abortion, anti-gay rights and anti-European Union though none of these issues was given a particularly high profile.

Although the CP was described by Hargreaves as 'non-denominational Christian', its doctrinal basis was significantly narrower than that of the CPA. It may be that Hargreaves was simply insensitive to Catholic perceptions but the language was distinctly Protestant (and charismatic and Pentecostal Protestant at that). Catholics might be able to live with the first statement of faith: 'We believe in one creator God, eternally existent in three persons, Father, Son and Holy Spirit, as stated in the historic creeds of the Christian church'. But the phrase 'solely in accordance with biblical principles' has an anti-Catholic flavour and the assertion that 'Jesus Christ will come again to the earth, personally, visibly and bodily to consummate history and the eternal plan of God' would alienate a large body of Christians.

The difficulty of deriving a legislative programme from Christian principles is demonstrated by the Christian Party's manifesto for the 2007 Scottish Parliament elections, which was a curious document. By including items that were not within the remit of the Scottish parliament, the party betrayed its lack of preparation and, by failing to present a clear image of the party, it demonstrated its naivety. There was robust right-wing stuff: a referendum on the restoration of the death penalty; banning abortion; increasing tax on booze and fags; initiatives to bring personal responsibility to bear upon 'self-inflicted disease (such as alcoholism)'; zero tolerance on drug possession; and the reintroduction of the right of teachers to hit children. There were also some positions that are distinctly rum, even for a party pitching for the right-wing vote: curfews for under 11 year olds and 'mandatory intervention of child protection agencies in relation to any child ten years or younger that is found unaccompanied on the street after 9.00pm'.[14]

There were also a variety of conservative Christian items: greater observance of a weekly day of rest; the reintroduction of corporate readings from the Bible in all Scottish state schools; public health campaigns to discourage homosexuality alongside excessive drinking and the use of addictive substances; promotion in school of chastity before marriage; reinstatement of Section 28 of the 1988 Local Government Act (the clause prohibiting the 'promotion' of homosexuality; known in Scotland as Section 2a); provision of Christian religious education on a mandatory basis, with no obligation to promote other faiths; and a Creationist science curriculum.

Finally, there was a ragbag of oddities. The Christian Party wanted the standard of 'beyond reasonable doubt' in criminal trials to be replaced by the 'more biblical' evidence of two or three reliable witnesses. It wanted the practice of addressing women as 'Ms' to be discouraged. It was opposed to the (hardly frequent) practice of altering birth certificates to reflect gender confirmation surgery. And – the only economic item in its platform – it wanted 'limits around coastlines to preserve stocks of fish and sand eels'!

The Welsh manifesto also seems to have been compiled from every candidate's wish-list. Predictably the education section asked for Darwinism to be 'balanced' with 'Creation/Design in the Universe' but it also asked for Greek and Latin (but not Welsh) to be taught in every school. It proposed selling off the entire NHS and it wanted the dragon removed from the Welsh standard because it was Satanic.

Given the almost infinite variety of political positions that could be generated from even a conservative Christian faith, it is predictable that what the Christians actually stood for would have been very heavily influenced by events. That is, the campaigns were based on a largely opportunistic selection of themes to fit whatever the right-wing press seemed most interested in promoting. The main difference between the first CPA interventions and those of the CP (and afterwards the CPA–CP Alliance) was that notions of reconciliation and justice got ditched in favour of anti-immigrant sentiment, homophobia and Islamophobia. The concerns over immigration and Islam grew as the CPA and CP recruited in London (and won council seats in the same sorts of areas where the BNP was successful). In their statements candidates were formal. Bob Handyside, for example, complained that 'minority groups are privileged and preferred before the majority'.[15] David Booth elaborated the concern about the power of Islam:

> some of our cities will become predominantly Muslim in a relatively short time, and they will be naturally seeking political representation for their

faith in some form or other, as Islam is more of a political ideology than a faith.... Islam will assert its values and expectations.... Already, it has been estimated that there are some 90+ Sharia courts operating in the UK, in a parallel legal system, which has been given the force of law by the UK government, where it does not contravene parliamentary laws ... this will eventually open the door to a fuller implementation of Sharia laws in the UK, by Sharia courts, possibly leading to punitive justice (a somewhat worrying prospect!).[16]

In less guarded moments, the xenophobia was more pungently expressed. At a hustings in the Vale of Glamorgan during the 2010 general election, the Christian party candidate said: 'I have heard that there are more white British people leaving this country to live elsewhere and more people coming in who do not actually want to integrate themselves – especially the Pakistani community. Shouldn't these people just go home?'.[17]

The homophobia seems to have been adopted in a particularly opportunistic manner for the Scottish elections of 2007. In 2000 the Scottish Parliament moved to repeal Conservative legislation that had made it an offence to promote homosexuality as an acceptable lifestyle in schools. Wealthy businessman and conservative Christian Brian Soutar funded a pressure group 'Keep the Clause' and there was much heated talk about targeting MSPs, but it came to nothing. Four years later gay rights again became an issue when a bed-and-breakfast provider in Wester Ross refused a booking from two gay men and provoked a long-running debate in the media over the government's equality agenda. Seeing the opportunity for a great deal of free press coverage, Hargreaves stood in the Glasgow region so that he could confront Patrick Harvie, the openly bisexual leader of the Green party in Scotland.

It is worth adding that many candidates seemed little interested in the manifesto or in electioneering. Like the NFOL supporters of the 1970s, they viewed their moral crusade as an old-fashioned evangelistic opportunity. David Griffiths in Clwyd West said:

> In my speech after the count I appealed to the heart of all parties that this election was not about politicians, not about parties but about our nation, a nation that had turned away from Jesus Christ. It was about HIS LORDSHIP.[18]

Navaid Syed, told the people of Bolton South East: 'It is time for the people to turn to the Great Healer Jesus. It is time for us to wake up and realise that with Jesus there is a hope and a future and there is real healing.'[19] Heidi Simmonds, candidate for Maidstone and the Weald, was typical of those who used their election literature profile to testify for the Lord. She began: 'My name is Heidi, I'm 23 years young, and I love God with all my heart. He really is my Everything.'[20]

Party activists

We can infer a great deal about the CPA and the CP from the characteristics of those who volunteered to stand as candidates. From the lists of those who stood in the general election of 2010, the European Parliament election of 2009, and the London Assembly election of 2008, I was able to identify 139 CP and CPA election candidates in England and Wales. Scotland will be discussed separately. Although the list is not exhaustive, it is long enough to be representative. For some of these, I could ascertain only the name, which sometimes reveals ethnicity. For most I was able to ascertain ethnicity, occupation, and gender. For many I was also able to identify the person's sect or denomination.

Of the 135 candidates whose gender is known, 32 per cent or just over two-thirds were female. As 21 per cent of all party candidates at the 2010 general election were female, the Christians were fielding an unusually high number of women.[21] Two explanations suggest themselves for what, given the otherwise conservative orientation of the CPA and CPA, is an unexpected disparity. First, the candidates were drawn from church circles, which are overwhelmingly female. Second, because the movement was new and election was unlikely, there was little competition for places. Hence there was not the usual circumstance of men being more successful than women in gaining a valued asset. Indeed far from competition for places, two things suggest that party leaders had to engage in a fair amount of elbow twisting to fill the lists. In many cases candidates had no plausible connection with the constituency or region in which they stood: one woman whose candidate forms gave a London address stood at various elections for Glasgow, the North East of England and the North West. Secondly, there was an unusually high number of husband and wife pairs.

Ethnic minorities are generally under-represented in British political parties. In 2005 there were only 15 non-white MPs, which at 2.3 per cent is less than half of the ratio for the population at large.[22] The proportion of non-whites is usually higher in candidate lists than in lists of winners; for example in the 2009 England and Wales local authority elections, 3.3 per cent of candidates were non-white.[23] Set against those proportions, the ethnic composition of the CPA/CP candidates was highly unusual. Of the 107 people whose ethnicity could be determined, 57 per cent were White British and 8 per cent were Black British. The most significant deviation from the norm was the very high proportion of African and Asian candidates: 13 per cent in both cases. The majority of the former were Nigerian in origin; the majority of the latter were Pakistani.

This unusual pattern may be partly explained by the London-centric nature of the CP and CPA. Although non-whites made up only 3.3. per cent of 2009 local authority candidates for the country as a whole, they were 16 per cent of those standing in London boroughs. Religion is also a consideration. Nigerians are a disproportionate part of the church-going population of London and the South East.

Not surprising, given the movement's ethos, almost every actual (as distinct from purely nominal) candidate who made any sort of presentation self-identified as a Christian and many also mentioned the seriousness of their religious commitment and their involvement in church activities. For 57 candidates it was possible to identify a specific affiliation, which is summarised in Table 8.1 below. For comparison I have placed alongside the rough proportions of those churches in the English and Welsh population as a whole.

That the rank order in one column is almost the reverse of that in the other graphically illustrates the reliance of the CP and CPA on religious minorities. Anglicans, Methodists and Catholics are grossly under-represented. Three small sections of British Christianity are equally over-represented: Pentecostal churches that primarily recruit people from African backgrounds, independent evangelical churches, and charismatic fellowships. The absence of Catholics is especially noteworthy given the very high proportion of Catholics in the Pro-Life Alliance, from which the CPA drew a lot of its original support. I was able to identify the religious affiliation of eight of 22 CPA candidates in 2004: all of them were Catholic and almost all of them worked for anti-abortion organisations. At least four of the five CPA candidates in Wales in 2007 were Catholic. In contrast, the four Welsh Christian Party candidates whose denomination is known were all Protestant: two Charismatics, one Independent Evangelical, one Baptist and one Pentecostalist. In brief, the Christian parties in England and Wales draw their activists primarily from two minor tributaries of British religious life.

Information on the occupations of candidates is scarce and the proportion whose occupation is unknown is so large that we should hesitate to make too much of the data, but what is known is interesting. As with all political parties, manual workers (4 per cent of Christian candidates) were under-represented. But so too (at just 9 per cent) were the higher managerial and professional classes who make up the majority of candidates in the mainstream political parties. There was only one lawyer and the five university or college lecturers all seem to be relatively junior. Skilled white-collar workers, teachers especially, were 22 per cent and routine white-collar workers (often NHS, social work and local government administrators) were 19 per cent of the total. Given that populist

Table 8.1 Denominational profile of CP/CPA activists and church members, England and Wales, 2008–10

	Activists (%)	Church members (%)
Anglican	5	28
Catholic	8	27
Other	2	9
Methodist	0	9
Pentecostal	31	9
Baptist	11	8
Charismatic	23	5
Independent Evangelical	20	5
Total	100	100

parties have often relied heavily on self-employed businessmen and women, it is worth noting that relatively few of the Christian candidates were self-employed (13 per cent) and with one exception their businesses were single-person or family operations.[24]

By far the most significant feature of the job profiles of the Christian candidates was the extraordinary number of clergymen and women. Nationally clergy formed only 0.15 per cent of the employed population in 2010 but they were at least 25 per cent of those CP and CPA candidates whose occupation is known.[25] What makes the clerical representation even more unusual is that only three were Anglican clergy (and one of those described his congregation in ways that suggested it was charismatic). The vast majority were Pentecostal preachers. As with religious affiliation, some of this over-representation may be explained by the movement's novelty: Hargreaves and other founders mobilised their colleagues in clergy networks. But as I will suggest below, that so many activists were pastors does tell us something important about the limited appeal of an avowedly Christian intervention in British elections.

It would be revealing to augment the social class data with information about the sectors in which the activists worked. Unfortunately the data is too thin to make solidly founded comparisons with the population at large, but there is one observation worth making. In addition to the full-time clergy, there was a considerable representation of people employed in promoting Christian causes and values. For example, many of the routine white-collar workers are employed by Christian charities and pressure groups and many of the teachers specifically mention being in 'Christian education'. The obvious parallel is with trade union officials in the Labour party: the CP and CPA were recruiting people whose commitment to Christian values was already strengthened by being employed in Christian causes.

One reason for identifying shared social characteristics of party activists is to highlight salient parts of a party's agenda and to infer how well agenda items are likely to play to the electorate at large. We suppose that activists are in some sense the distilled essence or embodiment of the party's intended appeal: not typical of intended voters but exemplifying something they value. In this case the status of candidates as representatives of the movement's ideological core is exaggerated by its novelty. It had not yet grown sufficiently to recruit much beyond the personal reach of the founders. For example, at least three of the party's candidate in the West Midlands came from one congregation. Most political parties begin as 'supply' rather than 'demand'. The founders create the appearance of demand for their product in the hope that their stand will prove them to be correct by attracting others who share their vision. Initially activists are likely to become involved for reasons other than, or additional to, strongly sharing the movement's platform: supporting a friend or a spouse, for example, or working for an organisation with cognate goals. Only once the movement has grown beyond the initial phase of calling in favours and twisting arms can we suppose it represents what the promoters hope will be the enduring interface of their ideals and public support. However, given that almost a decade separates the founding of the CPA and the 2010 elections, it does seem reasonable to draw some broad conclusions about the general appeal of its mission from the characteristics of those who were willing to go forward as candidates.

The first and most obvious point is that the typical English or Welsh churchgoer is not attracted by the claim that Christian beliefs require, or that Christian interests are best served by, a separate party. As we will see in Chapter 10, the majority of Britons, even of those Britons who attend church regularly, are not in favour of religion enjoying greater political prominence. That so many CPA/CP candidates were Nigerian (and hence familiar with a political culture in which religious leaders are prominent) reinforces that point.

Second, we can see the limited value of trying to mobilise Christians with the threat of Islam. There may be a great deal of general disquiet about Islamic extremists. There are popular local campaigns against visible signs of Islam (such as the building of mosques). But the vast majority of British Christians clearly do not feel that Islam represents such a threat that they should put their religious identity before the complex of other interests that produced their previous political preferences. Hence the CP and CPA have become reliant to an unusual degree on people from backgrounds that are shaped by enduring competition with Islam: Nigeria and Pakistan and, in one case, Bosnia.

Third, we can infer something from the absence of mainstream Christian clergy. Despite the complaints of senior Anglican clergy that the Christian voice has been neglected by a government keen to court non-Christian minorities, mainstream clergy are generally well-connected to central and local government bodies and often play important roles in their wider communities. As well as already providing some of what the CP and CPA hope to gain through electioneering, that acts as something of a constraint on getting involved with what, so long as it is polling only as many votes as the Monster Raving Loony party, will look like dangerously narrow enthusiasm. Mainstream clergy are often called upon to play the role of community 'master of ceremonies'. They are the ones who speak to the media when a gunman runs amok in Cumbria or two young girls are murdered in a Cambridgeshire village. In a largely secular society, the clergy are well aware that they can only perform such roles if their religion is seen as a guarantor of a generally benign and inclusive attitude and not as a special interest that is being promoted. Hence they are reluctant to be associated with a narrow partisan view of Christianity.

It may also be that mainstream church clergy have sufficient experience of the difficulties of translating value preferences into effective action to make them wary of the notion that there is a Christian political agenda that can be pursued without serious risk to their pastoral position. Finally, we can note that most mainstream clergy will have little sympathy for the secular right-wing elements of the CP and CPA platforms. Kenyan-born pastor James Gitau was campaigning for the BNP just three weeks before he was selected to stand for the Christian Party. In his justification he said he had always rejected racism but had supported the BNP because it was the only party that was against sodomy.[26] It is hard to imagine any Methodist minister making the same choices or being happy standing alongside someone who did.

The Pentecostal and charismatic pastors who support the CPA and CP are typically outsiders with little public engagement or role beyond their own congregations. Almost all are entrepreneurial leaders (and founders) of independent congregations who do not have to answer to a larger church organisation and who do not have to be much concerned about their relationships with people outside their own congregation. Especially if their base is a relatively insulated ethnic minority, they are more likely than their mainstream counterparts to combine a poor feeling for British political sensibilities with a high opinion of their own self-importance.

The Scottish activists

Scotland is different and needs to be considered separately. In the 2007 election to the Scottish Parliament, the Christian Party fielded 76 candidates and the CPA fielded 15. It proved to be more difficult to profile the Scottish candidates because, while all the CPA's candidates were sufficiently involved to provide personal details on the party's website and in election literature, a large proportion of the CP candidates were purely nominal.

There were proportionately fewer women on the Scottish than the England and Wales lists: 19 per cent of the CP and 20 per cent of the CPA. There were also far fewer candidates from ethnic minority backgrounds. I decided to leave out three London residents out of the CP calculations. Of the remaining 73, all but two were White British, the vast majority of them Scots. Two may have been Asian. The story is the same for the CPA: all White British, apart from one who came from what he knew as Southern Rhodesia and one Glaswegian of Pakistani parentage.

It was only possible to identify the occupations of 42 per cent of the sample so we should be wary of making too much of what is known but the Scots activists seem to be markedly higher-status than the English and Welsh. For the CP, about 10 per cent were senior managers and professionals with retired doctors and head teachers making up a large part of that group. Some 43 per cent were skilled white-collar workers, with teachers again being prominent. There were proportionately fewer self-employed business people. There were also a lot of clerics: 29 per cent of those who occupations were known. Such a high proportion may well be a result of the large number of unknowns. Because pastors tend to get mentioned on websites, my Google searching probably identified all of those who were religious officials while it failed to identify those with more humble or private occupations. However, even if there were no more clergy among the unknowns and we expressed the clergy presence as a proportion of the entire cadre, at around 12 per cent it would be lower than in the Christian parties in England and Wales but still be vastly greater than in the Scottish population at large.

The CPA social class profile was interestingly different. Over 40 per cent were senior professionals and managers, one-quarter were skilled white-collar workers (with teachers again being prominent) and a similar proportion were self-employed business people. However, there was only one religious official: an ordained Catholic deacon. The lack of clergy in the CPA is a reflection of the religious profile of the two parties, which was markedly different.

Again one has to be cautious of the low numbers but of 21 CP activists whose church connection is known, a disproportionate nine were members of charismatic fellowships. There were four independent evangelicals, two Free Church, one Baptist, one Episcopalian, and three Catholics. There were no members of the mainstream Church of Scotland. The CPA had no clergy candidates because it was overwhelmingly Catholic: a reflection of the centrality to the CPA in Scotland of the abortion issue. Many of the CPA candidates had been active in anti-abortion organisations and many had previously stood for election as Pro-Life Alliance candidates.

The candidate profiles match the campaign issues. The CP and CPA in England (and to a lesser extent Wales) were increasingly concerned with Islam. With a far smaller Muslim population in Scotland, the Scottish CP concentrated on gay rights and the Scottish CPA focused on abortion. That the former was essentially Protestant and the latter Catholic may explain some of the ill feeling between the two parties that was a feature of this period.

Electoral performance

It is somewhat tedious to list every election at which Christian candidates did not do well but it is important to evaluate performance in a sufficiently large number of varied types of election so that we can be confident we are seeing a reflection of popular interest.

Hargreaves attracted a great deal of media attention but very few votes. In 2004, he contested Birmingham Hodge Hill at a by-election and won just 90 votes. In the 2005 general election he stood in the more promising seat of the Western Isles. The last strongholds of conservative Presbyterians who reject the liberalism of the Church of Scotland, the Outer Hebridean islands of Lewis and Harris are probably the most conservatively religious parts of Great Britain and the conservatives have been politicised by losing campaigns to prevent flights and ferries on the Sabbath. In addition, something of an opportunity has been created by the collapse of the Conservative party in Scotland. The liberal economic reforms of the Thatcher government in the 1980s were particularly damaging to Scotland and her decision to trial an unpopular reform of local government funding in Scotland cost the Conservatives dearly, as did their opposition to devolution. Twenty years later the party has still not been able to shift the widespread perception that it is an English party and that potentially leaves conservative voters with no obvious home. Despite those advantages, Hargreaves won only 7.6 per cent of the vote. The following year he contested a by-election in the far less promising industrial lowland constituency of Dunfermline and West Fife where he gained 1.2 per cent of the vote. The 2008 by-election in the Humberside constituency of Haltemprice and Howden was an even less attractive proposition. The popular sitting MP David Davis had resigned so that he could use the by-election to make a point and would always win the votes of Conservatives and social conservatives. Hargreaves found just 76 supporters.

It is always a little dangerous to infer popularity of a value position from the performance of a single candidate. We might guess that Ram Gidoomal attracted voters in the London mayoral elections for reasons (such as his winning personality, his ethnic background and his business success) other than the intrinsic appeal of the movement's platform. We might similarly guess that whatever Hargreaves gained by his success in attracting media attention may well have been lost by his naivety and extremism.[27] Hence it is important to consider aggregate performance of a large number of candidates in the elections the CPA and CP have fought.

In the 2004 European Parliament elections, the CPA, CP (under the title of Operation Voice) and the tiny Christian Democratic party together gained 0.5 per cent of the votes cast. Five years later a far larger number of candidates were fielded but the result was disappointing. In Scotland the vote went down. Only in London did the total get out of the basement of great British eccentrics but the change from 2.4 to 2.9 per cent seems trivial given the opportunity to mobilise against the supposed heightened fear of Islam.

In the 2010 UK general election, the CPA/CP alliance took 0.1 per cent of the vote. As it fielded only 71 candidates, its votes-per-candidate ratio is more informative: 262. And it lost its only elected representatives in England. As part of a concerted effort to crush the British National party, the Labour party made strenuous efforts to mobilise its vote in those London boroughs where the BNP had shown signs of gaining a foothold. It succeeded to the extent that in the local elections that accompanied the general election, the CPA lost its three council seats in the London Borough of Newham.

With a larger churchgoing population, the two votes system of proportional representation, and a very weak Conservative party, Scotland offers Christians as fertile an environment as they are going to find but as we see from Table 8.3, the CP and CPA failed to make anything much of it. There was a significant

Table 8.2 Christian vote, European Elections, 2004 and 2009

Region	2004 Candidates	2009 Candidates	2004 (%) vote	2009 (%) vote
North East	0	7	0	1.2
North West	5	25	0.5	1.6
Eastern	7	24	0.3	1.5
East Midlands	0	17	0	1.5
West Midlands	0	18	0	1.3
London	8	51	2.4	2.9
South West	0	21	0	1.4
South East	13	35	0.8	1.5
Yorkshire	0	16	0	1.4
Scotland	7	16	1.8	1.5
Wales	4	30	0.7	1.9
Overall	44	260	0.5	1.6

boost in 2007 when Hargreaves and the Scottish Christian party joined the CPA and a hint of impact in Central and Glasgow (with large Catholic populations) and in the Highlands and Islands (the last redoubt of evangelical Presbyterianism) but far from building on those results, the parties lost momentum. Replacing Hargreaves as party leader with an Inverness doctor gave the SCP a more indigenous feel but cost it a great deal of publicity and in some regions paper candidates with London addresses had to be fielded to make up the numbers. The CPA fielded candidates in only two of eight regions. Overall the vote was less than half of its 2007 level, which must mean that many of those who voted Christian then did not repeat the experience in 2011.

Conclusion

There are some good reasons why the UK does not have a tradition of Catholic-inspired Christian Democracy. Unlike most Catholic countries, our left–right division has not coincided with and reinforced a secular–religious divide: as Chapter 6 demonstrated, serious Christians have been found across the political spectrum. In many European countries the pre-1939 right-wing parties were so discredited by their support for totalitarian dictatorships that after 1945 Christian Democratic parties were able to find a large space for a politics that was conservative on social and moral issues but centrist and sometimes even progressive on economic issues. There was no corresponding space in British politics because the main conservative party had not been discredited. Or to be more precise, what it lost by appeasement in the late 1930s, it regained through Churchill's leadership of the war effort. The UK's native Catholic population was very small and its Irish immigrants were concerned, in the early twentieth century, with arguments around the status of Ireland. When that was settled they followed their economic interests and became active in the Labour movement. The division of the Protestant population into supporters of the state churches and dissenters (which roughly mapped on to Conservative and Liberal parties in the nineteenth century) prevented any hope of a Christian Democratic party emerging from those bases. And as the Church of England shrunk and lost social

Table 8.3 Combined Christian party votes in Scottish Parliament elections, 1999–2011

Region	1999 (%)	2003 (%)	2007 (%)	2011 (%)
Central	0.8	–	3.6	1.4
Glasgow	0.9	1.3	2.7	0.7
Highlands and Islands	–	–	3.9	2.0
Lothians	0.3	0.2	1.0	0.5
Mid-Scotland and Fife	0.2	0.4	0.9	0.6
North East Scotland	–	–	1.1	0.8
South of Scotland	–	–	1.1	0.7
West of Scotland	1.0	1.4	2.5	0.9
Overall	0.4	0.4	2.3	0.9

prestige over the twentieth century, the social bases of clergy recruitment changed so that by the Thatcher era, its political heart was well to the left of centre. Thatcher's brand of conservatism went down even less well with the Church of Scotland, whose clergy had to sit in silence while she lectured the 1988 General Assembly on the real meaning of the parable of the Good Samaritan (which was that he was only able to help because his wealth had not been taken from him by an incompetent state).

When the CPA was formed, any historically aware observer would have been sceptical of its chances of creating a viable party along the lines of the German Christian Democratic Union. What the above account of the CP and CPA has shown is that neither was able to create a Christian *party* (as distinct from a pressure group that claimed Christian justification for an ad-hoc and shifting set of complaints). They failed miserably to attract mainstream Christians to the cause, and their reliance on minority religious traditions – the charismatic churches for the CP and the Catholic Church for the CPA – confirmed the public impression that these were oddball movements staffed by swivel-eyed zealots rather than serious parties. As we have seen, the anti-abortion stance was well out of line with public preferences. The same is true of homophobia. A major survey in 2008 showed that only 19 per cent of the unreligious respondents thought 'homosexual sex is always or almost always wrong'. Only a third of the larger group of somewhat religious respondents agreed with that sentiment. And, as with abortion, even the religious respondents were far more tolerant than the Christian parties required: only half thought that homosexuality was always wrong.[31] That both parties recruited heavily from ethnic minorities simply reinforced the general perception that these were fringe enterprises.

Furthermore they were fringe enterprises that drew on two fringes with a not-entirely-dead history of conflict. As I argued in Chapter 4, the salience of Protestant–Catholic religious animosities was eroded by the absence of matching underlying significant social and political differences. In contrast to the situation in Northern Ireland, in Britain sectarianism is no longer a social force. However, it remains an abiding interest for core members of the 'sects' in question. Charismatic and evangelical Protestants on the one side and conservative Catholics on the other are quite capable of treating each other civilly in mundane daily social interaction but if the issue is Christian truth, then each side will deny it to the other. In Holland in the 1970s the Catholic party and the Reformed Protestant party could first form an alliance and then merge because, as broad-spectrum political parties, their religious inspiration was not at the forefront of their agenda or their activities. On most issues, their positions were indistinguishable. The CP and CPA are not broad-spectrum political parties with secular agendas inspired by religious traditions. They are pressure groups that aim to mobilise activists and voters with religious justifications for provocative social positions. So long as their religious motivation is primary, and it is that rather than some secular value that is being punted to the electorate, there is always the danger of the underlying tension coming to the fore, as it did in the Scottish parliament elections of 2007. The replacement of Teresa Smith as leader of the CPA does not change the fact that, outside of the Greater London area, the CPA drew heavily on pro-life activists, almost all of whom were loyal Catholics while most of the CP were committed Protestants and at least one of the Scottish activists had been involved in demonstrating against the 2010 papal visit.

Despite the overwhelming evidence that popular involvement in religion in Britain is still declining, it is becoming increasingly fashionable to talk about religious resurgence, de-secularisation and the post-secular society. The formation of the CP and the CPA is seen by their members as proof that Christians are becoming increasingly influential. This seems a perverse interpretation. Christians did not have to stand in elections as Christians when the churches were popular and when their values were taken for granted. It is precisely because they have lost social power that a handful of conservative Christians, bank-rolled by a few millionaire backers, have taken the opportunities created by new electoral systems to advertise their faith.

9 Religious minority politics

Introduction

It is now difficult to write or say anything about Muslims without being accused of either a lack or a surfeit of political correctness.[1] In the academy such sensitivity often takes the form of challenging the propriety of making any assertions about the nature and consequences of Islam. So before I turn to the substance of this chapter I need to engage in some ground clearing.

Conventional social scientists suppose that religions such as Christianity and Islam exist in the same sense that tribes or clans or social classes exist; they are of course the product of human action but they are not solely the mental projections of any one group of people and thus cannot be readily imagined away. The edges of any 'imagined community' of adherents may be fuzzy but we assume that they have enough of what phenomenologists call 'facticity' for us to think of them as having effects. Max Weber, the founder of sociology, wrote extensively on the social, economic and political causes and consequences of the major world religions.

As part of the post-modern challenge to conventional social science, some scholars 'deconstruct' entities such as Islam and Hinduism.[2] There are generally two lines of argument: the case from social construction and from internal variation. The construction criticism is that if, for example, we can show that the codification of the idea of Hinduism was the ideological work of some agent (such as a government, keen to order its subjects) the thing itself does not really exist and cannot be the cause of anything. The obvious retort is that the post-modern critique applies equally well to every other concept and depiction we use, including those used in justifying post-modern deconstruction.[3] The first page of a British government study of religious beliefs demonstrates a charming naivety about language when it announces that 'the actual term "religion" is an invented or constructed category', as if there were some contrasting category of abstract nouns that, like rain in Scotland, occurs naturally.[4] The social constructionist mistake is to confuse discovery and creation. When we say that Newton discovered gravity, we do not mean that previously people had trouble adhering to the earth's surface. The development of words and ideas may indeed shape how we see social phenomena but that does not prevent us assuming that, at certain times and places, the things described by words exist independently of how we or anyone else thinks about them.

In a more moderate form, it is also argued that there is no monolithic Hinduism or Islam: there is only a number of different 'Hinduisms' and 'Islams'. For example, in a blog discussion about the relative tendency to violence of various religions, an anthropologist argued:

> I am sorry that I have to repeat myself: religion in itself does not exist. Yesterday and today (although less today) people who declare themselves Muslims of different groups, Christians of different sects, Jews of different sects, Hindus of different sects, Buddhists of different origins and sects, kill others and justify their actions in many ways, some of which involve religion.[5]

The rebuttal of the internal variation case for deconstruction is simple. If smaller groups (such as 'Hindus of different sects') can be meaningfully identified then there can be no principled objection to identifying larger entities such as Hinduism: the only issue is accuracy. That is, we should take care to impute shared characteristics only to those who share them. Only the ill informed would suppose that all British Christians (or even all British Roman Catholics) obey the Pope or that all Muslims obey the Grand Mufti. Nonetheless it seems perfectly proper to allow the possibility that groups of people share beliefs, attitudes, and values. Most Mormons have things in common that distinguish them from non-Mormons. They share a common identity that they routinely signal in many ways, including most obviously using the term 'Mormon' to refer to themselves. Although scholars who promote the deconstruction of terms such as 'Muslim' or 'Hindu' present themselves as being on the side of those whom they would save from being falsely 'essentialised', the denial of a shared identity to people who assert it seems as great an imposition as imputing a common identity to those who have little or nothing in common. When people routinely describe themselves as Muslim, subscribe to beliefs promoted by Muslim organisations, regularly attend worship at mosques, read and learn the Qur'an, attend to the judgements of Islamic scholars, and demand that they be accorded rights as a religious minority, it seems strange to deny that there is a religion which we and they call Islam.[6]

It is important to be accurate and it is sometimes important to be precise about details. Just how much detail is appropriate depends on the matter in hand. In discussing general voting preferences in the nineteenth century, a distinction between Anglican and Nonconformist will generally suffice but to understand the role of religion in the early days of the Labour movement we will probably want to distinguish between, for example, Unitarians, Methodists and Baptists and we may even need to note differences between Wesleyan and Primitive Methodists. But that does not mean that terms such as Christian and Nonconformist cannot sometimes be used to explore the social consequences of different religious beliefs.

As well as improperly dismissing the value of group labels, the blogging anthropologist quoted above makes a second common mistake in supposing that, as not all adherents to religion A support X all the time, and as adherents of other religions also support X some times, we cannot ask the question: 'Do religions differ in their support for X?' Internal and temporal variation are not necessarily the same as complete chaos. Especially as most religious adherents themselves think that their religion has a degree of cohesion that distinguishes it from alternatives, I see no reason why analysts should not at least explore the possibility that religions differ systematically and non-accidentally in their consequences. It seems perverse to exempt religions from questions that we would not hesitate to ask of other social forms. We know that Christian Democratic policies in Germany have varied since 1945 and we know that the German CDU is not identical to the Belgium Christene Volkspartij but neither fact prevents us distinguishing Christian Democracy from socialism or exploring the connection between core ideas and specific policies within those two competing political ideologies.

The point of the above ontological digression is to justify what I have been doing throughout this book: exploring the political consequences of forms of religion. For admirable ethical reasons, commentators are now acutely sensitive about inappropriately imputing vices to adherents of religious minorities. I take the view that, provided we are properly concerned with accuracy, there is nothing in principle objectionable about that exercise. Just as I have discussed the political correlates of different strands of Christianity in Britain, it is reasonable to explore the nature and effects of non-Christian religions. This chapter will consider the challenge posed by non-Christian religions to church–state relations, the shift from race relations to religious identity politics, the rise of Islamist extremism, the social isolation of non-Christians communities, and the extent of Muslim alienation.

Are non-Christians different?

Attitudes to the topics discussed in this chapter have become so polarised in the last decade that it is important to begin by restating the obvious: the non-Christian religions in Britain have a number of characteristics that, even if the host society were entirely free of xenophobia, would explain why arguments over the nature and public place of religion now have a prominence they have not enjoyed since debates over the 1829 Catholic Emancipation Act. These can be summarised as difference, demonstrativeness, and commitment.

First and most obviously, irrespective of their internal variations, Islam, Hinduism and Sikhism differ from Christianity vastly more than the Baptist strand of Christianity differs from the Presbyterian or Roman Catholic. Responses to the building of a mosque, temple or gurdwara will be many and varied but they will not be the same as reactions to the building of a new church. The former are exotic; the latter is commonplace.

Second, Islam, Hinduism and Sikhism are orthoprax rather than orthodox religions. That is, they differ systematically from Christianity (especially in its

Protestant form) in requiring certain rituals and ways of life. Of course correct action requires a substrate of belief but what is apparent and hence public is the need to conform to a distinctive set of behavioural requirements: in the case of Islam, the sharia. In contrast salvation for Christians is found largely in having the correct beliefs. This is an important difference because it may have implications for the ease with which believers adapt to a largely secular public sphere. Adherents to 'orthodox' religions may be annoyed that their religion is not accorded the honour of a prominent public position, but pique aside, there is little that is required of a Baptist that is compromised by living in a secular society. However, adherents of religions that make conformity to a series of behavioural requirements essential to salvation may find public secularity not just offensive but practically constraining. The pious Baptist car assembler can pray while working; his Muslim co-worker has to stop work at specific times to pray. Very few Christians believe that their religion mandates a particular diet or dress code. Many Muslims believe that certain foods prepared in particular ways are to be avoided; many Sikhs believe they must dress in a particular way. We need not suppose that orthodox and orthoprax religions are entirely different in the demands they make of the public sphere. In all religions we find zealots who will insist that their sensitivities justify being awkward and imposing on others. So we can match the stories of zealous Muslim taxi drivers refusing to have dogs in their cabs with stories of Christian hoteliers refusing bookings from gay or unmarried couples. My point is not that orthoprax religions are a public nuisance and orthodox religions are not; it is that the former have more behavioural requirements that they take more seriously. And that tendency is compounded by the familiarity with settings in which the orthoprax religion is dominant and its behavioural requirements are imposed on the society at large. British Muslims, Hindus and Sikhs may have first-hand experience of living in Pakistan, Uttar Pradesh or Punjab and thus may bring to the British setting the expectation of being able to be religious in the style which is required in the old world but is awkward in the new. That many Muslims, Hindus and Sikhs are distinguished from other Britons by religiously inspired characteristics is not an invention of those who dislike non-Christians; it is confirmed by organisations such as the Islamic Human Rights Commission (IHRC) which campaign for such differences to be 'recognised' by the state.

That non-Christian religions are in theory more demonstrative than Christianity does not mean that their adherents cannot moderate their claims. Many Sikhs now meet the need to be bearded and carry a sword by wearing a trimmed beard and carrying a very small ornamental dagger. Islam can be described as a long list of 'religious needs' but the IHRC position of wishing the state to allow 'dual space' with alternate and complimentary legal systems is a long way from trying to create an Islamic culture and society.[7] Nonetheless it is very unlikely to be accepted by any liberal democracy. As described in Chapter 1, religious minorities in Britain have been fighting for the last two centuries to remove religious discrimination, not to increase it, and they have argued on the grounds of individual, not group, rights. The British state has reluctantly accepted that strongly held religious beliefs should be accommodated. For example, during periods of military conscription, it permitted pacifists to serve in non-combat support roles and it allows parents to withdraw their children from school religious assemblies. But it is hard to imagine our grudging tolerance of religious differentiae evolving into the principle that religious minorities should be governed according to their own wishes. Apart from more profound concerns about equity, such distinction would require the state to decide what counted as a religion worthy of accommodation. The IHRC asks for all *major* religions to be permitted dual space but it is hard to see the consistent grounds on which we could preclude Scientology or the Church of Gay Nazis for Christ from demanding the same privileges as Christianity and Islam.[8]

It is worth adding that, as with any negotiations between competing interests, people's reactions are largely explained not by the current demands that the other party makes but by estimates of what the other party 'really' wants. We are naturally reluctant to concede one demand if we suppose that the new status quo will be taken as the base line for further demands. There is a clearly a great deal of hysterical over-reaction in the hostility of right-wing commentators to Muslim religious sensibilities, but there is one major difference between Islam on the one hand and Hinduism and Sikhism on the other that explains why even people who are not *Daily Mail* readers have more reservations about accommodating the first than the latter two. Islam, like Christianity, is a conversionist faith. Hinduism and Sikhism have acquired small numbers of non-Indian and non-Punjabi converts but they are still essentially ethnic religions. Though it has been greatly shaped by non-religious elements of the ethnic cultures that carry it, Islam is not an ethnic religion. Only some Muslims hope to convert Europe to Islam and even fewer support the particular vision of a Caliph ruling an expanded unified 'Islam-dom' but the religion still has the capacity to legitimate an ambition for growth, which concerns all of those who do not share that religion.

The third quality that distinguishes non-Christian religions from Christianity in the West is that its adherents are generally more committed to their faith. This needs to be broken down into two separate observations: proportions of populations and personal commitment. Most Muslims, Hindus and Sikhs came from (and retain ties with) cultures that were considerably more religious than that of Britain and while some quickly reduced their levels of personal religiosity to the British norm, most did not. A rough rule of thumb is that in surveys two-thirds of nominal Muslims, Hindus and Sikhs will say they are religiously observant while only one-third of British nominal Christians says the same.[9] I should add that this is patently an exaggeration of Christian religiosity; were it so, church-going would be twice as popular as it is. Secondly, and this takes us back to the earlier orthodox–orthoprax contrast, those Muslims, Hindus and Sikhs who are observant have more to be observant about. As I have argued at great length elsewhere, secularisation not only involves a decline in the proportion of people in Britain who are Christian; it also involves an internal erosion of what is distinctive about Christianity so that many members of mainstream Christian churches are now little distinguished from their non-religious fellows.[10]

Together these features create a number of problems for British church–state (or to be more precise religion–state) relations.[11] Much misunderstanding stems from the fact that the secularity of the British public sphere differs from that of France or the USA in being based on tacit understandings and precedent rather on than formal constitutional principles. Nonconformists reduced the power of the state churches to the point where they could comfortably live with it and then called a truce, which left the Church of England and the Church of Scotland with a variety of privileges that were tolerated on the understanding that they would not be used to increase partisan advantage. The same principle applies to nonreligious people's attitudes to the residual privileges of religion. For example, the privileged access that churches have to the BBC is accepted because nonbelievers can turn off the radio and because the BBC itself ensures that religious broadcasters do not aggressively proselytise or criticise other faiths. To strengthen its case for Islam to be given various forms of official recognition, the IHRC exaggerates the salience of residual elements of Christian domination. For example it justifies its demand for Sharia law by noting that the Church of England still has church courts.[12] Such courts now govern only a tiny fraction of the business of the Church of England and have no impact outside the church. That they are trivial is clear from the fact that most English people will have never heard of them. The IHRC also notes that 'only the Christian faith is protected by blasphemy laws'[13] without adding that such laws only survived because they were not used. The last Scottish conviction for blasphemy was in 1843. There were only a handful of prosecutions in England after that date and the last one was in 1921. Mary Whitehouse mounted a private case against *Gay News* in 1977 because the state refused to prosecute. The case provoked such ill ease that when representatives of other faiths argued that they should enjoy the same protection as Christianity, the government restored parity between religions in the other direction: the common-law offences of blasphemy and blasphemous libel were abolished in England and Wales in 2008. The state funding of Church of England schools was tolerated because there was little about them that was specifically Anglican or even Christian. The funding of Catholic schools was more contentious because they were more culturally distinctive but that distinctiveness has been eroded by secularisation. Since the 1960s the decline of the Christian Brothers and a general shortage of pious Catholic teachers has forced many Catholic schools to employ non-Catholics and the decline in the number of Mass-attending Catholics has further weakened the church ethos of many such schools. Anglican and Catholic schools have become popular since the 1980s with middle-class parents in London but this has little or nothing to do with a wish to have their children socialised into the Christian faith: it is a strategy of class (and ethnic) avoidance.

In brief we can think of the secularisation of British public life as a process that stopped short, leaving the *appearance* of popular support for the institutional privileging of Christianity when in reality such privileges as did remain were welcomed by few and tolerated by the rest only so long as they were not used in a partisan fashion. This is the background that makes the migration of a significant number of non-Christians to Britain awkward. The state is pushed by the requirement of fairness either to extend the same privileges to non-Christians (and to new Christian bodies) or to complete the process of secularising the public sphere.

If difference, demonstrativeness, and commitment are three features of non-Christian religion that challenge the current fudge of UK church–state relations, there is a fourth difference that currently applies exclusively to Islam. For a wide variety of reasons, either directly (as in the invasion of Iraq and Afghanistan) or indirectly (in the former Yugoslavia or in the Indian sub-continent) Britain and its allies have been or are involved in conflicts that have religious elements. We may not see our involvement in foreign politics as a repeat of the Crusades but some Muslims do.

From race to religion

Thanks to the marvel that is YouTube it is now possible to see clips of *Till Death Us Do Part*, a late 1960s BBC sitcom. It featured Alf Garnett, an East End of London working-class patriarch who spends most of each episode arguing with his daughter and son-in-law. The writer Johnny Speight created a memorable character: a working-class conservative-voting reactionary who lauded the Queen and railed against the Labour party, the welfare state, long hair, pop music and 'Coons' and 'Pakis'. It may just be selective memory but I cannot recall Garnett complaining about alien religions as such. The main targets for his grossly offensive racist remarks were skin colour and smelly food. Likewise with the routines of comedians such as Bernard Manning who came to TV and radio from the working men's clubs. Through the 1970s and 1980s xenophobia was secular as was the reaction to it. Gangs of working-class white youth engaged in 'Paki-bashing', not Muslim-mugging. Government responses took the form of 'race' relations legislation. West Indians and Asians formed common fronts to fight racism and to campaign for equal rights and well-meaning pop musicians organised *Rock Against Racism* tours. Activists in the Asian Youth Movement 'were not necessarily atheists. But religion never shaped their politics'.[14]

Given the considerable differences in culture between West Indians and Asians, and between Asians from different countries, it may be that such an alliance was always precarious, but critics of government policy such as Munira Mirza argue that the shift from race to religion was at least in part a result of changes in the attitudes of British left-wing groups and in government policy.[15]

In Chapter 2 I suggested that Muslim, Hindu and Sikh politics had much in common with the earlier experiences of the Irish in Britain and in the USA. Despite their conservative culture, they found a home on the political Left because the Labour party represented their class interests and the Conservative party was more firmly opposed to immigration.[16] There is a further parallel in the role of clannishness. Even before local councils and central government developed the formal policy of dealing with religio-ethnic minorities through self-styled community leaders (and the multicultural rationale for so doing), the Labour party in some British cities had developed its own version of New York's infamous Tammany Hall, with the clan replacing the unions and immigrant associations.[17] Pervaiz Khan tells the story of his uncle who came to Britain in the 1950s and by the 1960s was a shop steward for the Transport and General Workers' Union. He developed strong ties to the Labour party leadership in Birmingham.

> He was never an elected councillor but he was treated as if he was. He had his own office in the council building, a pass and a parking space. He effectively acted as a 'whip', making sure that other Asian councillors voted the 'right way'. In return he got council grants for the Asian community, for community centres and other projects'.[18]

The Labour party courted community elders who could deliver large numbers of votes by instructing their people how to vote. Such a system was encouraged by the relative isolation of some migrant communities, low levels of education, poor English language skills, and the subordination of women. Brokers mediated between minority communities and government agencies. Such brokers lost their influence as immigrants and their children became effective representatives of their own interests but in both legal and illegal forms clannishness remains a political force. In June 2004, six leading Birmingham Muslims (including Muhammad Afzal, a city councillor for 23 years) used forged postal ballots to steal an election for Labour.[19] In 2009, six Pakistani men in Slough received prison sentences for vote-rigging: this time in the Conservative interest.[20] The same year, five Muslim Tories in Bradford were found guilty of forging postal ballots in the Bradford West Westminster seat.

In these examples, community leaders were arguably reinforcing secular politics in delivering votes to mainstream parties: it is integrationist corruption. Minority politics became less integrating over the course of the 1980s. The Thatcher government shifted the centre of British politics to the right. Partly as a result of the decline of British industry and partly as a result of anti-union legislation, the trade unions lost power. This hastened a change in left-wing thinking that had been in train since the student demonstrations of the late 1960s. With the working class shrinking and no longer willing even to audition for the role of leader of the revolution, hope shifted to what the French called 'new social movements'[21] and then to identity politics. Gay rights, environmentalism, and feminism became more popular sites of radical activism and the stress shifted from campaigning against discrimination to campaigning for recognition of, and 'respect' for, identity.

Local government was central to the promotion of religio-ethnic identity politics. Between 1981, when Labour gained control of the Greater London Council, and 1986 when the Tories abolished it, 'the GLC pioneered a new strategy of making minority communities feel part of British society. It arranged consultations with them, drew up equal opportunities policies, established race relations units, and dispensed millions of pounds in grants to minority groups'. The GLC promoted a new notion of racism, which now meant

> [not] the denial of equal rights but the denial of the right to be different.... Black people, so the argument went, should not be forced to accept British values or adopt a British identity. Rather, different peoples should have a right to express their own identities, explore their own histories, formulate their own values, pursue their own lifestyles.[22]

As Gita Saghal and Nira Yuval-Davis of the Southall Black Sisters concluded, the GLC reduced the fight against racism to 'preserving the "traditions and cultures" of the different ethnic minorities'.[23]

The GLC model was borrowed by other Labour councils. Birmingham City Council created nine groups to act as channels of representation between it and the city's minorities: the African and Caribbean People's Movement, the Bangladeshi Islamic Projects Consultative Committee, the Birmingham Chinese Society, the Council of Black-led Churches, the Hindu Council, the Irish Forum, the Vietnamese Association, the Pakistani Forum, and the Sikh Council of Gurdwaras. By funnelling money and influence through these organisations, it encouraged people to claim membership of one of these putative interest groups and it encouraged the minorities to compete with each other. As Malik puts it: 'In applying multicultural snake oil to the problems of Birmingham, the council created rifts between communities where none had previously existed and exacerbated tensions that had previously been managed.'[24] The same story could be told for Bradford and for Sheffield and once Labour won the general election of 1997 the same multicultural approach was applied by central government. The tendency to privilege religio-ethnic identity was, of course, not simply a consequence of Labour party policy. The natural tendency of migrants to settle alongside their fellow countrymen and co-religionists had already laid the foundation for what Amartya Sen has called 'plural monoculturalism' but, as Sen argues, the British enthusiasm for 'recognising' cultural differences exaggerated the very problem it was designed to solve.[25]

There is evidence to support this claim. The Pew Forum's 2006 survey of Muslim attitudes in 13 countries showed that Muslims in Britain were more critical than those in France, Spain and Germany, despite those countries making far less effort to accommodate minority sensibilities. When asked 'Is there a conflict between being a devout Muslim and living in a modern society?', 47 per cent of British Muslims but only 36, 28 and 25 per cent in Germany, France and Spain respectively answered 'Yes'.[26] When asked to say if relations between Muslims and Westerners were generally good or bad, 'bad' was chosen by 62 per cent of British Muslims, 60 per cent of German Muslims, 58 per cent of French Muslims and only 23 per cent of Muslims in Spain. There are, of course, so many other differences between the Muslims of these four countries that we should hesitate to ascribe the more negative attitudes of British Muslims solely to the government's multiculturalism policy, but we can minimally say that the policy has not been an unalloyed success.

Radicalisation and Rushdie

The shift in emphasis from race to religion was accompanied by a crucial change in the nature of British Islam: the challenge to the Barelwi tradition from the more 'purist' and radical forms of Deobandi and Wahhabi Islam. Most of Britain's Asian Muslims were Barelwis: moderate Sunni Muslims whose reverence for Muslim saints and for the person of the Prophet showed the influence of the Sufi movement. 'Their easy-going Islam (in matters of doctrine and worship; they are even more puritanical on matters of sex than other Muslim sects) is also reflected in attitudes to politics.'[27] The Deobandis (named after the Indian town which was home to the central college) are radicals who see themselves as ridding Islam of superstition, who stress the study of the Qur'an and the law, and who seek to impose on every facet of everyday life through the issuing of fatwas.[28] The Afghani Taliban were products of the Deobandi tradition. The puritanical Wahhabi version of Islam came from Saudi Arabia and like the Deobandi tradition, it regarded the veneration of saints and holy places as idolatry. Although notions of 'moderate' and 'radical' involve a great deal of simplification, they are sufficient for our purposes. The key point is that for a variety of quite different reasons, the more moderate Islamic traditions of the first generation of British Muslims have been partly displaced by more radical versions. One cause of the shift is organisational. While the Barelwi tradition is local and self-reproducing, the Deobandis concentrate on creating networks of schools to produce a cadre of religious leaders who export their message; the success of that initiative can be seen in the fact that the majority of British mosques are now run by Deobandis. Another cause of the shift is wealth. Whatever its intrinsic appeals, the Wahhabi mode has benefited immensely from Saudi oil wealth, which has paid for imams, mosques, books and other teaching materials.

In late 1988, the increasingly radical nature of elements of British Islam was brought abruptly to the attention of a wider public by responses to a novel. In September, the Anglo-Indian novelist Salman Rushdie published *The Satanic Verses*. Very quickly Muslims condemned the fictional work as blaspheming the Prophet. The book was banned first in India, where Rushdie was already unpopular because of his previous works, and then in a range of other Muslim countries such as Bangladesh, Sudan, and Sri Lanka. Collets and Dillons bookshops in Charing Cross Road, London were bombed and there were explosions in York and High Wycombe. Unexploded devices were found at Penguin stores in Guildford, Nottingham, and Peterborough. In January 1989, the Bradford Council of Mosques (one of the bodies set up by Bradford city council as part of its multi-culturalism policy) organised a mass burning of copies of the book. An already unprecedented reaction to a work of fiction was amplified by Iran's Supreme Leader, Ayatollah Ruhollah Khomeini, who pronounced the following Fatwa:

> In the name of God the Almighty. We belong to God and to Him we shall return. I would like to inform all intrepid Muslims in the world that the author of the book Satanic Verses, which has been compiled, printed, and

published in opposition to Islam, the Prophet, and the Qur'an, and those publishers who were aware of its contents, are sentenced to death. I call on all zealous Muslims to execute them quickly, where they find them, so that no one will dare to insult the Islamic sanctity. Whoever is killed on this path will be regarded as a martyr, God-willing.[29]

In case the reward of martyrdom was insufficient, Iran offered a considerable bounty. In March 1989, the United Kingdom broke off diplomatic relations with Iran. Although Rushdie was to survive nine years of police protection and frequent moving, his translators were less fortunate. The Japanese translator was killed in 1991. The Turkish language translator was the intended target in the events that led to the Sivas massacre in July 1993, which resulted in the deaths of 37 people. The Norwegian publisher barely survived an assassination attempt in 1993.

In Britain, several Muslim leaders endorsed Khomeini's decision. Other leaders, while supporting the Fatwa, claimed that British Muslims were not allowed to carry out the Fatwa themselves. Prominent amongst these was Dr Kalim Siddiqui, head of the Muslim Parliament. After his death in 1996, his successor Ghayasuddin Siddiqui maintained support for the Fatwa, even after the Iranian leadership had moderated its position. That some Muslims supported murdering a novelist was troubling but what shook many British non-Muslims was the absence of Muslims who were prepared to defend the right to free speech.

The notion of disaffected youth is a cliché but its underlying truth is relevant to understanding the growth of Islamic militancy in the UK. As Will Herberg showed in his classic study of migrants to the USA *Protestant–Catholic–Jew*, the second and subsequent generations of migrants have to choose a posture towards the culture of their parents and grandparents.[30] Ineffectively socialised into the religious culture of the first generation, many young British Muslims rejected the Indian subcontinental Islam of their parents: 'not only were they segregated from the wider social world, they were also cut off from the traditional institutions and structures of Islam.'[31] Ed Hussain explains the growing rift with his pious but old-fashioned father caused by his attraction to radical Islam:

> Eventually his father gave him an ultimatum: leave Islamism or leave my house. Hussain decided to leave his house. He stole out in the middle of the night and crept down to the East London mosque, which was controlled by the Jamaat-influenced Islamic Forum. He was taken in by 'the brothers' and treated like a 'family member'. For people like him, Hussain observes, 'cut off from Britain, isolated from the Eastern culture of our parents, Islamism provided us with a purpose and place in life.[32]

Given the notoriety of Osama Bin Laden and the easy availability of materials encouraging jihad, it may well be that young men such as Ed Hussain or the London tube bombers would have led themselves to the political postures they adopted, but it is a curious feature of 'the rise of British jihad'[33] that the liberal culture that jihadis so despise offered a remarkable opportunity for hearing radical preachers. In a world where conspiracy theories abound there is no shortage of explanations of what seems like undue tolerance. Journalist Richard Watson believes that MI5 and other security agencies engaged in a Faustian pact. Tabs would be kept on them but Muslim radicals would be left alone provided they did not encourage attacks on British targets. Whatever the reason, the UK has given sanctuary to Islamic extremists who face punishment in Muslim countries. Omar Bakri Mohammed, who was responsible for recruiting 'most of the extremists at the heart of the British jihad'[34] sought asylum in Britain after being expelled from Saudi Arabia in 1986. He had previously been expelled from Syria. Despite his known radicalism, he was allowed to remain in Britain where he not only regularly addressed a Muslim youth club but was invited to lead a religious assembly in a Crawley secondary school 'in the name of religious inclusion. We didn't know about his background or views. ... There was a kind of collective naivety about radical Islamic lecturers then'.[35] He was excluded only when a holiday in Lebanon allowed the Home Secretary the easier route of preventing his re-entry. Abu Hamza was an Egyptian who became a British citizen in 1981 after marrying an English woman and who was injured by explosives in Afghanistan. From 1997 to 2006 when he was convicted for inciting religious hatred, he very publicly promoted jihad from his base at the large Finsbury mosque in London. Although wanted in Yemen on suspicion of terrorist crimes, he was allowed to remain because the UK will not extradite people to countries where they may face execution. In 2008 the Home Secretary approved his extradition to the USA to face terrorism charges but to date he has been successful in appealing against the extradition. Abu Qatada arrived in the UK in 1993 on a forged passport and was granted asylum on grounds of religious persecution. He became known for his sermons arguing that non-Muslims and mainstream Muslims who did not support jihad were legitimate targets for murder. He was arrested in 2005 and won an appeal against deportation to Jordan, where he was wanted for terrorist crimes. On 8 May 2008 he was granted bail by the Special Immigration Appeals Commission but he was returned to prison for breaking bail conditions.

Abdullah el-Faisal (born Trevor Forest) is a Jamaican convert to Islam who was trained in Saudi Arabia before becoming an imam at the Brixton mosque in 1991. His taped sermons demonstrate that he regularly preached the virtue of murdering Jews, Hindus, Christians and Americans. For example, he said: 'should we hate Jews and when we see them on the street, should we beat them up? You have no choice but to hate them. How do you fight the Jews? You kill the Jews.'[36] In 2003 he was convicted of incitement to murder and served four years before being deported to Jamaica.

Reliable numbers are hard to come by but those who were involved in recruiting young British Muslims have claimed that hundreds of young men went to fight in Afghanistan and Pakistan and they were just the most active of a much larger number attracted to Islamic extremism in one form or another. Watson believes that some 4,000 young British Muslims were regarded as a threat to national security.[37]

Quite what explains receptivity to the jihadi cause is not at all clear. Extensive efforts to find common factors in the backgrounds of those who killed themselves in terrorist operations or were convicted of such actions have failed to identify any narrow set of characteristics that they share.[38] Some came from relatively deprived homes and their actions could be explained as compensation for frustration, but others came from very comfortable backgrounds. Some were converts, presumably driven by a desire to prove their new allegiance but others had been raised as Muslims.

What the diverse backgrounds show is that is misleading to suppose, as both critics and supporters do, that the jihadis are either the tip of the Islamic iceberg or the epitome of its essence. Just which position within a wide spectrum 'truly' represents Islam is a theological question; what the social scientist can do is ask about typicalities and norms. It is clear that the British jihadis are abnormal both in their support for jihad and in their previous relationship to Islamic religious culture and institutions. Probably the majority were less than averagely religious before they were attracted to the cause. They became involved against the wishes of family and friends. In many cases, they were rejected by informal groupings and formal organisations for their extremism. For example, in 2010 Muslims in Cardiff contacted police to express concerns about some young men. Saleem Kidwai, secretary general of the Muslim Council for Wales, said: 'there was a group of 15 boys that the community was aware of, they were going to have a meeting and they were rejected by all the mosques. Their views are extremist.'[39]

Despite the atypicality of the British jihadis, the government response focused on British Muslims as a whole. If an IHRC survey is at all reliable, many Muslims see this as victimisation on a parallel with the 1970s assumption that the way to suppress the IRA was to police the Irish.[40] The government could defend its actions on the grounds that, as the jihadis had nothing in common other than being British Muslims, efforts to reduce their number should be directed at the Muslim population. In defence of the government it should be said that partisan groups such as IHRC are patently in the cake-having and cake-eating business: they object to the demonisation of the Muslim population but assert its integrity as a community with community, not individual, rights. And the government response to Islamic terrorism has not been solely or even primarily one of securitisation. As well as introducing a raft of security legislation, the Labour government devoted a great deal of prestige and public money to addressing issues of representation both through its traditional method of flattering community leaders and through schemes to encourage Muslims to become more involved in mainstream party politics.

Worlds apart?

The view is not confined to writers such as Richard Watson and Kenan Malik, who document the background to Muslim extremism, but those working in that genre are agreed, as are many parts of government, that the relative isolation of religio-ethnic minority communities is a problem.[41] Watson wrote of the Muslims of Savile Town in Dewsbury, a small town south of Leeds: 'Four decades since they arrived in England they are even more isolated, both geo-graphically and culturally, from the rest of the town.'[42]

Many forces combine to keep ethno-religious minorities together. The ori-ginal chain migration pattern of settlement, exclusion from large parts of the council housing stock, the preference for keeping family close, desire for proximity to community resources such as Asian groceries and places of worship, and the fear of racist conflict combine to create a considerable degree of segregation. 'At the regional and at the micro-level the grass-roots pattern is one of ethno-religious completeness rather than ethno-religious mixing'. We can quantify residential segregation and express it with an Index of Segre-gation (IS) with values ranging from 0 (none at all) to 100 (complete separa-tion). In 2001 the average Muslim IS for ten large English urban centres was 54; for Sikhs and Hindus it was 48 and 38 respectively. But those averages conceal considerable local variation. In Oldham the Muslim figure was 70; in Burnley 66; the average was brought down by London. Its low score of 36 is explained not by London's Muslims being more evenly spread amongst non-Muslims but by the large number of small Muslim communities, each of which is separate.[43]

One major source of isolation is relative poverty. British Muslims, Hindus and Sikhs differ considerably in income and prosperity. Hindus are the most affluent and Muslims the poorest with Sikhs occupying an intermediate position. In 2001 unemployment rates for Muslims aged 25 and over were just under 14 per cent compared with 6 per cent for Sikhs, 5 per cent for Hindus and 4 per cent for the population of England as whole.[44] Some of that difference comes from circum-stances prior to immigration. 'For example about a third of the Indian population comes from the professionalised middle class East African Asian population forced out by Africanisation policies in the 1960s and 1970s'.[45] Much of the rest of the difference stems from cultural preferences. One of the major sources of economic marginality for Muslims is the low representation of women in the labour force. That is a result of 'traditional South Asian values of protecting women's honour ... together with relatively early and almost universal marriage for young women, early onset of childbirth and large family size'.[46] Less than 30 per cent of Muslim women aged 25 and over were economically active, compared with 60 per cent of all women and 62 per cent of Hindu and Sikh women.[47]

Relative isolation is a political problem because it limits opportunities for social advance. One reason why liberals who are not principled secularists oppose single-faith schools is that they tend to be less effective educationally than the state schools. The Dewsbury Markaz mosque, one of the largest in Britain, supports a school. In 2005 an Ofsted inspection faulted the school for poor academic standards of achievement and – the two cannot be unrelated – for spending too much time teaching Islam and not enough time on the national cur-riculum subjects that will allow entry into higher education.[48]

Isolation is also a problem because it is the structural basis for the creation and maintenance of distinctive worldviews. The introversion and narrow-mindedness that creates the highest chance of a distinctive religious culture being maintained and successfully transmitted from one generation to the next also encourage a debilitating sense of collective victimhood. When interviewed for a TV documentary, Iqbal Sacranie, head of the Muslim Council of Britain, asserted that '95–98 per cent of those stopped and searched under the anti-terror laws are Muslims'. The actual figure was around 14 per cent, which is close to their proportion in the population of London, where most stop-and-searches took place.[49] The IHRC survey showed a large proportion of Muslim respondents thinking that other Muslims were being oppressed by the police, though they themselves had not had any such experience: a common example of myth displacing experience.[50] The most extreme example of self-pity displacing rational thought is the refusal to believe that acts claimed by Islamic terrorists were actually the work of Muslims. A disconcerting proportion of British Muslims – 45 per cent in one survey and 56 per cent in another – appear to believe that the 9/11 World Trade Center attacks were not the work of Muslims.[51] Dr Mohammad Naseem, the chairman of Birmingham's Central Mosque told a BBC2 documentary that he found *The Ripple Effect* more plausible than the official accounts of the London tube bombings. *The Ripple Effect* is a 56-minute video (widely available on the internet), which asserts that the government, security services and Israelis collaborated to kill Londoners and blame it on Muslims in order to bolster support for the war on terror. Naseem freely distributed copies.[52]

It is easy to suppose that high levels of minority residential segregation and unemployment are associated with the growth of a shared oppositional culture but it is less easy to demonstrate that this is the case or to gauge its extent. Particularly since the 2001 World Trade Center attack and then the 2005 London Underground bombings, there have been a great many surveys of Muslim opinion. but there are many reasons for being cautious about taking the results at face value. In the first place, the timing of such research is likely to produce distorted responses. Asking people to respond to acts committed by their co-religionists at a time when public hostility is understandably high may well have produced exaggerated responses because the very setting is something of an implied challenge.

One important observation is that the assessment of some survey results would benefit from having a comparison group. One poll asked for views on the statement 'It is never justified for anyone to attack British civilians because of Britain's activities in Iraq and Afghanistan'. Seventy-three per cent of Muslims agreed and 10 per cent disagreed, which might seem like a lot of Muslim support for terrorism – and it was trumpeted in the press as such – until one knows that 7 per cent of non-Muslims also disagreed.[53] Much is often made of apparent Muslim support for Sharia. For example, one poll showed that 59 per cent of Muslims would prefer to live under British law, compared to 28 per cent who would prefer to live under Sharia law; a figure that rose to 37 per cent for Muslims aged 16 to 24.[54] It is worth considering what proportion of churchgoing Christians would say that they would like to live under 'Christian law'.

Beyond technical concerns about the quality of small polls based on hastily prepared questions, I have two general concerns about making inferences from most attitude surveys. The first is the obvious one that if you invite people to complain they may well express more unhappiness than they normally feel; how else do we explain the finding that half of university lecturers find the job stressful?[55] The second is a more nebulous suspicion that we may misrepresent poll respondents if we fail to appreciate the complexity of beliefs, attitudes and motives. My concern may be clearer if I identify some anomalies in survey results. Almost three-quarters of Muslims aged 16 to 24 agreed that 'I prefer that Muslim women choose to wear the veil', and the responses were similar for men and women. Yet very few young Muslim women in the UK actually wear the veil even though, for many, there is little stopping them. According to a 2004 survey, 47 per cent of British Muslims 'would prefer to live in a foreign (preferably an Islamic) country'[56]. Yet they do not leave. Almost half the sample claimed to pray five times a day and two-thirds agreed that 'My religion is the most important thing in my life'.[57] Yet two-thirds paid interest on a loan or mortgage, half had bought a lottery ticket, almost a quarter consumed alcohol, and 20 per cent had gambled.

Knowing what people really think is difficult but I suspect that to take at face value what people say when asked such questions is to fail to allow for the gap we often find between aspiration and likely or actual action. We know from research that compared what Americans said to pollsters about their rate of churchgoing with actual counts of church attendance, that churchgoing Americans exaggerate considerably how often they go to church.[58] We know from studies of American teenagers who pledge themselves to chastity before marriage and then fall pregnant that verbal commitments are no sure guide to behaviour.[59] Catholics will often venerate saints but come nowhere close to emulating such saintly standards in their own lives. My point in these three examples is not that religious people are deluded or hypocritical. It is that, as in many secular walks of life, people with varying degrees of piety can imagine exemplary performance and admire it in one mental compartment while their behaviour is shaped by more mundane standards and concerns. That is, professions made in attitude surveys may tell us what the speaker in some sense admires (and that admiration may be a relatively transient response to particular questions) without it being the case that the speaker will emulate that which is admired.

In summary there is evidence that Muslims, Hindus and Sikhs are socially segregated to an extent that, in some places, deserves to be called isolation. Social-structural difference is accompanied by cultural separation. This is less the case for Hindus and Sikhs than for Muslims. Because their class profile, degree of involvement in the labour market, gender roles and patterns of family formation are closer to the UK norm, the first two are more integrated. They are also less culturally distinctive, because their religious differentiae are both less 'different' and less pressing. And finally, whatever identity problems young Hindus and Sikhs may suffer by virtue of being between two worlds, they do not have available a global conflict that can provide a potentially oppositional form of identity.

Reversing the image

Field concludes a thorough review of surveys of Muslim attitudes with the following gloomy assessment:

> Polls ... reveal a community that ... remains ill at ease with the majority British culture and apprehensive about its future. As last one in twenty, disproportionately young Muslims, are so disaffected as to be willing to contemplate complete rejection of mainstream society and the use of violence against it. A further 15% are partially alienated, to the extent of finding Western values decadent, experiencing no great sense of loyalty to Britain, feeling that Muslims have allowed themselves to become too integrated into British culture and sympathizing with the motives of those who take up arms for Islam. A further third co-exist with British society but consider themselves more Muslim than British and seek to retain Islamic identity through education, marriage and other social institutions.[60]

But that leaves almost half of Britain's Muslims who are not in one of the delineated groups. To the extent that alienation has a social structural base, we can expect it to diminish. Improved education has the potential to make the disaffected simply more articulate in their disaffection but as we have already seen with Britain's Sikh community, it also has the potential for upward social mobility, a decline in average family size, greater involvement of women in work outside the home, a weakening of clan and caste ties, more frequent marrying-out, and greater integration.[61] Although the proportion of Muslim women working is low, the majority of those who do work full-time 'feel comfortable practising their religion at work'.[62]

What tends to get missed in the current concern about Islamic extremism is the extent to which religious minorities are already politically well integrated. Fears of minority community alienation have created the common perception that electors from ethno-religious minorities are less likely to vote in general elections than other electors. Research published in 2007 showed that, on the contrary, registered South Asian electors were more likely to have voted than the norm. This was slightly offset by the fact that South Asians adults 'are less likely to be registered to vote than the rest of the population, partly because a larger part of the population is born in ineligible countries'.[63] And rather than community isolation being associated with abstention, turnout was actually higher 'in areas where South Asians are more likely to be from lower social classes than in areas where more middle-class South Asians live'. The researchers explain this as a function of community leaders being effective at delivering the vote, and critics have been quick to present the finding as proof that ethno-religious minorities have not yet grasped the nature of democracy.[64] The interesting point is that Muslims are as likely to be critical of clan politics as secular liberals. A Bradford Muslim who was active in the 2010 general election rebuked the local parties for selecting candidates for their ability to deliver a religio-ethnic bloc rather than potential to work for the city as a whole and criticised council candidates for a narrow vision of their responsibilities: 'Council members are there to represent their constituencies; however they must do this in the context of the needs of the whole district and all communities, Muslim or otherwise.'[65]

Although religious minority representation is still short of par, it has increased considerably. In 1996 there were 160 Muslim local councillors: by 2001 there were 217.[66] More recent national figures are not available but we know the proportionate growth in numbers has continued in London. Over the three four-year council terms between 1998 and 2010, the percentage of Muslim councillors in London rose from 4.4 to 6.1 to 7.8 per cent, which is about par for the Muslim population of the city.[67] Westminster representation is lower but again it is increasing. In 2010, the number of Muslim MPs doubled from four to eight, and a significant first was recorded with the appointment of Baroness Sayeeda Warsi to the chair of the Conservative party with a seat in cabinet.

The Citizenship Survey is a household survey covering a representative core sample of 10,000 adults in England and Wales, with an ethnic minority boost sample of 5,000 and a Muslim boost sample of 1,200 each year. Maria Sobolewska used its data to test four indicators of political exclusion: trust in institutions, feeling of political efficacy, political participation, and a sense of belonging to Britain. Rather than Watson's bleak introverted community she found a mixed picture. While Muslims are more aware of religious prejudice, they seem satisfied with their political influence, they trust political institutions and they feel they belong. Indeed on some indicators they seem more content than 'white Christians' and 'white people with no religion'. She finds no evidence of increasing religiosity among Muslims: at 73.5 per cent, the proportion of Muslims born in Britain who describe themselves as practising their religion is slightly lower than the 76.2 per cent of their parents who make the same claim. Most importantly, religiously observant Muslims seem no more or less excluded or alienated than their non-observing counterparts.[68]

Conclusion

The formation in 2010 of a Conservative-led coalition government signalled the end to two decades of state-sponsored multi-culturalism. It is in the nature of Britain's unwritten constitution that changes are piecemeal and ad hoc but it seems clear that there will be no major restructuring of church–state relations of the sort desired by the Islamic Human Rights Centre. Adjustments will continue to be made to accommodate the sensibilities of non-Christian religious minorities but, as such accommodations generally provoke corresponding claims from Christians, resolution will continue to follow the pattern we saw with the blasphemy laws. Rather than being expanded in remit, they were dropped. Equality will continue to trump diversity.

What is clear from the multitude of culture clashes that are now routinely reported is that friction generally occurs and becomes a cause célèbre because one or more party is being deliberately bloody-minded. The Muslim who took a job in a Tesco warehouse and then complained because he was asked to move pallets of alcohol was clearly looking for a fight and the employment tribunal was properly unimpressed by his claim that he did not know Tesco sold alcohol. The Muslim woman who took a Christian hotelier couple to court for apparently abusing her religion was a recent convert whom the court decided had been looking to be insulted. Where those involved (such as the Hindu who wished to cremated on an open-air funeral pyre) are pragmatic, resolution is almost invariably possible. Opposition to such accommodation often seems equally spurious and bloody-minded: it is hard for example to take seriously the English Defence League's commitment either to Christian culture or to the principles of liberal democracy.

Sami Zubaida makes an important point when he reminds us that much of the frustration and alienation that experienced by young Muslim men results 'from class and race factors that are part of the British landscape, and their reactions (drugs, crime, dissent, religion, reform) are familiar. Only, unlike other British groups, they have the option of a religious identity, one that is prominent and problematic on the world stage, in terms of which they can speak'. He adds: 'This identity also adds to the dimensions of racism against them. The jihadis are one (extreme) reaction to these dilemmas.' Zubaida also notes that many Muslims are as 'Muslim' as their compatriots are Christian.

> Why are all Pakistanis, Bangladeshis, Arabs, Iranians, Indonesians, always 'Muslim', while Europeans are English, French, Italian, Dutch, but not 'Christians'? Behind the pious declaration of universal Muslim identity we know that there are many prejudices: of Pakistanis towards Bangladeshis, Arabs towards south Asians, Iranians towards Arabs.

Zubaida explains this obsession with religion as just another version of 'the old "orientalist" assumption that the Islamic religion is the essence, of which all other social and cultural traits of Muslims are mere manifestations'.[69] I think he is wrong. First, the assumption that religion is central is, as Zubaida's own examples show, as likely to have been made by non-Westerners as by those whose ancestors created the Empire and its orientalist justifications. Secondly, to the extent that members of the non-Muslim public read points of conflict as 'Islamic' they are usually doing no more than accepting the claims of the Muslim side of the argument. They may well be as ill-informed about Muslims as the Muslim respondent to the IHRC survey who asked why terrorist policing was directed at Muslims and not at Irish Republicans was about the history of British anti-terror legislation, but they are not making something out of nothing.

However, Zubaida is right that 'if Muslims are to be seen as "normal" fellow citizens, with diverse social and cultural characteristics which are unrelated to religious identity or adherence', liberals and democrats have to question this 'totalising concept of Muslims'. Such questioning is certainly not helped by our right-wing press's fondness for hyping every trivial disagreement about how to handle some religious sensitivity into evidence of imminent 'dhimmitude' (to use the old Ottoman empire term for a Muslim state's treatment of religious minorities). Nor is it aided by the media's treating all demographic data as raw material for predicting the year that Muslims form a majority of the population.

Relations between Britain's Muslim minorities and the wider society are delicately poised. Given that there are well-funded and well-organised Islamist groups that work to increase Muslim disaffection, increased alienation is a possibility if influential actors such as the mass media and the government's agencies do not do more to damp down anti-Muslim prejudice. That the political editor of the *Daily Telegraph* was willing to document and denounce violence against Muslim targets is as much a hopeful sign as the vitriolic responses from parts of his readership is a cause for concern.[70] In the end, I suspect that the future tenor of Muslim politics in Britain will depend as much on what happens in North Africa, the Middle East and South Asia as on anything domestic. The social, economic and political health of Egypt, Tunisia, Lebanon, Syria, Jordan, Libya, Pakistan and Bangladesh may not be 'causes' of British Muslim alienation in any mechanical or immediate sense but the well-being of Muslim societies is, in the ideological and romantic sense, a cause to which Muslims in Britain can become more or less attached. If most or even just some of those countries can replace their sclerotic and corrupt dictatorships by regimes sufficiently democratic to enjoy popular confidence and sufficiently competent to ensure stability and the possibility of economic growth, a major encouragement to domestic extremism will be reduced. If democratisation fails and if economies do not grow sufficiently quickly to absorb the youthful population, migration to Europe will increase rapidly and, irrespective of their role, Western powers will be blamed for those failures.

10 The public place of religion

Introduction

As the Christian churches in the United Kingdom have declined in size, they have also declined in power. They can no longer plausibly command the population at large and indeed have difficulty exercising discipline over their own members. Although Bryan Wilson often pointed to a decline in such indices of personal religiosity as church attendance and church membership as evidence of secularisation, he actually defined it in terms of influence: as the decreasing social significance of religion.[1] One important element of that loss of significance is the retreat of religion from the public sphere. The details differ interestingly from country to country but most modern democracies have evolved a distinction between the private and public worlds. Two things go hand-in-hand. We have become increasingly tolerant of religious deviation in the private sphere, as a personal preference. Now that paganism has been recognised by the armed forces as a legitimate religion, we have to conclude that the phrase 'religious deviation' is passé. At the same time, we have come to expect the public sphere to be largely secular. Many faith-based choices that were commonplace 200 years ago would now be regarded as unacceptable discrimination.

There are two analytically separable elements to religion's loss of public presence: the loss of social functions and the loss of political power. A common characteristic of modernisation is the expansion of the state's activities in important social fields such as health care, social welfare and education. This expansion has generally been secular, either because churches have been unable to expand such provision or because religious diversity prevented any one church being able to act as a viable and legitimate conduit for state-funded expansion. Where religious organisations have continued to provide social functions such as education and nursing care, the specifically religious content has generally diminished so that the education provided by Catholic and Anglican schools in Britain, for example, differs little from that provided by state outlets. We give money to the Salvation Army to provide social care for the homeless; we do not expect that money to be used to evangelise either the general public or the Salvation Army's homeless clients.

The second common characteristic of modernisation is the expansion of universal rights or, to put it the other way round, rights are no longer allocated on the basis of religious identity. Governments of modern liberal democracies may encourage churches as important actors in civil society but churches generally exercise very little political power. Furthermore, where religious organisations retain public influence, their officials are usually conscious of the anachronistic nature of their position and go out of their way to present their actions as serving universal goods. The Church of England still has 26 seats in the House of Lords for its bishops, a privilege that will end when the currently partial reform of the second chamber is completed. Insofar as that is defended, which is not much, it is with the claim that the bishops promote the spiritual interests of people of all faith and none. No bishop would now assert that the Church of England deserves a place in our legislature because it is the sole representative of the Creator in this kingdom.

In brief, modernisation has generally been accompanied by the *privatisation* of religion. It is worth adding, because it is relevant to our guesses about how or why the process might be reversed, that the privatisation of religion was not always a result of secularist animus towards religion. Scholars such as Talal Asad, who wish to argue that contemporary church–state relations are a product of conscious secularism, base their conclusions on too selective a history of the current public–private divide. They concentrate on the confrontations between church and progressive forces in Catholic countries and overlook the conflict between state church and dissenting sects in Protestant settings.[2] The absence of a state church in the USA, for example, owes very little to the work of secularists and far more to the fact that the early colonies differed in their dominant churches. Had the founding fathers wished a national church, they would not have been able to agree a candidate. Similarly in the UK the gradual loss of power and influence by the state churches was hastened by there being two different state churches and a great deal of religious dissent. The liberal case for a secular state tended to follow, rather than precede, the failure of theocratic imposition. Or, to be more precise, although there had long been the odd liberal voice arguing for toleration, it was only when competing religious groups accepted that none could dominate, and hence that their interests would be best served by the removal of religious impositions, that a largely secular state became accepted as most people's second preference.

If religious pluralism is one driver of a secular public sphere, the other (which church leaders conveniently neglect to mention when they complain about their current impotence) is the shrinking pool of the faithful. Even the once-hegemonic churches can appreciate that their claims to power cannot not be sustained now that they have been abandoned by the majority of the population.

The de-privatisation of religion

Almost all indices of involvement in organised religion have declined across Europe since Wilson published his classic statement of the secularisation paradigm *Religion in Secular Society* in 1966.[3] And they are now showing decline in the USA, where the consensus is that a figure of around 20 per cent is a more accurate representation of the proportion of the population that regularly attends church than the 40 per cent that was regularly reported in the 1980s. Yet as secularisation has proceeded apace, the sociological secularisation paradigm has been increasingly criticised by sociologists of religion.[4] Some of that criticism has been based on caricatures of what the secularisation paradigm requires. More sensible attempts at refutation have concentrated on evidence for an enduring interest in religion (or spirituality) despite the decline of the churches. For example, Davie has argued that Britons are 'believing but not belonging', and Heelas and Woodhead have claimed that holistic spirituality is taking the place of religion.[5] However, until recently most critics of the secularisation paradigm – Peter Berger and Rodney Stark, for example – have accepted the general thrust of the privatisation observation.[6]

However, this too is now being questioned. One text that is frequently cited in the argument is Jose Casanova's *Public Religions in the Modern World*, which brought together the rise of Islamic fundamentalism and Catholic liberation theology to make the case that since the 1980s religion has been reasserting a public presence.[7] One can question the relevance of Islamic fundamentalism to this debate. Most Muslim countries were never secular in terms of popular religiosity or the social functions of religious institutions. Such privatisation of religion as they displayed was the result of imposition by an unrepresentative elite pursuing modernisation by imitating those elements of Western secularity that suited their political strategies. More to the point is Casanova's argument that since the Catholic Church ceased to claim unique theocratic authority it has been effective in the public sphere as a representative of general human rights. But as Casanova's point can readily be rephrased as saying that religious organisations can be effective in the public sphere when they play by secular rules, that seems to confirm, rather than refute, the privatisation point.[8]

There are two further reasons to see (or anticipate) de-privatisation: religious demography and religious migration. Eric Kaufmann, and Pippa Norris and Ronald Inglehart have suggested one way in which secularisation may be self-defeating.[9] In Europe (for Kaufmann) and globally (for Norris and Inglehart) an important demographic change is in train: religiously liberal and secular families generally have fewer children than conservatively religious families. Hence the number of those who hold that religious beliefs and values should permeate all of life, rather than be confined to the domestic sphere, is growing relative to the number of those who are comfortable with the privatisation of religion. As I have argued elsewhere, this case depends on demographic projections that are at the extreme end of what is likely and on a genetic view of religion.[10] All panda cubs become pandas but not all children born to Catholic parents become or remain Catholics. Were religious cultures passed from one generation to the next intact, as Kaufmann supposes, we would be as religious as were our great grandparents. We are patently not.

The second putative cause of de-privatisation is immigration. Kaufmann and much of Western Europe's right-wing press suggest that the migration to the West of significant numbers of Muslims challenges the secularist accommodation that Western societies have evolved over the last hundred years. Conservative Muslims turn the logic of liberal democracy against the culture it has produced by claiming the freedom, for example, to maintain inequitable gender roles, to preserve their beliefs from public ridicule or criticism, and to make public displays of their faith. Of itself the movement of people from conservative religious cultures in the global South and East to the West will not reverse secularisation: the numbers are too small. Hence the importance of the next part of the equation: the assertiveness of conservative Muslims will encourage Christians to become correspondingly demanding.

It is certainly the case that some British church leaders have taken to complaining that the government is overly respectful of Muslim concerns and indifferent to Christian ones. The following is a selection of British stories from 2009: a Christian Registrar refused to administer the civil partnership ceremonies for gay couples; a Christian bus driver refused to drive a bus that displayed an advert for agnosticism; an air hostess defied her airlines injunction against the wearing of conspicuous jewellery in order to display a crucifix; and a Christian social worker refused to vet gay couples for adoption. As Steve Kettell has pointed out, Christian church leaders have two very different stories about the public sphere.[11] They disavow any interest in theocracy and claim they want no more than a voice proportionate to their numbers in the general population (though when setting a figure on that voice they do prefer the 71 per cent who ticked the Christian box in the 2001 census to the less than 10 per cent who regularly attend church services). Yet when they have lost some issue on numbers, they claim the right to ignore the result on the grounds of religious privilege. For example, in 2010 the Pope criticised the British government's equality legislation on the grounds that his God said Christians should discriminate against homosexuals.[12]

Before we take such special pleading as representing a large body of popular Christian grievance, we should note two things. First, much of the appearance of a groundswell of complaint comes from right-wing media outlets that uncritically report false stories and inflate true stories of Muslim 'aggression' and from a small number of campaigning organisations that fund court cases. That is, there is obvious top-down inflation. Second, as we saw in the previous chapter, the failure of the Christian Party and the Christian People's Alliance to attract more than 100 or so voters in any constituency suggests a lack of popular support for the assertion that Britain is close to being over-run by Muslims. To get a clearer sense of public attitudes (and how they may have changed) we need independent evidence.

Kaufmann's prediction of a conservative Christian backlash is obviously shared by some (but not all) conservative Christians. They hope that Christianity will regain influence as atheists and marginally Christian people react to Islamic assertiveness by becoming believers or becoming more active in their faith. As yet there is no evidence of such a revival in the ranks of the Godly but there is no doubt that religion has become contentious and newsworthy in a way that has not been the case in most of Western Europe since the nineteenth century.

Polarisation?

A Dutch study of attitudes towards the public place of religion has some bearing on these related questions. Although Achterberg *et al.* do not claim to identify a Christian revival, they find an interesting pattern in recurrent international survey data. The Christian desire for religion to have a greater public role is highest in countries where Christians are relatively least numerous. Furthermore, data covering the period 1970 to 1996 suggest that the decline in the number of Christians in the Netherlands has coincided with 'a strengthening of the call for public religion among the remaining faithful' and with 'increased polarisation about this with the nonreligious'.[13]

That polarisation suggests an alternative to de-privatisation. It is always possible that religion becoming contentious may encourage the faithful to become more assertive and may even shift a few marginal Christians into the committed Christian camp, but it seems unlikely that any significant number of people who were not socialised into Christian beliefs and practice in childhood and hence who do not share a Christian perspective on public affairs will react to Islamic assertiveness by espousing a faith for which they have previously shown no interest or inclination. Instead of distinguishing between good and bad religion, it seems more likely that they will take the view that any religion taken too seriously is a threat to public order and become consciously committed to the public–private divide. It may well be, as Achterberg *et al.* suggest, that an increasing proportion of the diminishing number of Christians will wish to cancel 'the secularist truce' with its 'anything in private and very little in public' solution to diversity but the unaligned majority of the population may become increasingly committed to the privatisation of religion.

It is worth stressing that attitudes do not always translate into outcomes. People who in theory favour religion enjoying greater public prominence or social power may prefer other things more. That is, this particular desire may be less salient than competing ones. Second, those who welcome de-privatisation may be outnumbered by those who wish to see the privatisation of religion strengthened. Third, numbers may not settle the outcome. As with such other contentious issues as the death penalty, the will of a majority or a plurality may be over-ruled by the political elites. Nonetheless, as change in the status quo is very unlikely unless there is a considerable groundswell of public opinion behind it, it is worth exploring public attitudes.

The public profile of religion in the United Kingdom

Detailed tests of Davie's assertion that the British are 'believing but not belonging' have failed to find any support.[14] A more accurate assessment would be that the majority of Britons lack a personal faith but have a general sympathy for the idea of religion when it is seen as a source of comfort for the bereaved and as a source of moral values. This seems the best explanation of the fact that significant numbers of British people who are not themselves religious seem happy for religion to enjoy a presence not merited by its popularity. For example, people who never watch religious programmes on television nonetheless think that television licence holders should continue to be legally obliged to make and air such programmes.[15] Significant numbers of people who say they do not believe in God nonetheless think that schools should have daily prayers.[16] However, such altruistic support for religion disappears when respondents consider being constrained by the religiously-inspired values of others. The 2001 Scottish Attitudes survey (SSAS) asked for responses to the proposition that it was 'right for religious leaders to speak out on ...' and offered five options. As can be seen from Table 10.1 Scots were quite happy for religious leaders to opine on grand abstractions but as matters become more personal going down the options, the proportion in favour declines. Remarkably, when we divided the sample into those with no religious background or who had never attended church regularly, those who had once attended regularly but since stopped, and those who attended regularly, we found that the rank ordering was the same. For all three groups the more personal the item, the less likely they are to favour religious instruction.[17]

It would be convenient to have data from the nineteenth century, when the major changes that we gloss as the privatisation of religion began in Britain, but the earliest reliable surveys come from the post-war period. In 1947 Mass Observation summarised British attitudes to religion gleaned from a detailed sample survey of residents in a London suburb ($n=500$) augmented by the large body of material collected from regular Mass Observation respondents. The report found that:

> broad and uninterested tolerance of religion is common – much more so than hostile feelings.... Many people look upon religion as something quite harmless and purely personal – an innocuous hobby, like collecting stamps. One of the results of this attitude is that these same people often feel that

Table 10.1 Acceptability of religious leaders speaking out and religious practice, 2001

Per cent who think it is right* for religious leaders to speak out on ...	No religious background or never regularly attended	Stopped attending	Regularly attends
World poverty	76	85	91
Environment	61	66	73
Education	45	47	72
Abortion	32	35	62
Sexual behaviour	30	35	58
Sample size (min/max)	503/510	502/507	328/330

*The options were, it is 'Generally right', 'Generally wrong', or 'Can't choose'.

religion is exceeding its legitimate grounds if it 'interferes' with more practical matters. Religion to them is all right in its place, but shouldn't get involved in everyday affairs outside the private life of believers.[18]

The way the research is analysed and reported does not allow us to put a percentage on the proportion of respondents whose views are thus summarised but it seems a plausible account of the typical British attitude to religion in the 1940s.

Early Gallup polls contain a few relevant items. In 1956 Gallup asked 'should prominent members of the Church, like the Archbishop of Canterbury, take part in political matters or should they keep right out of politics?' The first option – 'should take part' – was preferred by 18 per cent, 10 per cent didn't know and 72 per cent chose 'should keep right out'.[19] A slight change of wording the following year – 'should the Church keep out of political matters or should they [sic] express their views on day-to-day social and political questions?' – softened the difference. 'Express views' was chosen by 36 per cent and 'Keep out' was chosen by 53 per cent. That change may be explained by the rewording from 'political matters' to 'social and political questions'; the former sounds like party politics while the latter sounds more like general virtues. It may also be explained by the omission of reference to the Archbishop of Canterbury, removing the reason that most Nonconformists would object to the proposition. The idea that church leaders should seek to shape public opinion became even more popular when all mention of politics was dropped and a contrast drawn with introversion. A 1963 poll asked 'should the churches be mainly concerned with the spiritual life of the individual or should they express their views on day-to-day social questions?' One-third of respondents thought the churches should confine themselves to the spiritual life; two-thirds thought they should express views on social issues.[20]

Just these few polls raise important methodological issues. First, it is obviously desirable to be able to distinguish the views of religious and non-religious people: a consideration that was absent from early polls. Second, it is obviously desirable either for questions to focus on general principles (rather than on the possible interventions of specific church leaders) or for there to be a battery of questions about a variety of church leaders that allow us to distinguish between being generally in favour of religion being more publicly prominent and being in favour of one's own religion being imposed on others. Gallup in 1956 should have realised that mentioning the Archbishop of Canterbury might polarise Anglicans and Nonconformists. The designer of the 2010 ComRes poll should have appreciated that, in a largely Protestant country, the proposition 'the Pope and other religious leaders have a responsibility to speak out on political issues they are concerned about' might have elicited very different responses had the first four words been omitted.[21]

Fifty years after those first Gallup polls, the context in which we form our attitudes to the public position of religion is very different. First, Britain has become markedly more secular. On every measure, there are few fewer religious people in Britain now than there were in the 1960s. Second, the growth of

Hindu, Sikh and Muslim minorities has changed what respondents can imagine when considering the public presence of religion. In the 1950s and 1960s, the religion that could be private or public was the respondent's actual or heritage faith or something like it. Baptists might not like the idea of the Church of England being more influential but the differences in what each would impose were slight. In 2010 what any respondent can imagine being imposed is considerably more exotic: the ritual slaughter of all food animals or a ban on beef or pork, for example. Third, the change in social and sexual mores since the late 1960s makes it likely that more people will see public religion as a challenge to their preferences. Although the attitudes of the major Christian churches have become more liberal, they still contain powerful voices that, on such issues as the propriety of sex outside the confines of marriage, contraception, abortion, divorce, and homosexuality, promote views greatly at odds with those of large parts of the population.

That the proper place of religion has become controversial since 1989 (to take the Rushdie Fatwa as our somewhat arbitrarily-selected starting point) explains why there have since been a great many opinion polls on the subject. Most have technical weaknesses and none allows a detailed exploration of correlations between respondent characteristics and stated attitudes, but it is worth noting the most consistent observations. First, there is still a strong preference in favour of religious leaders speaking out 'on political issues they are concerned about', though we cannot know if this reflects likely agreement with church views or a principled commitment to free speech.[22] Second, there seems little consistent patterning by age, gender, or class in such responses. Third, where we do find what seems to be a clear divide, it is in questions that directly address the public merits of religion. For example, a 2009 poll asked for reaction to the proposition that 'Religion has an important part to play in public life'. Though age, class, gender and regional differences were small, there was a considerable gulf between the responses of those who claimed a religious identity and those who said they had no religion. The half of the sample who identified as Christians divided 73 to 23 per cent in favour of the proposition. Those who claimed no faith divided 36 per cent in favour and 60 per cent against.[23] Finally we can note the responses to a refreshingly blunt question in a 2007 poll. Respondents were asked 'Do you regard the influence of religion on this country as beneficial, harmful or neither?' Only 17 per cent thought it beneficial, 27 per cent thought 'neither' and 42 per cent thought it harmful. The remaining 14 per cent couldn't choose among the three options.[24]

British social attitudes surveys, 1998 and 2008

To identify public attitudes to the influence of religion and any significant change in those attitudes, we need a large survey data set that contains the same questions at two points in time. The 1998 British Social Attitudes survey (hereafter BSA) contained a full module of questions on religion, as did the 2008 survey. The six questions relating to religion, politics and public life detailed in

Table 10.2 overlap in the two datasets. Detailed statistical testing shows that responses to the six items cohere sufficiently for them to be used to construct a single scale.[25] Responses to each item are scored from 1 to 5. For brevity's sake, I will call scores above the mid-point 'pro public religion' or PPR and those below it 'anti public religion' or APR.

Before we begin the detailed statistical analysis, it is worth looking at the first two items on their own. Table 10.3 shows two things very clearly. First, in both 1998 and 2008 a large majority of respondents were on the APR side. Three-quarters thought religious leaders should not try to influence voting and two-thirds thought that religious leaders should not influence government decisions. That is, at least these elements of the privatisation of religion were popular. Second, when we compare the 2008 responses with those of 1998, we find a clear decline in the PPR position and an increase in the APR view. Because the BSA is a sample survey rather than a panel survey, we are not looking at the same people twice; we are looking at two separate bodies of people, each of whom is as representative of the population as such survey management can ensure. So we cannot say that people have changed their minds to become more anti public religion but we can say the typical Briton in 2008 was less sympathetic to religious leaders being influential than the corresponding abstraction for 1998.

The 2008 BSA contained one item that was not used in 1998, but is nonetheless sufficiently interesting to be worth reporting. It asked, 'If more of our elected officials were deeply religious, do you think the laws and policy decisions they make would be ...?' and offered 'Probably worse', 'Probably better' or 'Neither' as possible responses. Twenty-nine per cent of the respondents chose 'Neither' or did not choose. Almost twice as many people thought decisions would be worse (45 per cent) than thought they would be better (26 per cent).

In Table 10.4 we can now see the results of the analysis of the mean scores of different groupings of respondents on the attitude scale, which was constructed from the six items listed in Table 10.2. The first and most telling observation from both the 1998 and 2008 survey data is that the mean score for the entire sample is less than the neutral or indifferent midpoint score of 3. That is, the general population was APR in both 1998 and in 2008. Crucially, although mean

Table 10.2 Religion, politics and public life in Britain (scale construction), BSA 2008 and 1998.

---

a. Religious leaders should not try to influence how people vote in elections
b. Religious leaders should not try to influence government decisions
c. Looking around the world, religions bring more conflict than peace
d. People with very strong religious beliefs are often too intolerant of others
e. How much confidence do you have in churches and religious organisations?
f. Do you think that churches and religious organisations in this country have too much power or too little power?

Table 10.3 The influence of religious leaders, BSA 1998 and 2008

Column percentages	(I) Religious leaders should not try to influence how people vote ...		(II) Religious leaders should not try to influence government decisions ...	
	1998 (%)	2008 (%)	1998 (%)	2008 (%)
Strongly agree/agree	73	76	65	69
Neither/undecided	12	12	14	17
Disagree/strongly disagree	15	12	21	15
Total	100	100	100	100
n =	793	1,952	791	1,930

scores are significantly higher for those people who say they attend services on a weekly basis or more often, they are still less than 3. That is, even the most religious bloc in the sample does not favour the de-privatisation of religion.

Second, scores on the attitude scale have remained static or, in the case of the middle group who attend worship monthly but not weekly, declined slightly. There is no evidence here that the increased notoriety of religion in the decade between 1998 and 2008 has produced any increase in the desire to see religion occupy a more prominent place in politics and public life, even among those who regularly go to services.

Although I will not report the detailed statistics here, the above conclusions were confirmed by multivariate analysis with the attitude scale from Table 10.2 as the dependent variable in a regression model that controlled for the gender, age-group and education level of respondents, took into account people's current religion as non-Christians and Christians (so as to allow for a shift in the relative size of those two groupings over the decade), and then gauged the relative effects of participation in organised religion on people's attitudes.

Table 10.4 Participation in organised religion and PPR–APR attitudes, BSA 1998 and 2008

Mean scores (1 → 5)	6-item scale 'Religion, politics and public life'	
	1998	2008
Not religious/never attend	2.1	2.1
Less often than monthly	2.4	2.4
Monthly but not weekly	2.6	2.5
Weekly or more often	2.9	2.9
Total	2.3	2.2
n =	763	1855
ANOVA F-test	54.31	113.26
p-value	<0.01	<0.01

In summary, analysis of the survey data from the 1998 and 2008 BSA surveys shows that most Britons were opposed to religion enjoying greater public prominence or influence. There was relatively little change over the decade. Such change as could be discerned was in the anti public religion direction.

Conclusion

The period between 1998 and 2008 saw the destruction of the World Trade Center in New York, the Iraq and Afghanistan wars, and the London Underground bombings. It also saw a large number of small disputes about the proper place of religion and increasing calls from church leaders for the government's attempts to placate the supposedly alienated Muslim minority to be matched by corresponding attention to Christian preferences. If there were going to be any significant corresponding change in attitudes towards the privatisation of religion, we would expect to see signs of it in the scale we constructed from BSA data in 1998 and 2008. We didn't. The British public is happy with the privatisation of religion.

These data, added to everything in the preceding chapters, suggest that talk of religious resurgence or post-secular society is merely academic novelty-seeking: the intellectual equivalent of the fashion rule that dictates perpetual revision. The unglamorous truth is that the secular trends we have seen through the twentieth century continue. As documented in the first chapter, migration has seen a change in the religious composition of the United Kingdom but it has not seen any increase in the power, persuasiveness or popularity of religion.

Notes

1 British Gods

1 *Reading Weekend Post*, 22 November 1996.
2 For general histories of the Christian Church in the British Isles pre-Reformation, see C. Harper-Bill, *The Pre-Reformation Church in England, 1400–1530*. London: Longman, 1996; J. E. A. Dawson, *Scotland Re-formed, 1488–1587*. Edinburgh: Edinburgh University Press, 2007; J. Watt, *The Church in Medieval Ireland*. Dublin: University College Dublin Press, 1998; D. Petts, *The Early Medieval Church in Wales*. Stroud: History Press, 2009.
3 For general histories of the Reformation in the British Isles, see P. Marshall, *Reformation England 1480–1642*. London: Hodder, 2003; F. Heal, *The Reformation in Britain and Ireland*. Oxford: Oxford University Press, 2005; D. MacCulloch, *The Later Reformation in England, 1547–1603*. London: Palgrave Macmillan, 2000; D. H. Fleming, *The Reformation in Scotland: Causes, Characteristics, Consequences*. Boston: Adamant Media, 2005; and G. Williams, *Renewal and Reformation: Wales c.1415–1642*. Oxford: Oxford University Press, 1993.
4 M. Lessnoff, 'Protestant ethic and profit motive in the Weber Thesis', *International Journal of Sociology and Social Policy*, 1 (1981), 5.
5 D. Martin, *On Secularization: Towards a Revised General Theory*. Aldershot: Ashgate, 2005.
6 J. Davies, *A History of Wales*. London: Penguin, 2007.
7 M. Lynch, *Scotland: a New History*. London: Pimlico, 1992.
8 E. Duffy, *The Stripping of the Altars: Traditional Religion in England, 1400–1580*. New Haven: Yale University Press, 2005.
9 The Solemn League and Covenant of 1643 was intended to bind Scots Presbyterians and English Independents against Popery. The state would support the true church and the church would support the state. The Covenanters were radical Scots who thought that the Church of Scotland was insufficiently reformed to merit their support. See W. Sime, *A History of the Covenanters in Scotland*. Edinburgh: Waugh and Innes, 1830.
10 www.lewrockwell.com/orig4/vance3.html. Accessed 2 January 2011.
11 For details of the changes in funding of the Church of Scotland, see J. N. Wolfe and M. Pickford, *The Church of Scotland: an Economic Survey*. London: Geoffrey Chapman, 1980. For the Church of England, see E. J. Evans, *Contentious Tithe: Tithe Problem and English Agriculture, 1750–1850*. London: Routledge and Kegan Paul, 1976.
12 J. Wolffe, *God and Greater Britain: Religion and National Life in Britain and Ireland 1843–1945*. London: Routledge.
13 E. F. Benson, *As We Were*. Harmondsworth, Middlesex: Penguin, 1938, 93–4.
14 These figures have been calculated from the data in P. Brierley, 'Religion', in A. H. Halsey and J. Webb, *Twentieth-Century British Social Trends*. London: Macmillan, 2000, 650–74.

15 W. K. Kay, *Pentecostals in Britain*. Carlisle: Paternoster Publishing, 2000, 1–36.
16 S. Bruce, *Secularization*. Oxford: Oxford University Press, 2011.
17 S. Bruce and A. Glendinning, 'When was secularization? Dating the decline of the British churches and locating its cause', *British Journal of Sociology*, 61 (1): 107–26.
18 S. Bruce, 'A sociology classic revisited: religion in Banbury', *Sociological Review*, 59 (2012): 201–22.
19 M. P. Hornsby-Smith, *Roman Catholics in England: Studies in Social Structure Since the Second World War*. Cambridge: Cambridge University Press, 1987; M. P. Hornsby-Smith (ed.), *Catholics in England 1950–2000*. London: Cassell, 1999.
20 T. Endelman, *The Jews of Britain, 1656 to 2000*. Berkeley: University of California Press, 2002.
21 On Muslims, see P. Hopkins and R. Gale (eds), *Muslims in Britain: Race, Place and Identities*. Edinburgh: Edinburgh University Press, 2009. On Hindus, see S. Vertovec, *The Hindu Diaspora: Comparative Patterns*. London: Routledge, 2000.
22 A, Bharati, *The Asians in East Africa: Jaihind and Uhuru*. Chicago: Nelson-Hall, 1972; J. Mattausch, 'From subjects to citizens: British "East African Asians"', *Journal of Ethnic and Migration Studies*, 24 (1998), 121–41.
23 P. Bachu, *Twice Migrants: East Africa Sikh Settlers in Britain*. London: Tavistock, 1985.
24 The 2010 ONS Integrated Household Survey (*n*=442,266) showed the Muslim population to have grown to 4.2 per cent; www.statistics.gov.uk/pdfdir/ihs0910.pdf. Accessed November 2010.
25 Home Office Citizenship Survey 2005, cited in R. Gale and P. Hopkins, 'Introduction', in P. Hopkins and R. Gale (eds), *Muslims in Britain: Race, Place and Identities*. Edinburgh: Edinburgh University Press, 2009, 10.
26 NOP Poll, 'British Muslims'; http://ukpollingreport.co.uk/blog/archives/291.
27 http://britishbornmuslims.wordpress.com/british-muslim-poll/.
28 P. Brierley (ed.), *Religious Trends 5*. London: Christian Research, 2005, table 2.21.
29 D. Voas, 'Intermarriage and the demography of secularization', *British Journal of Sociology*, 54 (2003): 83–108.
30 ONS www.statistics.gov.uk/STATBASE/Product.asp?vlnk=14275.
31 The very many arguments routinely deployed against this proposition (such as the claim that forms of alternative spirituality are filling the gaps left by the decline of the churches) are discussed at length and evaluated in Bruce, *Secularization*.

2 The politics of religion

1 S. Bruce, *Conservative Protestant Politics*. Oxford: Oxford University Press, 1998, Chapter 2.
2 Campbell explains that quote and his views of religion in an interview with Catherine Devaney in *Scotland on Sunday*, 9 November 2008.
3 P. Harris, 'Fight the good fight: Blair v Hitchens', *Observer*, 28 November 2010.
4 D. Hempton, *Religion and Political Culture in Britain and Ireland: From the Glorious Revolution to the Decline of Religion*. Cambridge: Cambridge University Press, 1996.
5 E. McFarland, *Protestants First: Orangeism in Nineteenth Century Scotland*. Edinburgh: Edinburgh University Press, 1990; D. MacRaild, *Culture, Conflict and Migration: The Irish in Victorian Cumbria*. Liverpool: Liverpool University Press, 1998.
6 J. Wolffe, *God and Greater Britain: Religion and National Life in Britain and Ireland 1843–1945*. London: Routledge, 1994.
7 J. H. Robb, *The Primrose League, 1883–1906*. Columbia University unpublished PhD thesis, 1942.
8 A. Seldon and P. Snowdon, *The Conservative Party*. Stroud: Sutton Publishing, 2004, 211.

9 'Bonar Law', The Freedom Party, at www.freedompartyuk.net/public/standardbearers/law.html. Accessed 2 January 2011.

10 G. Smith, 'Margaret Thatcher's Christian faith: A case study in political theology', *Journal of Religious Ethics*, 35 (2007), 233–57, argues that Thatcher had an active Christian faith that shaped her politics. What he actually shows is that her politics were informed by a series of secular attitudes that she inherited from her nonconformist father.

11 Speech to the Conservative Group for Europe, 22 April 1993. A 'pools filler' is not someone who fills swimming pools. It is someone who every week completes football pools coupons: a form of gambling, popular with the working class for most of the twentieth century, in which one tries to predict the outcome of every game in the football league. The very few who get them all right win the bulk of the small fee paid by every entrant. The Orwell quote is from *The Lion and The Unicorn*. London: Searchlight Books, 1941.

12 I. Fallon, *Billionaire: The Life and Times of Sir James Goldsmith*. New York: Little Brown and Co. 1992.

13 S. Bruce, *No Pope of Rome: Militant Protestantism in Modern Scotland*. Edinburgh: Mainstream, 1984; M. Rosie, *The Sectarian Myth in Scotland: Of Bitter Memory and Bigotry*. London: Palgrave Macmillan, 2004.

14 BNP manifesto, local government elections, 2003.

15 D. Williams, 'the BNP and Christianity', *Searchlight*, July 2006.

16 G. Walker, *A History of the Ulster Unionist Party: Protest, Pragmatism and Pessimism*. Manchester: Manchester University Press, 2003.

17 Until the 1990s, when the Conservative party allowed branches in Northern Ireland to affiliate, British parties refused to recruit in the province. Ulster Unionist MPs traditionally took the Tory whip at Westminster and the Alliance party was associated with the Liberal Democrats. It is eternally to the shame of the Labour party that in the 1970s it advised members who moved to Northern Ireland to join the Social Democratic and Labour party, a Catholic nationalist organisation, rather than the genuinely non-sectarian Northern Ireland Labour party, which folded in 1987.

18 D. Torrance, 'Letters reveal SNP crisis over "bigoted" president's anti-Catholic diatribes', *The Times*, 11 September 2010.

19 C. A. Davies, *Welsh Nationalism in the Twentieth Century: The Ethnic Option and the Modern State*. Westport, CT: Greenwood Press, 1989; Laura McAllister, *Plaid Cymru: The Emergence of a Political Party*. Bridgend: Seren, 2001.

20 S. Bruce, *Paisley: Religion and Politics in Northern Ireland*. Oxford: Oxford University Press, 2007, 193–201.

21 For an excellent general review of Catholic politics, see J. H. Whyte, *Catholics in Western Democracies*. Dublin: Gill and Macmillan, 1981.

22 J. Hannan, *The Life of John Wheatley*. London: Spokesman Books, 1988; Iain McLean, *The Legend of Red Clydeside*. Edinburgh: John Donald, 2000.

23 H. Ansari, *Muslims in Britain*. London: Minority Rights Group International, 2002, 19.

24 'Muslims favour Labour in elections, says poll', at www.muslimvote.org.uk/index.php?option=com_content&view=article&id=148:muslims-favour-labour-in-elections-says-poll&catid=59:election-news&Itemid=194. Accessed 3 March 2011.

25 Ansari, *Muslims*, 19. One reason for the broadening of religio-ethnic minority party support is that Hindus and Sikhs have become resentful of the attention which the Labour government has paid to Muslims; S. Meghani, 'Why Labour is losing the Hindu vote', *Labour Uncut*, 3 August 2010.

26 A. Heath, S. Fisher, G. Rosenblatt, D. Sanders and M. Sobolewska, 'Ethnic heterogeneity in the social bases of voting in the 2010 general election', unpublished paper.

27 D. W. Bebbington, 'Nonconformity and electoral sociology, 1867–1918', *Historical Journal*, 27 (1984), 636.

28 J. Howard, *A History of Wesleyan Methodism in Staithes*, Guisborough, 1967, 17.

29 K. D. Wald, *Crosses on the Ballot: Patterns of British Voter Alignment Since 1885*. Princeton, NJ: Princeton University Press, 1983.

30 Speech at Queen's Hall, London, July 1917. The daughter of a Tory peer, Royden was a suffragette and one of the first advocates of the ordination of women in the Church of England.

31 R. Worchester and R. Mortimore, 'The Catholic vote in Britain helped carry Blair to victory', from www.ipsos-mori.com/newsevents/ca/247/The-Catholic-Vote-In-Britain-Helped-Carry-Blair-To-Victory.aspx. Accessed January 2011.

32 IPSOS-MORI, 'Voting intention by religion, 1992–2005', www.ipsos-mori.com/researchpublications/researcharchive/poll.aspx?oItemId=2370&view=wide&view=print. Accessed January 2011. On Catholic voting, see D. Seawright, 'A confessional cleavage resurrected? The denominational vote in Britain', in D. Broughton and H.-M. ten Napel (eds), *Religion and Mass Electoral Behaviour in Europe*. London: Routledge, 2000, 45–61.

33 B. Clements, 'Religious affiliation and political attitudes: findings from the British Election Study 2009/10', *British Religion in Numbers* website; www.brin.ac.uk/news/?p=481. Accessed 5 November 2010.

34 L. A. Kotler-Berkowitz, 'Religion and voting behaviour in Great Britain: a reassessment', *British Journal of Political Science*, 31 (2001), 552. His case for the continued salience of religion is slightly exaggerated by treating the patterned preferences of non-religious people as 'religious' effects.

35 S. McAndrew, 'Religious faith and contemporary attitudes', in A. Park, J. Curtice, K. Thomson, E. Clery and S. Butt (eds), *British Social Attitudes: the 26th Report*. London: Sage, 2010, 87–113.

36 McAndrew, 'Religious faith', 100.

37 *The Boys Of Fairhill*, 1977. Mulligan LUN 014 LP.

38 K. Medhurst and G. Moyser, *Church and Politics in a Secular Age*. Oxford: Clarendon Press, 1988.

39 For details, see K. M. Wolfe, *The Churches and the British Broadcasting Corporation 1922–1956. The Politics of Broadcast Religion*. London: SCM Press, 1980.

40 H. Clark, *The Church under Thatcher*, SPCK, London, 1993.

41 S. Silvestri, 'Public policies towards Muslims and the institutionalization of "moderate Islam" in Europe', in A. Triandafyllidou (ed.), *Muslims in 21st Century Europe*. London: Routledge, 2010, 47.

42 John Madeley takes a different view: J. Madeley, 'European liberal democracy and the principle of state religious neutrality', in J. Madeley and Z. Enyedi, *Church and State in Contemporary Europe*. London: Frank Cass, 2003.

3 Religion and violence in Northern Ireland

1 G. Walker, *A History of the Ulster Unionist Party: Protest, Pragmatism and Pessimism*. Manchester: Manchester University Press, 2004.

2 For a good brief history of Northern Ireland, see M. Mulholland, *Northern Ireland: A Very Short Introduction*. Oxford: Oxford University Press, 2003. For the Troubles see D. McKittrick and D. McVea, *Making Sense of the Troubles*. London, Penguin, 2001.

3 A. Edwards, *The Northern Ireland Troubles*. Oxford: Osprey, 2011.

4 T. O'Neill, *The Autobiography of Terence O'Neill*. London: Hart-Davis, 1972.

5 D. McKittrick, S, Kelters, B. Feeney and C. Thornton, *Lost Lives: The Stories of the Men, Women and Children Who Died as a Result of the Northern Ireland Troubles*. Edinburgh: Mainstream 2004.

6 S. Bruce, *Paisley: Religion and Politics in Northern Ireland*. Oxford: Oxford University Press, 2007.

7 http://en.wikipedia.org/wiki/Constitution_of_Ireland. Accessed April 2010.
8 R. Rose, *Governing Without Consensus.* London, Faber and Faber, 1971.
9 A facsimile of the IRA proclamation is at http://en.wikipedia.org/wiki/Easter_Rising. Accessed 3 March 2011.
10 McKittrick et al., *Lost Lives.*
11 S. O'Callaghan, *The Informer.* London, Corgi, 1999.
12 M. Gethins, 'Catholic representation in policing Northern Ireland', unpublished PhD thesis, University of Aberdeen 2006, 258.
13 *Irish News*, 10 February 1989.
14 Gethins, Catholic representation, 213.
15 *Irish News*, 16 August 2001.
16 *Belfast Telegraph*, 26 October 1990.
17 For his account of Bloody Sunday, see E. Daly, *Mister, Are You a Priest?* Dublin, Four Courts Press, 2000.
18 B. C. Hayes and I. McAllister, 'Public support for political violence and paramilitarism in Northern Ireland and the Republic of Ireland', *Terrorism and Political Violence*, 17 (2005) 599–617.
19 P. Mitchel, *Evangelicalism and National Identity in Ulster, 1921–1998.* Oxford, Oxford University Press, 2003.
20 S. Bruce, *God Save Ulster: The Religion and Politics of Paisleyism.* Oxford, Oxford University Press, 1986 and *Paisley: Religion and Politics in Northern Ireland.* Oxford, Oxford University Press, 2007.
21 For example P. Marrinan, *Paisley: Man of Wrath.* Tralee: Anvil, 1973; E. Moloney and A. Pollak, *Paisley.* Swords: Poolbeg, 1986; and D. Cooke, *Persecuting Zeal: a portrait of Ian Paisley.* Dingle: Brandon, 1996.
22 *Protestant Telegraph*, 17 February 1973, 5.
23 On the UDA and UVF see S. Bruce, *The Red Hand: Protestant Paramilitaries in Northern Ireland.* Oxford, Oxford University Press, 1992.
24 Bruce, *God Save Ulster*, 79.
25 *BBC Northern Ireland News*, 26 October 1982.
26 *Belfast Telegraph*, 31 July 1981.
27 Cooke, *Persecuting Zeal*, 192.
28 *Irish News*, 18 December 1981.
29 *Irish News*, 10 July 1986.
30 All three were from County Armagh and were involved in arms offence related to their membership of Ulster Resistance.
31 Marrinan, *Paisley*, 144; Moloney and Pollak, *Paisley*, 138; Cooke, *Persecuting Zeal*, 149.
32 In quoting an extract from *The Red Hand* where I say something similar, J. McGarry and B. O'Leary, *Explaining Northern Ireland.* Oxford, Blackwell, 1995, 181, use an inserted '*sic*' and exclamation marks to imply that I am guilty of sexism. I am merely reporting the sexism of working class loyalist paramilitaries.
33 D. Lister and H. Jordan, *Mad Dog: the Rise and Fall of Johnny Adair and C Company.* Edinburgh: Mainstream, 2003.
34 M. Stone, *None Shall Divide Us.* London, John Blake, 2003, 277.
35 C. Crawford, *Inside the UDA: Volunteers and Violence.* London, Pluto, 2003, 144.
36 Crawford, *Inside the UDA*, 159.
37 *Irish News*, 28 November 1998.
38 I am obliged to Neil Southern for this felicitous expression.
39 R. Johnstone, 'British Israelism examined and its errors exposed', *Burning Bush*, March 1970, 3. This was the last of four long critical articles.
40 *Burning Bush*, January 2000: 1.
41 Hayes and McAllister 'Public support ...', 609.

4 Sectarianism in Scotland

1 *Daily Telegraph*, 22 November 2004.
2 *Daily Express*, 22 November 2004
3 *Scotsman*, 22 November 2004.
4 NFO Social Research, *Sectarianism in Glasgow – Final Report*. Edinburgh: NFO Social Research, 56.
5 Justice 2 Committee of Scottish Parliament; www.scottish.parliament.uk/official_report/cttee/just2–02/j202–4602.html#Col2317. The Convenor of the Committee later concluded 'the organisation's research did not stand up to any real cross-examination'; www.scottish.parliament.uk/official_report/cttee/just2–02/j202–4902.html#Col2438.
6 *Daily Record*, 7 May 2002.
7 *Sunday Mail*, 28 November 2004.
8 J. Handley, *The Irish in Scotland 1798–1845*. Cork: Cork University Press, 1945; *The Irish in Modern Scotland*. Cork: Cork University Press, 1947.
9 One can hardly blame Handley for not highlighting this feature of his two books but almost invariably, when some dilution of their cultural hegemony caused militant Protestants to protest, the changes went ahead anyway. The bigotry was eye-catching but it was also largely ineffectual.
10 I might add that I and other colleagues have repeatedly tried to persuade senior politicians, civil servants and church leaders to fund serious research. We have been rebuffed often enough for me to conclude that posturing is far more popular than investigation. An explanation for the popularity of the sectarian trope is given in S. Bruce, T. Glendinning, I. Paterson and M. Rosie, *Sectarianism in Scotland*. Edinburgh: Edinburgh University Press, 2004.
11 P. Walls and R. Williams, 'Sectarianism at work: accounts of employment discrimination against Irish Catholics in Scotland', *Ethnic and Racial Studies*, 26 (2003), 632.
12 Walls and Williams 'Sectarianism', 643.
13 Remarkably the paper passes over the one incontestable example of sectarian labour market discrimination: the right of Catholic schools to hire only Catholics for teaching posts.
14 Walls and Williams 'Sectarianism', 640–6.
15 Bruce *et al.*, *Sectarianism*.
16 L. Paterson, 'Salvation through education? The changing social status of Scottish Catholics', in T. Devine (ed.), *Scotland's Shame: Bigotry and Sectarianism in Modern Scotland*. Edinburgh: Mainstream, 2000, 145–57; *Scottish Education in the Twentieth Century*. Edinburgh: Edinburgh University Press, 2003.
17 E. Buie, 'Irish feel forced to hide roots', *Herald*, 11 April 2001.
18 W. W. Knox, 'Religion and the Scottish Labour movement *c.*1900–39', *Journal of Contemporary History*, 23 (1988), 609–30.
19 T. Gallagher, *Glasgow: The Uneasy Peace*. Manchester: Manchester University Press, 1987, 272.
20 M. Keating, R. Levy, J. Geekie and J. Brand, 'Labour elites in Glasgow', *Strathclyde Papers on Government and Politics*, 61 (1989), 19.
21 Handley, *The Irish in Scotland*, 311.
22 Gallagher, *Glasgow*, 57.
23 C. Brown, *Social History of Religion in Scotland Since 1730*. London: Methuen, 1987, 164.
24 J. H. Treble, 'The development of Roman Catholic education in Scotland 1878–1978', in D. McRoberts (ed.), *Modern Scottish Catholicism*. Glasgow: Burns, 1979, 111.
25 L. Paterson, *Scottish Education*, 40.
26 T. A. Fitzpatrick, *Catholic Secondary Education in South-West Scotland before 1872*. Aberdeen: Aberdeen University Press, 1986, 34
27 Gallagher, *Glasgow*, 103.

28 S. Bruce, *Secularization*. Oxford: Oxford University Press, 2011.

29 To avoid confusion, I should stress that in this late dating of the onset of decline, what is being cited is membership taken in isolation. As a proportion of the available adult population, Scottish church membership had been falling since 1905 and attendance had been falling since at least 1851.

30 E. Kaufmann, 'The dynamics of Orangeism in Scotland: social sources of political influence in a mass-member organization, 1860–2001', *Social Science History*, 30 (2006): 263–92.

5 Protestantism and democracy?

1 F. Halliday, 'The politics of Islamic fundamentalism: Iran, Tunisia and the challenge to the secular state', in A. S. Ahmed and H. Donnan (eds), *Islam, Globalization and Postmodernity*. London: Routledge, 1994, 96.

2 B. Lawrence, *Defenders of God: the Fundamentalist Revolt Against the Modern Age*. London: I.B. Tauris, 1990, 46.

3 E. Said, *Orientalism*. London: Routledge, 1978.

4 S. P. Huntington, *The Clash of Civilizations and the Remaking of the World Order*. London: Simon and Schuster, 1996.

5 M. Weber, *The Protestant Ethic and the Spirit of Capitalism*. London: George Allen and Unwin, 1930.

6 M. Smyth, *Stand Fast*. Belfast: Orange Publications, 1974, 4.

7 D. Martin, *Tongues of Fire: The Explosion of Protestantism in Latin America*. Oxford: Basil Blackwell, 1990.

8 M. Rosie, *The Sectarian Myth in Scotland: Of Bitter Memory and Bigotry*. London: Palgrave Macmillan, 2004.

9 S. M. Lipset and E. Raab, *The Politics of Unreason Right-Wing Extremism in America, 1790–1970*. New York: Harper and Row, 1970.

10 Matthew, ch. 22, v. 21.

11 G. Maddox, *Religion and the Rise of Democracy*. London: Routledge, 1966, 4.

12 My knowledge of the Scottish church comes from the excellent three volume history: J. Drummond and A. L. Bulloch, *The Scottish Church 1688–1843*; *The Church in Victorian Scotland 1843–1874* and *The Church in Late Victorian Scotland 1874–1900*. Edinburgh: St Andrew Press, 1973, 1975 and 1978.

13 E. Gellner, *Thought and Change*. London: Weidenfeld and Nicholson, 1965; *Nations and Nationalism*. Oxford: Basil Blackwell, 1983; *Nationalism*. London: Weidenfeld and Nicholson, 1997.

14 For the record, this is a modified version of the case made in E. Halévy, *A History of the English People in 1815*. London: Penguin, 1937. Instead of claiming that Methodism prevented an English revolution, I am making the weaker and more general point that Catholicism's resilience to democratic innovation ensured much greater polarisation.

15 E. Gellner, *Plough, Sword and Book: The Structure of Human History*. London: Collins Harvell, 1988, 107.

16 Martin, *Tongues of Fire*.

17 Maddox, *Religion and the Rise of Democracy*, 18.

18 A. Thompson, *Historical Sketch of the Origins of the Secession Church*. Edinburgh, A. Fullerton and Co., 1848, 164.

19 Gellner, *Sword, Plough and Book*, 107.

20 A. Stott, *Hannah More: the First Victorian*. Oxford: Oxford University Press, 2003.

21 R. Robinson, *Islam and Muslim History in South Asia*. New Delhi: Oxford University Press, 2000, 77.

22 S. Bruce, *Conservative Protestant Politics*. Oxford: Oxford University Press, 1998, 98–142.

23 S. Bruce, *Fundamentalism*. Oxford: Polity, 2000.
24 S. Bruce, *Politics and Religion*. Cambridge: Polity Press, 2003, 209–13.
25 S. Bruce, *Secularization*. Oxford: Oxford University Press, 2011.
26 D. Martin, *The Dilemmas of Contemporary Religion*. Oxford: Basil Blackwell, 1978, 1.

6 Methodism and socialism

1 P. Snowden, *Autobiography*. London: Ivor Nicholson and Watson, 1934, 22.
2 M. Worley, *The Foundations of the British Labour Party*. Aldershot: Ashgate, 2009, 131.
3 Published in 1906 as 'La naissance du méthodisme en Angleterre', and translated by Bernard Semmel as *The Birth of Methodism in England*. Chicago: University of Chicago Press, 1971.
4 Halévy, 'Birth of Methodism', 77.
5 For a review of responses to the Halévy thesis, see E. S. Itzkin, 'The Halévy thesis: a working hypothesis', *Church History*, 44 (1975), 47–56.
6 G. Parkinson, quoted in H. Beynon and T. Austrin, *Masters and Servants. Class and Patronage in the Making of a Labour Organization. The Durham Miners and the English Political Tradition*. London: Rivers Oram Press, 1994, 44.
7 J. Bullock, *Bowers Row: Recollections of a Mining Village*. Wakefield: EP Publishing, 1976, 121.
8 *Population (Great Britain): Religious Worship (England and Wales), LXXXIX (1852–3)*, cciii.
9 J. Benson, *British Coalminers in the Nineteenth Century: a Social History*. New York, 1980, 143.
10 J. Stephenson, *A Pocketful of Coal Dust: Reflections on North-east Folk Life*. Self-published, 1979, 3.
11 R. Wilson, 'The coal miners of Durham and Northumberland: The habits and diseases: A paper read before the British Association for the Advancement of Science, at Newcastle 1st of September, 1863'. *Transactions of the Tyneside Naturalists Club*, 1863–4, vol. VI, 14.
12 W. M. Patterson, *Northern Primitive Methodism*. London: Dalton, 1909, 283.
13 T. Eden, *Durham vol 2*. London: Hodder and Stoughton, 1953, 591.
14 H. Pelling, 'Religion and the nineteenth-century British working class', *Past and Present*, 27 (1964), 128–33.
15 S. Chaplin, 'Durham mining villages', in M. Bulmer (ed.), *Mining and Social Change*. London: Croom Helm, 1978, 64.
16 R. Wearmouth, *The Social and Political Influence of Methodism in the Twentieth Century*. London: Epworth Press, 1957, 111.
17 N. Emory, *The Coalminers of Durham*. Stroud: Alan Sutton, 1992, 61.
18 Wearmouth, *Social and Political Influence*, 117.
19 J. Wilson, *Autobiography of Ald. John Wilson, JP, MP. A Record of a Strenuous Life*. London: T. F. Unwin, 1910. British Library shelfmark 10855.df.19.
20 Wearmouth, *Social and Political Influence*, 118.
21 In a system where men were paid by weight of coal extracted, the honesty of the company's weighing was often contested. The checkweighman, who was elected and paid by the miners, checked the weighing.
22 *Account of Money and Members in the Thornley Circuit of the Primitive Methodist Connexion*. Durham Records Office M/Th 6 (37–48).
23 Moore, *Pitmen*, 70–71.
24 In the 1851 Census of Religious Worship Catholic attendances in Easington district totalled 470 and the most popular services were attended by 280 people so the number of Catholic attendees must lie between 235 (if everyone attended twice) and 280 (if no-one did).

25 In theory Anglican communicants and Methodists members need not be two discontinuous bodies. Some Wesleyan Methodists remained sufficiently sympathetic to the Church from which they had been expelled to take communion periodically. However, very few Primitive Methodists, who generally outnumber Wesleyans by two to one in the pit villages, would have communicated in the Church of England.

26 Examples can be seen in the display of historical artefacts in the Newbiggin chapel.

27 C. J. Hunt, *The Lead Miners of the Northern Pennines in the Eighteenth and Nineteenth Centuries*. Manchester: Manchester University Press, 1970, 228.

28 Hunt, *Lead Miners*, 198.

29 R. Moore, *Pitmen, Preachers and Politics: the Effect of Methodism in a Durham Mining Community*. Cambridge: Cambridge University Press, 1974. For a detailed critique see E. P. Thompson, 'On history, sociology and historical relevance', *British Journal of Sociology*, 27 (1976): 387–442. See also J. Halpin, 'Mining in the Deerness Valley', www.durham-pa.gov.uk/miner/projects.nsf/vwebtitle/mining+in+the+deerness+valley+area+%28part+3%29. Calculating penetration requires reliable baseline population figures. To achieve an area that fitted a unit for which we have population data, I added to Moore's Esh Winning, Waterhouses, Quebec and Cornsay Colliery, the pit villages of New Brancepeth, Ushaw Moore, Langley Moor, Brandon, Broompark and Bearpark.

30 H. L. Neal, *The Story of Bearpark*. Self-published, 1956, 21.

31 *Centenary Brochure, New Brancepeth Methodist Church 1877–1977*, 12.

32 Quoted in Hunt, *Lead Miners*, 228.

33 Bulmer, 'Mining', p. 162.

34 As both Methodist and Anglican figures are proportions of the same total population, changes in one figure by definition has some impact on the other but given that a large majority of the population were not involved in any form of organised religion, we can view the two sets of data as relatively independent.

35 R. Currie, A. D. Gilbert and L. Horsley, *Churches and Churchgoers: Patterns of Church Growth in the British Isles since 1700*. Oxford, 1997, tables A3 and B10.

36 R. Moore, 'The Deerness Valley: Population and religion', unpublished paper, 5.

37 Minutes of meeting of the St John's Methodist Church Society, *Sacriston*, 20 September 1964, Durham Records Office M/DDV 340.

38 G. Evans, *Miners on the Move: The Settlement of Incomers to the Cannock Chase Coalfield from Northumberland and Durham*. Stafford: Stowefields Publications, 2002.

39 Evans, *Miners*, xiv.

40 Evans, *Miners*, 16.

41 *The British Workman* was a temperance magazine that promoted the construction of alcohol-free rivals to the public house. Joseph Love funded a British Workman pub in Durham close to his New Connexion chapel. In Eggleston the British Workman funded an extension to the Baptist chapel with its own entrance that was used by Methodists as well as Baptists.

42 W. J. Morgan, 'The Miners' Welfare Fund in Britain 1920–1952', *Social Policy and Administration*, 24 (1990), 199–211.

43 *Durham Diocese Visitation Returns 1982*. Durham University Library Special Collections, AUC 4/7.

44 For a very detailed account of the shift from the Liberals to Labour in the Deerness Valley, see Moore, *Pitmen*, Chapter 7.

45 Beynon and Austrin, *Masters and Servants*.

46 J. Kent, *Jabez Bunting The Last Wesleyan: A Study in the Methodist Ministry after the Death of John Wesley*. London: Epworth Press, 1955; Bullock, *Bowers Row*.

47 J. E. Williams, *The Derbyshire Miners: A Study in Industrial and Social History*, London: Allen and Unwin, 1962, 78.

48 This is explained at length in S. Bruce, *Secularization*. Oxford: Oxford University Press, 2011.

49 Data helpfully supplied by the Director of the National Coal Mining Museum.
50 Moore, *Pitmen*, 149.

7 Opportunity structures and culture wars

1 Whitehouse had been involved in Frank Buchman's Moral Re-Armament, an anti-communist evangelical movement; G. Lean, *Frank Buchman. A Life*. London: Constable 1985.
 2 R. Wallis, *Salvation and Protest: Studies of Social and Religious Movements*. London: Frances Pinter, 1979, 107
 3 Wallis, *Salvation and Protest*, 107.
 4 A. Howard, 'Cathy come home', *Independent*, 3 November 2006.
 5 M. Palin, *Diaries 1969–1979: The Python Years*. London: Weidenfeld and Nicholson, 2006.
 6 J. Capon, *And There Was Light: The Story of the Nationwide Festival of Light*. London: Lutterworth, 1972; A. C. Whipple, 'Speaking for Whom? The 1971 Festival of Light and the search for the "silent majority"', *Contemporary British History*, 24 (2010), 319–39.
 7 Wallis, *Salvation and Protest*, 133–4.
 8 Wallis, *Salvation and Protest*, 163.
 9 Wallis, *Salvation and Protest*, 160–1.
10 Moral Majority advertising brochure, 1983.
11 S. M. Lipset and E. Raab, *The Politics of Unreason*.
12 The Bob Jones family, whose Bob Jones University, Greenville, South Carolina, was a key institution in this world, were never persuaded and continued to argue that both entanglement with the world and the belief that social reform was Biblical were threats to salvation: the first through contamination; the second through distraction.
13 J. M. Penning, 'Pat Robertson and the GOP: 1988 and beyond', in S. Bruce, P. Kivisto, and W. H. Swatos Jnr (eds), *The Rapture of Politics: The Christian Right as the United States Approaches the Year 2000*. New Brunswick: Transaction, 1995, 105–22.
14 L. Barnett, 'The electability test', *Time*, 29 February 1988, 13.
15 D. W. Brady and K. L. Tedin, 'Ladies in pink: religion and political ideology in the anti-ERA movement', *Social Science Quarterly*, 56 (1976), 564–75.
16 M. Riesebrodt, *Pious Passion: The Emergence of Modern Fundamentalism in the United States and Iran*. Berkley: University of California Press, 1993, makes an excellent case for the modern challenge to traditional gender roles being at the heart of both the Protestant and the Islamic fundamentalist response to modernity.
17 S. E. Finer, *Comparative Government*. Harmondsworth, Middlesex: Penguin, 1982, 227–8.
18 For details of rules and history see O. Gay. 'Party election broadcasts'. House of Commons Standard Note SN/PC/03354 13 January 2010; www.parliament.uk/documents/commons/lib/research/briefings/snpc-03354.pdf.
19 L. Paterson, *The Autonomy of Modern Scotland*. Edinburgh: Edinburgh University Press, 1994.

8 Christian parties

1 It is worth adding that opinion in Northern Ireland was not as far behind that in Britain as the Ulster opt-out suggests. The anomaly was tolerated because it was relatively easy for women in Northern Ireland who wished terminations to be referred to British providers. In contrast legislation on homosexuality, which was also initially not applied to Northern Ireland, was eventually brought into force: the

obvious difference being that the restrictions on homosexual residents of Northern Ireland were more debilitating because they could not be redressed by a brief visit to Britain.

2 Scottish Parliament Information Centre, Scottish Parliament election results, 6 May 1999.

3 *The Economist*, 19 March 2005.

4 S. McAndrew, 'Religious faith and contemporary attitudes', in A. Park, J. Curtice, K. Thomson, E. Clery and S. Butt (eds), *British Social Attitudes: The 26th Report*. London: Sage, 2010, 94.

5 One was David Alton, Catholic Liberal MP for various Liverpool constituencies 1979 to 1997 who had consistently campaigned against his party's abortion position and eventually resigned over the issue.

6 www.cpaparty.org.uk/?page=about_us. Accessed 26 August 2010.

7 *Christian Democrat Voice*, edition 2, 2002, 2.

8 In 1991 Newham was the second most deprived local authority area in Britain according to G. Smith, 'Ethnicity, religious belonging and interfaith encounter; some survey findings from East London', *Journal of Contemporary Religion*, 13 (1998), 333–51. In 2005, it was the eleventh most deprived borough in England and Wales according to K. Harriss, *Muslims in the London Borough of Newham*. Oxford: Centre on Migration, Policy and Society, 2005. It was the site for a detailed study of health problems among ethnic minorities: S. Salway, L. Platt, P. Chowbey, K. Harriss and E. Bayliss, *Long-term Ill-health, Poverty and Ethnicity: A mixed methods investigation into the experiences of living with a chronic health condition in the UK*. Bristol: Policy Press, 2007.

9 *Herald*, 13 March 2007.

10 I. Dey and B. Marlow, 'Philip Richards: The hedge fund star who crashed to earth. RAB Capital's Philip Richards has lost his once-golden touch', *Sunday Times*, 14 September 2008; http://business.timesonline.co.uk/tol/business/industry_sectors/banking_and_finance/article4747922.ece. Accessed 3 December 2010. Details of party funding are available from the Electoral Commission's website.

11 *Private Eye*, 16 May 2010.

12 CPA, *European Union Manifesto*, London: CPA. www.cpaparty.org.uk/resources/EUManifesto.pdf. Accessed June 2009.

13 The above summary is from the CPA, *Mayflower Declaration*.

14 http://christianparty.homestead.com/l_manifesto.pdf. Accessed September 2010.

15 Christian Party, 'Bob Handyside: Your man for real change', Press release, 1 August 2008.

16 'David Booth – Christian Peoples Alliance: I think that we have reached a point in time, where it is worth a re-think of the current popular politics and parties, as to whether they are really serving the interests of Christians', http://blog.echurchwebsites.org.uk/2010/03/26/david-booth-christian-peoples-alliance-reached-point-time-worth-rethink-current-popular-politics-parties-serving-interests-christians/. Accessed 7 November 2010.

17 *Guardian*, 27 April 2010.

18 http://blog.echurchwebsites.ork.uk/2010/05/07/christian-candidates-election   results. Accessed 7 November 2010.

19 www.christianparty.org.uk/candidates.html. Accessed 2 November 2010.

20 www.christianparty.org.uk/candidates.html. Accessed 2 November 2010.

21 Centre for Women and Democracy, *Election 2010: Where the Women Candidates Are*. Centre for Women and Democracy, 2010, 2. www.cfwd.org.uk/uploads/pdfs/WomenCandidatesApril2010.pdf. Accessed November 2010. Generally speaking, the more prestigious the position and the better the chance of winning, the more male candidates there are. In recent decades there have been more women candidates in council elections than in parliamentary elections. The CP/CPA gender profile is that

of a no-hope movement in council elections rather than that of a serious party in a Westminster election.

22 B. Jones, D. Kavanagh, M. Moran and P. Norton, *Politics UK*. London: Pearson, 2007, 415.

23 C. Rallings, M. Thrasher, G. Borisyuk and M. Shears, *2009 Local Election Candidates Survey*. London: IDEA, 2010; www.idea.gov.uk/idk/aio/15289960.

24 I mention this because historically conservative populist parties have drawn heavily on the petit bourgeoisie; see M. Canovan, *Populism*. New York: Houghton Mifflin Harcourt, 1981.

25 Office of National Statistics, 'Labour Force Survey: employment status by occupation and sex, April–June 2010', www.statistics.gov.uk/STATBASE/Product.asp?vlnk=14248. Accessed November 2010. We might want to moderate that figure by noting that a few pastors also mention other occupations but, in the other direction, we should also note that a high proportion of those who occupation is not known listed religious activities which could well have been full-time.

26 *Guardian*, 12 April 2010.

27 In August 2008 Hargreaves starred in a Channel 4 reality TV programme called *Make Me a Christian*, in which he attempted to convert a sad group of apparently mentally unstable people.

28 In the 2004 election the PLA stood in North West, Eastern and South East; the CPA stood in London and South East; the Christian Democratic Party stood alone in Wales; and Operation Christian Voice stood in Scotland. In 2009 all the English regions were contested by the CP–CPA alliance. The Christian Party of Wales stood alone in Wales and the Scottish Christian party stood alone in Scotland.

29 The parties are CPA and Operation Voice, etc.

30 S. McAndrew, 'Religious faith and contemporary attitudes', in A. Park, J. Curtice, K. Thomson, E. Clery and S. Butt (eds), *British Social Attitudes: the 26th report*. London: Sage, 2010, 98.

9 Religious minority politics

1 In case this is thought an exaggeration a Belgian sociologist who had been invited to respond to a public lecture on secularisation I gave in Antwerp in 2009 accused me of oppressing Muslims by being an empirical social scientist. Even though I had barely mentioned Muslims my generally positivistic orientation meant that by Foucauldian logic I was part of the oppression of religious minorities.

2 R. King, *Orientalism and Religion: Post-colonial Theory, India and the Mystic East*. London: Routledge, 1999.

3 S. Bruce, 'Defining religion: a practical response', *International Review of Sociology*, 21 (2011), 105–18.

4 Home Office. *Religion in England and Wales: Findings from the 2001 Home Office Citizenship Survey*. London: Home Office, 2004, 1.

5 G. Marranci, Blog *Islam. Muslims and an Anthropologist*. http://marranci.wordpress.com/2008/07/03/the-dog-the-hat-the-police-and-muslims-in-dundee/. Accessed 17 January 2011.

6 The incompatible arguments that to ascribe any property to Islam is falsely essentialising orientalism and that Muslims have rights as members of a religious minority are often made by the same people; see S. Vertovec, 'Islamophobia and Muslim recognition in Britain', in Y. Y. Hassad (ed.), *Muslims in the West: From Soujourners to Citizens*. Oxford: Oxford University Press, 2002, 19–35.

7 S. R. Ameli, B. Faridi, K. Lindahl and A. Merali, *British Muslims' Expectations of the Government: Law and British Muslims: Domination of the Majority or Process of Balance?*. London: Islamic Human Rights Commission, 2006, 87.

8 Before anyone cites the apparently similar judgements already made by Charity Commissioners, I should point out that it judges the public benefit of some activity, not the religious rectitude of its promoters.

9 R. Gale and P. Hopkins, 'Introduction', in P. Hopkins and R. Gale, *Muslims in Britain: Race, Place and Identities*. Edinburgh: Edinburgh University Press, 2009, 10. Almeri *et al.*'s sample is more religious: 16.6 per cent described themselves as 'Highly practising', 70.2 per cent said 'practising' and 13.1 per cent described themselves as 'secular' or 'cultural' Muslims and 0.5 per cent said they 'don't care about Islamic values at all'. Almeri *et al.*, *British Muslims' Expectations*, 31.

10 S. Bruce, *Secularization*. Oxford: Oxford University Press, 2011.

11 It has to be said that many academics are far from even-handed in their treatment of this issue. Hall, for example, takes it as axiomatic that the Sikhs she studies have a right to preserve their distinctive culture but she treats non-Sikh reluctance to see British society change as pathological; K. D. Hall, *Lives in Translation: Sikh Youth as British Citizens*. Philadelphia: University of Pennsylvania Press, 2002.

12 Ameli *et al.*, *British Muslims' Expectations*, 20.

13 Ameli *et al.*, *British Muslims' Expectations*, 20.

14 K. Malik, *From Fatwa to Jihad: the Rushdie Affair and its Legacy*. London: Atlantic Books, 2009, 51.

15 M. Mirza, A. Senthilkumaran and Z. Ja'far, *Living Apart Together: British Muslims and the Paradox of Multiculturalism*. London: Policy Exchange, 2007.

16 J. Rex, 'The urban sociology of religion and Islam in Birmingham', in T. Gerholm and Y. Lithman (eds), *The New Islamic Presence in Western Europe*. London: Mansell, 1988, 206–18.

17 On the politics of Tammany Hall, see G. Myers, *The History of Tammany Hall*. Michigan: Scholarly Publishing Office, University of Michigan Library, 2005 and R. Ashby, *Boss Tweed and Tammany Hall*. Boston: Blackbirch Press, 2002.

18 Malik, *From Fatwa*, 69.

19 N. Britten and G. Jones, 'Judge lambasts postal ballot rules as Labour 6 convicted of poll fraud', *Daily Telegraph*, 5 April 2005.

20 D. Kennedy, 'Six jailed for postal vote fraud over rigged election in Slough', *The Times*, 2 May 2009.

21 S. Waters, 'New social movement politics in France: The rise of civic forms of mobilisation', *West European politics*, 21 (1998), 170–86.

22 Malik, *From Fatwa*, 58–9.

23 Malik, *From Fatwa*, 62.

24 Malik, *From Fatwa*, 70.

25 A. Sen, 'The uses and abuses of multiculturalism', *New Republic*, 2 July 2006.

26 Pew Global Attitudes Project, *The Great Divide: How Westerners and Muslims View Each Other*. Washington, D.C.: Pew Forum, 2006, 3.

27 T. Modood, 'British Asian Muslims and the Rushdie affair', *Political Quarterly*, 61 (1990), 151.

28 Modood, 'British Asian Muslims', 150.

29 http://en.wikipedia.org/wiki/The_Satanic_Verses_controversy.

30 W. Herberg, *Protestant–Catholic–Jew: an Essay in American Religious Sociology*. Chicago: University of Chicago Press, 1983.

31 Malik, *From Fatwa*, 102.

32 Malik, *From Fatwa*, 102.

33 R. Watson 'The rise of the British jihad', *Granta*, 103 (2008), 86–7.

34 Watson, 'British jihad', 86–7.

35 Watson, 'British jihad', 47.

36 *Independent*, 25 February 2003.

37 Watson, 'British jihad', 82.

38 For a review, see R. Simcox, H. Stuart and H. Ahmed, *Islamist Terrorism: The British Connections*. London: Centre for Social Cohesion, 2010; www.socialcohesion.co.uk/uploads/1278089320islamist_terrorism_preview.pdf. Accessed 1 January 2011.

39 *Daily Star*, 22 December 2010.

40 Ameli *et al.*, *British Muslims' Expectations*.

41 T. Cantle (ed.), *Community Cohesion: a Report of the Independent Review Team*. London: Home Office, 2001; http://resources.cohesioninstitute.org.uk/Publications/Documents/Document/DownloadDocumentsFile.aspx?recordId=96&file=PDFversion. Accessed 9 March 2011.

42 Watson, 'British jihad', 78.

43 J. A. Beckford, R. Gale, D, Owen, C. Peach and P. Weller, *Review of the Evidence Base on Faith Communities*. London: Office of the Deputy Prime Minister, 2006, 44.

44 Beckford *et al.*, *Review*, 16.

45 Beckford *et al.*, *Review*, 16.

46 All these data are from Beckford *et al.*, *Review*, 16–18.

47 Office for National Statistics, 'Labour market: Muslim unemployment rate highest'. London: ONS, 2006; www.statistics.gov.uk/cci/nugget.asp?id=979. Accessed 6 February 2011.

48 On language acquisition, see C. Julios, *Contemporary British Identity*. Aldershot: Ashgate, 2008.

49 Malik, *From Fatwa*, 133.

50 Ameli *et al.*, *British Muslims' Expectations*.

51 C. Field, 'Islamophobia in contemporary Britain: the evidence of the opinion polls, 1988–2006', *Islam and Christian–Muslim Relations*, 18 (2007), 468.

52 BBC 2, *The Conspiracy Files 7/7*. Broadcast, 30 June 2009.

53 Anthony Wells, 'One year on': http://ukpollingreport.co.uk/blog/archives/265. Accessed 1 September 2009.

54 Mirza *et al.*, *Living Apart Together*, 5.

55 P. Baty, 'Stress levels on the rise, UCU survey indicates', *Times High Education Supplement*, 10 July 2008.

56 Field, 'Islamophobia', 467.

57 Mirza *et al.*, *Living Apart Together*, 37–9.

58 C. K. Hadaway, P. L. Marler and M. Chaves, 'What the polls don't show: A closer look at US church attendance', *American Sociological Review*, 58 (1993), 741–52.

59 M. Regnerus and J. Uecker, *Premarital Sex in America; How Young Americans Meet, Mate, and Think about Marrying*. New York: Oxford University Press, 2010.

60 Field, 'Islamophobia', 469.

61 A. W, Helweg, *Sikhs in England*. Delhi: Oxford University Press, 1986, 152–212.

62 Ipsos MORI, 'Muslim women survey', 25 March 2009; www.ipsos-mori.com/researchpublications/researcharchive/poll.aspx?oltemid=2357.

63 E. Fieldhouse and D. Cutts, *Electoral Participation of South Asian Communities in England and Wales*. York: Joseph Rowntree Foundation, 2007, Summary.

64 www.bnp.org.uk/news/democracy-new-conservative-style. Accessed 10 January 2011.

65 M. Shabbir, 'Is clan-based politics a major barrier to progress?', *Muslim View*, 19 August 2010.

66 H. Ansari, *Muslims in Britain*. London: Minority Rights Group International, 2002, 19.

67 E. Tatari, 'Muslim councillors on the increase in London', *Muslim News,* 25 June 2010; www.muslinnews.co.uk/paper/index.php?aricle=4682.

68 M. Sobolewska, 'Religious extremism in Britain and British Muslims: threatened Citizenship and the role of religion', in R Eatwell and M. Goodwin (eds), *New Extremism in Britain*. London: Routledge, 2010, 32–64.

69 S. Zubaida, 'The "orientalist" assumption', *Open Democracy*, 27 October, 2005; www.opendemocracy.net/conflict-terrorism/responses_2970.jsp.

70 P. Oborne, 'Hatred of Muslims is one of the last bastions of British bigotry', *Daily Telegraph*, 21 January 2011. Responses can be found at http://blogs.telegraph.co.uk/news/peteroborne/100074414/if-youre-looking-for-islamophobia-try-the-comments-under-my-article-about-baroness-warsi/. Accessed 1 February 2011.

10 The public place of religion

1 B. R. Wilson, *Religion in Secular Society*. London: CA Watts, 1966, xiv.
2 T. Asad, *Genealogies of Religion: Discipline and Reasons of Power in Christianity and Islam*. Baltimore: Johns Hopkins University Press, 1993.
3 D. Voas, 'The rise and fall of fuzzy fidelity in Europe', *European Sociological Review*, 25 (2009): 155–68.
4 For a book-length explanation of secularisation and critique of the criticisms, see S. Bruce, *Secularization*. Oxford: Oxford University Press, 2011.
5 P. L. Berger, G. Davie and E. Fokas, *Religious America, Secular Europe? A Theme and Variations*. Aldershot: Ashgate, 2009; P. Heelas and L. Woodhead, *The Spiritual Revolution: Why Religion is Giving Way to Spirituality*. Oxford: Blackwell, 2004.
6 Berger *et al.*, *Religious America, Secular Europe*, 13–4; R. Stark, 'Secularization RIP', *Sociology of Religion*, 60 (1999): 249–73.
7 J. Casanova, *Public Religions in the Modern World*. Chicago: University of Chicago Press, 1994.
8 The separate issue of why religious leaders are often invited to perform important secular roles is discussed in S. Bruce, *Politics and Religion*. Cambridge: Polity Press, 2003, 139–42.
9 E. Kaufmann, 2006 'Breeding for God', *Prospect*, 128; www.prospectmagazine.co.uk/2006/11/breedingforgod/; P. Norris and R. Inglehart, *Sacred and Secular: Religion and Politics Worldwide*. Cambridge: Cambridge University Press, 2004.
10 Bruce, *Secularization*, 2011.
11 S. Kettel, 'On the public discourse of religion: an analysis of Christianity in the United Kingdom', *Politics and Religion*, 2 (2009): 420–43.
12 R. Butt, 'Your equality laws are unjust, Pope tells UK', *Guardian*, 2 February 2010.
13 P. Achterberg, S. Aupers, P. Mascini, D. Houtman, D., W. de Koster and J. Van Der Waal, 'A Christian cancellation of the secularist truce? Waning Christian religiosity and waxing religious deprivatization in the West', *Journal for the Scientific Study of Religion*, 48 (2009): 687–701, 867.
14 D. Voas and A. D. Crockett 'Religion in Britain: neither believing nor belonging', *Sociology*, 39 (2005): 11–28.
15 In 2000, the Independent Television Commission organised a series of focus-group studies of religious broadcasting. I was an expert witness for a Glasgow group, the members of which were remarkable for their unanimity both that religious programming was socially beneficial and that they never watched any.
16 S. Bruce and T. Glendinning, 'Religious beliefs and differences', in C. Bromley, J. Curtice, K. Hinds and A. Park (eds) *Devolution – Scottish Answers to Scottish Questions*. Edinburgh: Edinburgh University Press, 2003, 86–115.
17 Details of the survey are given in Bruce and Glendinning, 'Religious beliefs'.
18 Mass Observation, *Puzzled People: A Study in Popular Attitudes to Religion, Ethics, Progress and Politics in a London Borough*. London: Victor Gollanz, 1947, 84.
19 G. H. Gallup Jr. *The Gallup International Public Opinion Polls: Great Britain 1937–1975, Vol 1*. New York: Gallup, 1978, 378.
20 ABC Television, *Television and Religion: a Report Prepared by Social Surveys (Gallup) Ltd on behalf of ABC Television*. London: University of London Press, 1964, 123.
21 ComRes opinion poll, 17–18 February 2010; www.comres.co.uk/page190146516.aspx.
22 ComRes opinion poll, 17–18 February 2010; www.comres.co.uk/page190146516.aspx.

23 ComRes, *Religion Survey for the BBC*. 18–19 February, 2009; www.comres.co.uk/page16583232.aspx.

24 YouGov, *Survey for John Humphries*. 1–5 February 2007; www.yougov.com/archives/pdf/Humphrys%20Religion%20Questions.pdf.

25 Higher scores represent sympathy for religion and lower score represent antipathy. Scale construction via reliability analysis: 6-item scale = $(a+b+c+d+e+f)/6$; Cronbach's $\alpha=0.72$, $N=1880$ in 2008 and $\alpha=0.72$, $N=769$ in 1998. (i.e. $\alpha=0.7$ for both the 1998 and 2008 BSA datasets).

Index

Page numbers in *italics* denote tables.